THE

COUNTRY OF THE MOORS.

A MOOR OF BARBARY.

PREFACE.

Respected Reader,

I AM led to hope that you will feel a certain interest in the subject which is my excuse for trying your patience again. I have endeavoured to sketch the existing state of a portion of the country of the Moors, the race — to me the most interesting of all — which shed the light of civilisation on the Dark Ages of Europe. These notes are the result of two journeys into the region where the remnant of the Moors have their present abodes. I cannot hope, save perhaps in the case of the city of Kairwân, to convey much original or novel information.

A peasant once presented himself at the Third Section, or Secret Police Department, in St.

Petersburg, and demanded a hundred roubles as the price of a certain communication. The money was promised on condition that the facts were not already known to the police. When the peasant had finished, the agent called his secretary from behind a screen, desiring him to bring such and such a document, and to read it aloud. It was the peasant's story word for word. Well, I can't make that out, he said aghast, as he went out: for I invented the story myself. The secretary had written behind the screen while the peasant spoke. In like manner, though I can take no credit for inventiveness, I am inclined to fear that the reader, turning to his bookshelves, may find much of the information I have to give, more solidly conveyed.

To several gentlemen I am much indebted for kind recommendations : Messrs. Rye, Stephens, Wright, Newsome, Fraser, Young, and especially Mr. Murray and his son, who have contributed to make my task a pleasant one. Colonel Playfair also helped me most kindly. I have to recognise the indulgence of the reviewers of a former account of very different scenes—from those who encouraged me to write again, to the one who remarked : We do not know any young man who has travelled so much as Mr. Rae, and seen so little.

My journey was a solitary one. I had not the hardy and invaluable companion of Arctic expeditions, or the genial friends who have cheered so many rambles elsewhere. The journey was easy enough. To Kairwân alone I should not recommend a visit, without various precautions and a certain respect for the prejudices of the unaltering Faith of Mohammed. Even then, it is not unlikely that an accident might happen.

Briefly, kind Reader, as the old geographer Leo says in closing his Chronicle : These are the things memorable and woorthie of knowledge seene and obserued by me Eduard Rae in the Countrey of the Mores : wherein whatsoeuer I sawe woorthie the obseruation, I presently committed to writing : and those things which I sawe not, I procured to be at large declared vnto me by most credible and substantiall persons, which were themselves eie-witnesses of the same : and so hauing gotten a fitte opportunitie, I thought good to reduce these my trauels and studies into this one volume.

Claughton,
    Birkenhead.
  October 1877.

THE
COUNTRY OF THE MOORS,

*A Journey from Tripoli in Barbary
to the City of Kairwân.*

BY EDWARD RAE, F.R.G.S.
Author of 'The Land of the North Wind.'

MAP AND ILLUSTRATIONS.

LONDON:
DARF PUBLISHERS LIMITED
1985

First Published 1877

New Impression 1985

ISBN 978 1 85077 030 5

WITH RESPECT AND LOVE I DEDICATE THIS BOOK TO MY DEAR MOTHER AND SISTER.

CONTENTS.

CHAPTER I.
                                                                    PAGE
Provence—The *Junon*—Sail for Malta—Storm—Passengers—
Sambo—Valetta—Franciscan Priest—Sail for Tripoli—The
Circe—Expectations 1

CHAPTER II.
The Tripolis—Its Origin and History—The Romans—Vandals—
Saracens—Spaniards—Knights of Jerusalem—Ottomans—The
Beys 9

CHAPTER III.
Trablus Gharb—The City—Bazaars—Leo Africanus—Prepare for
Journey to Lebda—Recommendation—Annibale and Giovanni . 16

CHAPTER IV.
Set out from Tripoli—Among the Palms—The Dellou—Tadjoura
—The Desert—Ras al Hamra—We reach Djefâra—Reception—
Accommodation—The Kaïd—The Plagues of Barbary—Taphra
—A Rencontre—Sidi Abd el Atti—Syrian Landscape—Weir—
Country of the Bedouins—Ruins—Homs 25

CHAPTER V.

Received at the Castle—The Kaïd—Murderers—Our Quarters—Ride to Lebda—Débris—Columns—Heat—Wadi Lebda—Group of Ruins—Temples—Severus—The Evil Eye—Triple Arch—Depredations—*Lepide*—Its Origin and History—A Legend of Leptis—The Gulf of Syrtis Major 35

CHAPTER VI.

Return to Homs—A Deputation—The Kaïd's Hospitality—Copper Coins—The Dead City—Start for Tripoli—Wearisome Journey—The Gharian—A Wedding—Djefâra in the Twilight—The Owl-slayer—Continue Journey—Great Heat—The Mecca Caravan—A Bargain—Tadjoura—The Hermitage—Frederick Warrington—The Times of the Beys—The Harbour—Mussulman Fanaticism—The Bazaars 49

CHAPTER VII.

The Pasha's Gardens—Ostriches—John Leo on the Naturall Historie of Barbarie—Tombs and Coins—Giovanni incorruptible—The Triumphal Arch of Aurelian—Roman Numerals—Prayers for Rain—Offering to the God of Rain—Alteration of Plans—Cyrene in Prospect—The Cyrenaïca 62

CHAPTER VIII.

Evening Ride—Esparto Grass—Black Families—An Ingrate—The *Allegra*—Usury, Caravans, and the Slave Trade—The Pashalik of Tripoli—Resources—Fall of the Leaf—Charity—Arab Home—Outer Bazaars—Love Charms—The Sheikh el Biled . . 74

CHAPTER IX.

Djemma 'l Basha—Djemma 'l Gordji—Djemma 'l Sheikh Bel Ain—Djemma 'l Sidi Dragut—Panorama—The Crescent City—Delusions—Productions and Misfortunes—Voiage of the *Iefus*—The Genowaies 89

CONTENTS. xiii

CHAPTER X.
PAGE

The Jews' Quarter—The Place of Stoning—The Dyers—An Austere Sentry—Bab el Djedîd—Jewish Reception—The Synagogue—The Murderer—The Dutch Consul—The Black Village—In the Palm Groves—Orange Garden—Essence Distilling—Fruit and Blossom—The Castle—A Roman Lady—Boûba—The *Circe*—The Last of Tripoli 98

CHAPTER XI.

Malta—Cape Bon—Tunny Fishery—Goletta—Perruquier—The City of Verdure—Preparations for Kairwân—Sketch of Tunis—Purchases in the Bazaars—Scenes in the City—Rose Buds and Orange Blossoms—Adopt a Young Moor—Braham the Silversmith—Thê Bardo—The Great Aqueduct. 109

CHAPTER XII.

Bakkoush—His Antecedents, Career, Characteristics, and Accomplishments—Old Times—Mosaics—Stroll through the City—Panorama—The Diamond Market—Sanctuaries—The Mosqu of the Olive Tree—Departure from Tunis 126

CHAPTER XIII.

Sail for the East Coast—Susa—Bazaars—The Sahel—Adrumetum—The Port of Kairwân—The Revolution—Monastir—Lepti Purva—Ras di Mas—Mehdia—The Patriarke of Cairaoan—Salectum 138

CHAPTER XIV.

The Barbary Coast—The Khassîr—Kerkeneh—The Flying Camp—Djerba—The Lotos Eaters—Skull Pyramid—Gulf of Kabes—Palus Tritonis 150

CHAPTER XV.

PAGE

Arrival at Sfax—Gale—A Mistake—A Deaf Mute—The Quarters of Sfax—Mosques—A Caravan of Dates—The Bazaars—Gracefulness of Sfaxins—Environs—The City of Twelve Thousand Gardens—Slave Caravans—Street Auction—Costumes—The Great Mosque—A Tragedy—The Silversmiths—Bakkoush at Home—An Eccentric Dervish—A Modest Marabout—Ruins of Lebda . 161

CHAPTER XVI.

Embark on *Corsica*—Privations—Facts about Sfax—Sail for the North—Sponges of the Lesser Syrtis—The Oulad Azim—Octopi—Sponge Culture and Chicken Manufacture—Mehdia—Sardines—Arab Cemetery—Port of Mehdia—Turris Hannibalis—Relics of El Djem—A Moslem Companion—Monastir—Collectors—Susa 180

CHAPTER XVII.

Of the Great Citie of Cairaoan—Hutmen—Hucba—Muse—Conquest of Andaluzia and Castilia—Site of Kairwân—Decline—Dr. Shaw on Kairwân and its Mosque—Origin of Name—Its Sacredness and Exclusiveness—Plans and Preparations—A Recommendation—Outfit—Disappointment 196

CHAPTER XVIII.

Departure from Susa—The Sahel—Bedouins—A Discovery in Natural History—Drought—M'seken—The Great Plain—Footprints of Pilgrims—The Great Minar—The Walls—Enter Kairwân—Observations—Maledictions 210

CHAPTER XIX.

The Year of the Hejra 1292—The Kaïd's House—Sidi Mohammed el Mourâbet—Hospitality—A Pervert—Supper à l'Arabe—Fanatical Mosquito—Visit the Kaïd—The Bazaars—Curiosity and Precautions—The Tunis Gate—A Horse Sale—My Bodyguard—Progress to Citadel—Soldiers—Civility—The Walls—Rough Usage 221

CHAPTER XX.

The Great Mosque—Sketches—The Khasinah—Decaying City—Its Former Size—The Bazaars—Slippers—Marabouts—The Mosques—Tombs of the Saints—Curiosity—An Aspiration—The Suburbs—Djemma 'l Zitûna—*Yahudi*—Postern Gate . 236

CHAPTER XXI.

Moorish Calendar—Chronicles of the City—Okhbah—Conquest of Spain—Ibn Aghlab—The City's Decline 246

CHAPTER XXII.

The Frenchman—Servants—Soldiers—Ride round Walls—A fine Barb—The African Mecca—The Haj—The Kaïd's Predecessors—Colleges—The Renegade of Kairwân 268

CHAPTER XXIII.

The Bazaars—A Bargain—Mosque of the Three Gates—Tombs—
—Measure the Great Mosque—Fanaticism—Details of Exterior—Sacred Well of Kafâyat—The Minar—The Courtyard—The Prayer Chamber—Its Interior—Columns of the Great Mosque—An Intrigue—Writing on the Wall 281

a

CHAPTER XXIV.

Foundation of Kairwân—Its Mosque and Kibleh—Its Vicissitudes —Cordova—Constructions—Raccadah—The Last of the Aghlabites—The New Mecca 292

CHAPTER XXV.

The Gate of Greengages—Measure the City—Ruined Bastion— Call to Prayer—The Citadel—A Mob—Leylet al Moolid—Elmawahel—Imprecations—Form of City—An Incident—Opinion of the Bazaars—Prepare to Leave—Farewell to the Kaïd—Last Night in Kairwân 304

CHAPTER XXVI.

Issue from the City—Traverse the Plain—Camp of Bedouins— Interview with Bedouin Ladies — Halt under Olive Trees— Ruined Tomb—Nablus—Hammamet—The Foudoûk of Birloubuïta—The Dakkhul Promontory—The Lead Mountain—Suleiman—Gulf of Tunis—Hammam 'l Anf—Rhades—Enter Tunis . 314

CHAPTER XXVII.

A Hammam—A Negotiation—Leave Tunis—Footsteps of Bruce— A Touch of Nature—Sad News—The Last of Perruquier— Cape Carthage—The Malta Channel—A Swell—Cagliari— Amphitheatre—Antiquarian Museum—A Visit from Sards— The Colony of Tunis—Leghorn—An Incident—Genoa—Paris . 323

LIST OF ILLUSTRATIONS.

———+———

A MOOR OF BARBARY . . . . . . *Frontispiece*
  Etched by Léon Richeton.

RUINED MONUMENT AT LEBDA . . . *To face p.* 36
  Photographed and Etched by the Author.

RUINS BY THE RIVER OF LEPTIS , . . . ,, 40
  Etched by Edwin Edwards from the Author's Photograph.

TRIPLE GATEWAY AT LEBDA . . . . ,, 44
  Photographed and Etched by the Author.

PALMS BY THE SEA. TRIPOLI . . . . ,, 104
  Drawn and Etched by the Author.

THE GREAT MOSQUE OF KAIRWÂN . . . ,, 236
  Etched by Léon Richeton from the Author's Sketch.

SKETCH PLAN OF THE GREAT MOSQUE . . ,, 288
  Engraved from the Author's Drawing.

SKETCH PLAN OF THE CITY OF KAIRWÂN . . ,, 306
  Engraved from the Author's Drawing.

MAP . . . . ,, 334

Errata.

Page 11, line 20, *for* Zobeir *read* Ibn Zobeir.
,, 39, ,, 14, *for* Windsor *read* Virginia Water.
,, 83, ,, 24, *for* knows *read* admires.
,, 146, ,, 5, *read:* Barth says Leptis means port. There is a Hebrew root *lapat*, to enfold or encompass; but no such word, I think, in Greek or Latin.
,, 210, ,, 3, *for* Arab *read* Moorish.
,, 218, ,, 13, *for* Arab *read* Arabic.

For *foudoûk* in several places, read *fondoûk*

Rae's Barbary.

THE

COUNTRY OF THE MOORS.

CHAPTER I.

Provence—The *Junon*—Sail for Malta—Storm—Passengers—Sambo—Valetta—Franciscan Priest—Sail for Tripoli—The *Circe*—Expectations.

IT was a lovely morning as we entered Provence. It was the early spring: green leaves were sprouting, and the almond-trees were thick with blossom. Beside us was the swift Rhone, and eastward were the purple mountains with snow on them. We passed Orange and its beautiful Roman arch, Arles and its noble Colosseum: and finally whirled into the busy town of Marseilles. In the train was a pleasant Englishman, also on his way to the Hôtel du Louvre and to Malta.

We walked down to the steamship office, and learned that the *Junon* would not sail until the following evening. We engaged our berths, and went down to see the steamer.

On the second afternoon we went on board the *Junon*, and for two hours watched the last cases marked *Malte*, *Alexandrie*, lowered into the hold by a terrible steam crane. At dusk we moved slowly out of the Joliette harbour, rounded the lightship, and were on our way over the luminous waters of the Central Sea. It was a dead calm: the sky looked very threatening. We steamed under the Château d'If, and left the twinkling lights of the city behind.

Towards midnight the wind burst upon us in a hurricane: the sea became wild and mountainous, great waves broke over our stern, and water poured in sheets down into our cabin. The doors and windows of the deckhouse were nailed up, and covered with boards and canvas. After a miserable night in the dark stuffy state-room, daylight came. Great green seas were sweeping aloft, breaking in a furious mass of foam, and burying the *Junon's* stern as if she could never rise again.

It was scarcely dawn when we went on deck: the sky was bare of all but stars, every cloud seemed blown out of it. The gale was violent, the seas were prodigious. The wind, fortunately aft, drove us along fast, though we could hoist no sail. Nothing could be put upon the table: our negro steward, from Martinique, was in despair, his woolly hair stood straight on end as the plates and glasses clattered and smashed. His white teeth glittered as he clenched them, and he ground out *sacrés* as if he had been educated in France.

We were but few passengers, and if some of us had had a second opportunity of sailing in the *Junon*, there would have been fewer still. We had asked at the agency after our fellow-passengers. There were two English officers, the agent said, Messieurs Cholmelée and Maquintôche. Mackintosh, an especially pleasant fellow, was Lieutenant in the 71st Highlanders, on his way to join his regiment; and Cholmeley, a powerful young Yorkshire squire, was to be attached to the regiment for a few months.

At daybreak on the third morning the gale had abated, and this day we could take our meals in the saloon.

The captain was a jolly good-looking Frenchman— a Legitimist: his political discussions with the other officers were very entertaining, and he was as much at home and familiar with us as if he had taken us to Malta a dozen times. This want of stiffness is a charm in a short acquaintance. A French story is told of an Englishman and a Frenchman, who met one rainy night in an inn, and sat before the fire drying and warming themselves. After one or two attempts at conversation, the Frenchman gave it up. Presently he stooped politely forward. 'I beg your pardon, sir,' he said: 'some of the ash of your cigar has fallen on your knee.' 'Well,' said the Englishman, 'I don't see that it concerns you. Why, the tail of your coat has been on fire for the last half-hour, and I said nothing about it.' The steward, Sambo, tells us tales of Martinique, but he refuses to sing us one of the old plantation songs. He has an excellent mouth for sugar-cane, but he says that it disagrees with him. As he eats the cane after sucking the sap, we are not surprised at this.

At length we sighted, towards noon one day, the Island of Gozo: and late in the afternoon we were steaming into the entrance of the Grand Harbour of Valetta.

I was glad to find the Tripoli steamers *Circe* and *Trablus Gharb* lying alongside of us, as we moored opposite to Fort St. Angelo. The *Trablus* had sailed, but put back, owing to the heavy weather, which had detained many vessels in Malta. I landed, and drove in one of the inexpensive light carriages up to Dunsford's Hotel.

It is a curious city: with its narrow tapering streets, and innumerable flights of steps, tall yellow stone houses, and their projecting green wooden bays, mediæval outlines of auberges and palaces—a sort of restored Rhodes. The bustling barefooted natives, with their yellow sunburnt skins, are the greatest busy-bodies in Europe. Accredited with the knowledge of all European languages, they scarcely know one. In their miniature world all mutual relations are defined in the shortest possible time, and with the most wonderful accuracy. They have been described as an ugly race of Catholic Arabs. English sentries were pacing in front of the guard-house: over which are the insignia of England, with the dedication—To the great and unconquered Britain the love of the Maltese and the voice of Europe confirms these islands. A.D. 1814. There were sailors with broad collars and blue shirts, but not English faces: quick parties of redcoats: sounds of fife, bugle, and drum: baskets of violets and other flowers, and piles of golden oranges—all in the warm sunny air of the Malta spring.

This City of the Knights, this surprising group of natural fortresses, is familiar to us all, but none the less remarkable and interesting. It is a magnificent possession for England, and probably will not be given up until the party who would have exchanged Gibraltar for Ceuta have acquired a little more importance.

Passing down to the Marina, to learn the hour at which the *Circe* was to sail, I chanced to enter the church of the Franciscans. There were large numbers of people and priests, and a strong odour of incense and lighted tapers. In the centre of the church, amid a crowd of kneeling men and women, flanked by two tall rows of candles, stood a high catafalque, covered with a black and silver pall. Upon this reposed, in full sacramental robes and hat, a Franciscan priest. His eyes were closed, and his hands clasped on his breast. Poor old man, he died on the previous day, and this was his funeral service. On my return I saw a crowd passing up the Strada Reale. The priest was being carried, just as he had lain in the church, to the catacombs of the Franciscans.

At ten in the morning, with all the bells in Valetta clanging for church service, we steamed slowly out of the harbour, and set sail for the Country of the Moors. Ahead of us was the Turkish boat, *Trablus Gharb*, an older but faster steamer than the *Circe*, also bound for Tripoli. It was a bright fresh day: and, light as the little steamer was, she rocked but little on the swell which remained from the gale. Mr. Saïd, who was agent for the *Circe* in Tripoli, was on board: and with Captain Kirkpatrick, a bright worthy little seaman, to whom the owners had very kindly recommended me, the day passed quickly. The passage is often a bad one, Tripoli harbour being almost inaccessible in northerly winds: and, instead of arriving in twenty-four or thirty hours, the steamers have to lie off for several days together, and even to return from within sight of the houses of Tripoli to Malta.

Lest it should be imagined that I could regard this journey in the light of a holiday and a diversion, I will mention some of the requests which reached me from friends and from strangers before I left England. I can only recommend any future traveller to Tripoli to conceal his destination from his nearest relatives. This was from an old friend and travelling companion :—

'Dear Rae: I send a list of a few things I wish you would get for me. Twelve inlaid hand mirrors, with mother-of-pearl and ivory: five or six essence cabinets, such as we found in Tunis and Cairo: two soft silk scarfs, of scarlet and plum colour: a set of coffee-cups and silver holders set in turquoise; must be old: any blue and white china worth having: whatever large pieces of silver-work—bracelets &c.—you don't want yourself. Some old embroidery. A brass Jewish lamp and a brass ewer and basin.'

The next was from a gentleman of whom I had not had the pleasure of hearing before :—'Sir: Hearing from a relative of yours that you are about to travel in Barbary, I venture to ask you to collect for me some shells and birds' eggs. Such and such shells exist in Barbary, and the eggs of such and such birds are to be met with. Pray be careful, in blowing the eggs, to do it only in the following way.' Then came a diagram of the only way in which I could be a successful blower of eggs. The next was from a gentleman distantly acquainted with a member of my family :—'Sir: As I understand you are just starting for the North Coast of Africa, I should feel extremely indebted to you if you would spend for me fifty or a hundred pounds in old Oriental embroidery. Then followed many excuses and no directions, the matter being unfortunately left to my taste.

One friend asked for ten pounds worth of attar of roses. One merely wanted me to spend ten pounds for him on something or other. One asked for an old Tripoline silver bracelet: one for a bottle-shaped gourd, to be set in silver filigree. Another modestly wished for a photograph of a lonely ruined column. I was asked to spend a hundred pounds in carpets: to bring ostrich feathers and a gazelle back with me: to proceed to the Atlas and report upon the Touâregs, one of the oldest races in Africa. Finally, I was very handsomely desired to buy for myself, as a present, the object which pleased me most in Tripoli. I can assure the reader that these commissions caused me much anxiety and uneasiness of mind.

CHAPTER II.

The Tripolis—Its Origin and History—The Romans—Vandals—Saracens—Spaniards—Knights of Jerusalem—Ottomans—The Beys.

OF the three capitals of the *Tripolis*—the region which obtained its name in like manner as the Decapolis and Pentapolis, and contained the cities of *Leptis*, or Neapolis, *Sabrata*, or Old Tripoli, and *Œa*, or New Tripoli —only the latter city remains. The cities of Leptis and Sabrata, one lying seventy miles east, and one forty-seven miles west from Tripoli, exist only as heaps of ruins. It is generally understood that, when the Phœnicians, driven from home by domestic strife, established these colonies on the northern coast of Africa, between the gulfs of the Greater and Lesser Syrtes—the country being more or less unproductive, the settlers had in view the creation of emporia for trade with the interior, in gold, gums, spices, ivory, and other precious articles. The frequency of oases in the country lying south of Libya Tripolitana, rendered it very suitable for such traffic, and its three seaports acquired wealth, refinement, and luxury.

The building of Tripoli proper is attributed by

some to the Emperor Severus: while the generally accurate geographer, Leo Africanus, declares that it was not built until after Old Tripoli had been captured by the Goths, and destroyed by the Mohammedans in the time of the Khalif Omar. This would injure Tripoli's claim to a decent antiquity, but the existence of a Roman arch of the period of Aurelian refutes Leo. Phœnician inscriptions of the same period also exist.

The founders of the Tripolis, as is well known, made settlements farther East—from Djerba to Algiers: and these Barbary provinces, having Carthage for their capital, flourished after the Pentapolis had begun to decay. The sun of Phœnician Carthage set on the fatal plain of Zama, but Roman Carthage rising from her ashes took the lead, and maintained it for six centuries. The limits of civilisation contracted as Roman power declined in Africa, and at length Valentinian called in the aid of the Vandal king. Those predatory barbarians gladly overran and occupied the country. A series of desolating wars followed, in which the brave and able Belisarius eventually recovered for Justinian, who reigned in Constantinople, these African dependencies: but their ruin was complete. Fresh wars under Solomon, the successor of Belisarius, had a similarly pernicious result: Africa was desolated. The Vandals, once numbering a hundred and sixty thousand warriors alone, were extirpated. Of Berbers an infinitely greater number perished. When Procopius, historian of the Vandals, landed in these parts of Africa, he was astonished at the population and prosperity of the cities and country. In less than twenty years the busy scene was converted into a silent solitude. It is said that five millions of human beings perished in the wars of the Emperor Justinian.

In the seventh century, during the rapid and astounding rise of Mohammedanism, the Arabians, called Saracens or Orientals—*Sharak*, East—turned their arms to the setting sun. Under the Khalîfat of Omar, Okhbah, at the head of the Mohammedan army, traversed the desert of Barca, destroyed Leptis : and in the year 647 appeared under the walls of New Tripoli. Gregory, the Carthaginian Prefect, appeared in relief of the city, and offered his daughter's hand and a hundred thousand pieces of gold for the Arabian Emir's head. On the Saracen side the same conditions were offered to the man who should slay Gregory, and in a bloody battle the Prefect fell. Zobeir, the Saracen chief who slew him, however, declared—probably after seeing the lady— that he laboured for a recompense above the charms of beauty or the riches of this transitory life. This may have been disinterested or not.

The Tripolitans purchased the withdrawal of the Saracens by the payment of six million dollars. For which step the government of Byzantium reproached and taxed them, so that on the reappearance of the Saracens in 668, they welcomed both their government and their faith. Okhbah then overran the northern part of Africa, from Djerba to the Atlantic, and from the Mediterranean to the Great Desert: establishing his capital in Kairwân, thenceforth the seat of Mohammedan splendour and learning. Once the aboriginal races rose —Kabyles, Touâregs, Berbers of the Atlas—and under their Queen Cahina, drove the invaders into Egypt: but as they then set to work to destroy whatever in the cities they considered tempting to an invader, the inhabitants invited the Arabians back, who definitely established their language and customs. After many vicissitudes, on the dissolution of the Khalifat, Tripoli became an independent Moorish state.

In the year 1510, it fell into the hands of Ferdinand the Catholic: but twelve years later Charles V. surrendered the city, together with Malta, to the Knights of St. John, whom the Turks had just expelled from Rhodes. The Ottoman Empire was in the zenith of its power: its corsairs infested the Mediterranean. The Knights strengthened and fortified Tripoli: but, after a short possession of less than thirty years, the Turkish corsairs, Sinan and Dragut, overcame them, and entered into possession of the city. Dragut Reis was made Pasha, and governed Tripoli as part of Sultan Suleiman's dominions.

VICISSITUDES OF TRIPOLI.

During the next century and a half, but little is known of the Regency or city. Pashas and Sanjaks, with a garrison for the castle, were sent from Constantinople to govern it, and its flag was a terror of the Inland Sea. After bombarding Goletta, Blake in 1655 imposed a treaty on the Tripolines: for a breach of which Sir Cloudesley Shovel and Sir John Narborough attacked it in 1655.

In the year 1714, Hamet Pasha the Caramanian, with the Moors of the city, rose, and put the Turkish garrison to death—three hundred of them—in one night. Hamet was proclaimed independent ruler, and, sending large tribute to the Porte, he received recognition. He invited foreigners to settle in Tripoli, exerted himself to improve manufactures and industry, made treaties with the various foreign powers, subdued the mountaineers of the Gharian, conquered Fezzân, reduced the Cyrenaïca, and acquired among his subjects the title of Great. Becoming blind, he is said to have shot himself, in the year 1745.

Hamet was succeeded by his son and grandson—the latter being Ali Pasha, a mild and well-meaning man, whose life was embittered by his sons. These were Hassan, Hamet, and Yussuf: the latter murdered Hassan in the presence of their mother, and fought again and again with Hamet. In this state of civil war, the Turks took the city, and Ali and his family had to escape abroad.

The Turkish governor, however, behaving with gross cruelty, was superseded, and Ali's family were re-established.

On the death of Ali, Yussuf became Pasha. Brute as he was, his views were broad and enlightened: he was anxious to remain on good terms with Europeans, and afforded them facilities for exploring the Regency. He captured Murzoûk, and established the slave trade, much to his own profit: he also entered largely into mercantile transactions. Tripoli had not yet washed its hands of piracy. Yussuf winked at it: indeed, his own fleet of eleven sail and a hundred guns did a good deal of business of the kind, under the command of the notorious Morat Reis—once Peter Lyle—a Scotch renegade.

In 1801, and thrice in 1804, American squadrons bombarded the city: on one occasion losing a frigate, the *Philadelphia,* which struck on the reef, and was captured by the Tripolines. In course of one desperate engagement the Moors fought splendidly—one half losing their lives: but the naval commander Mohammed Sous, for the loss of his ship, was paraded round the city on the back of an ass, and received five hundred strokes of the bastinado. In consequence of this unjust and brutal treatment, none of Yussuf's captains would put to sea.

Yussuf incurred debts, to enforce payment of which,

END OF YUSSUF'S GOVERNMENT.

Tripoli was successively bombarded by the Sardinians, Sicilians, and French. In 1832, Yussuf's sons rekindled the family feud: the city was besieged for a year: Yussuf abdicated in favour of his second son.

One day—May 20, 1835—a Turkish squadron entered Tripoli harbour. The Pasha was enticed on board of one vessel under promise of protection, and there presented to 'Mustapha Nedjib Pasha, Governor of Tripoli.' The Sublime Porte has since nominated the Pashas of Tripoli—generally with a four years' tenure of office.

CHAPTER III.

Trablus Gharb — The City — Bazaars — Leo Africanus — Prepare for Journey to Lebda — Recommendation — Annibale and Giovanni.

EARLY on the second afternoon we were off a white-walled town, having a black reef running out in front of it, over which the waves were breaking. We rounded the extremity of the reef, and cautiously entered the harbour, across the end of which the city wall stretches in almost a straight line, facing the rising sun. It has at one extremity the tall massive citadel, and on its seaward extremity a yellow fort, from which the reef extends to the north-east. Above the city wall stand flat-roofed houses, half-a-dozen minarets, and a single palm. In the harbour lay two steamers—the *Trablus*, and a Turkish war-steamer—and a dozen vessels of moderate size. Beyond the castle extends a white beach, with low walls and a few domes. Behind and beyond these, as far as the eye can reach, to the extremity of the little bay, stretches a vast and beautiful grove of palms. Thick, feathery, and green, they form a noble background to the city.

The pilot, a good-looking sunburnt man, came on

board, and we steamed slowly in through the treacherous passages, which admit vessels only drawing sixteen or eighteen feet. The wind came whistling in from the east, the sky grew grey and thick, the waves curled and crested: the pale yellow sand, where camels and white-robed Arabs were pacing, was caught up and filled the air: the palm trees swayed and stooped and became enveloped in dust. We had only got in in time. A boat came off, pulled by four Arabs in striped *cashabbiyehs*, the anchor was dropped, and we were fairly in the harbour of *Trablus Gharb*. This city is Tripoli of the West: Tripoli of Syria is *Trablus Shark*, Tripoli of the East.

A number of Tripolines were assembled on the little jetty to see us land, and we went through the comedy of passing the customs authorities, established in a shed. Captain Kirkpatrick pointed out to me a burly gentleman with a bronzed face. That is Mr. England, he said, who will be happy to receive you in his house. I made the gesture of remuneration. Certainly not, said the little captain: it would be an affront. Then I don't go, I said. You must, said the captain: there are no quarters available in the city. So I was introduced to my host, who expressed himself very hospitably: porters took my baggage on their shoulders, and we made our way through an old stone gateway up to the house, a few minutes' walk from the harbour.

Mr. England's household resembled Robinson Crusoe's: it consisted of a dog, a cat, a young goat, a few birds, an antelope, and a man Peppo. A Maltese gentleman, Dr. Camilleri, a very zealous antiquarian, lived with him. While all the news from Malta was being told, Mr. England's servant was preparing my room, the best in the house, which I was rather ashamed to monopolise.

In the afternoon we sallied forth into the city, which is of the form of a half moon, or half octagon, measuring eight hundred and fifty yards by a thousand yards. It is surrounded by a high wall, flanked by six bastions, and has at one tip the castle, at the other the half-ruinous forts. The sea face runs in a gentle curve round the end of the harbour.

Tripoli has three gates. Bab el Bahhr, the Sea Gate, by which we first entered: Bab el Meshîah, opening upon the sea beach under the castle walls: and Bab el Djedîd, the New Gate, behind the Jew quarter, and leading to the Jewish cemetery. All the houses of Tripoli are of Moorish character. The Europeans live chiefly in the quarter between the harbour gate and the centre of the city. Behind this lies the Jew quarter. Between the European quarter and the bazaars lies the quarter of habitations, chiefly of the better classes. The city is much smaller than Algiers or Tunis. The population of Tripoli has been estimated variously

A CITY OF THE MOORS.

at from twenty-five to fifteen thousand. Wars and plague have rendered the latter figure more probable: perhaps two thousand Turks, ten thousand Moors, two thousand Christians, and two thousand Jews, represent the approximate present population.

The bazaars occupy the southern end, under the wing of the castle. To reach them from the harbour gate, one traverses the European quarter and that of habitations. We entered the long blank white alleys of this neighbourhood, where flying buttresses overhead cast broad shadows whenever the sun is not in the zenith.

We came, after a few turns, to the Turkish bazaar, the chief and broadest thoroughfare of the city. White walls on either side carried a rude roof, under which vines trailed, and through which the sunlight streamed. Here was a low Moorish gateway to a khan or fondouk, of which the interior was colonnaded. Many of the shop-fronts were painted blue. Here were the barbers and grocers, the silk and cotton merchants. The crowd was a picturesque one, though falling far short of a Tunisian crowd. Jews in dark blue turbans, Moors in white turbans, Turks in the fez, Arabs in brown rough *barracans* of undyed wool, with bare brown legs, wandered to and fro. Turkish soldiers in Zouave dress and gaiters strolled hand in hand. The barbers' shops were especially neat, having gaily coloured racks for razors and combs, and clean matted divans. They had, too, old hand-mirrors, inlaid with ivory and mother-of-pearl, and jars of leeches. In the cafés sat Moors, with clean turbans of straw-coloured silk and white stockings, while the attendants moved quietly about with brass trays and the little cups of scalding coffee.

Parrots hung in cages, and leopard and jackal skins in some of the shops. Many houses had the Cairene wooden latticed windows, now, alas! disappearing in the Egyptian capital. In cooks' shops Arabs were devouring yellow cakes, fried, by perspiring negroes, in copper pans.

Next came the blacksmiths' bazaar, the entrance to the Djemma 'l Basha, and the apothecaries' bazaar. We watched the shops of dates and milk, one of the most common resorts of the poorer classes: who found there their breakfast, and too often their dinner. The dates were pressed in esparto paniers, and fresh milk was constantly arriving in vessels borne by asses. Honey stood in vast jars—much of it comes from Candia—esparto baskets stood full of raisins, beans, red pepper, and ground corn for kouskousou. In an oil shop stood prodigious jars of olive oil, like those of Ali Baba, and one had only to travel to the silversmiths' bazaar, to find the forty thieves. Much of the oil comes from Zleitûn and Imsellâtah, among the Gharian hills. Sellers of oil, having asses laden with skins, passed us.

Near the long colonnade of Djemma 'l Basha is the flower market. Close by was a café, and on seats placed along the white steps, a crowd of soldiers in white linen were enjoying themselves. Facing the mosque were shops of ironmongers, with sheep-shears, flat horse-shoes, tin powder-horns, primitive shot-pans, and strings of cowrie shells brought from Tomboûkto. Men were selling coarse quilted linen skullcaps; boys carrying baskets of mulberry leaves and blossom were crying out for proprietors of silkworms. In an apothecary's shop hung ostrich eggs: a little farther was a leather-worker.

We went out by the south-eastern gate on to the seashore. The great citadel wall at this point runs out like the bow of an ironclad ram, and forms the southern extremity of this city of the Moors.

We rambled back along the harbour wall, and called upon Mr. Said, my fellow traveller from Malta. I visited Mr. Hay, our consul-general, who received me very kindly. I mentioned my wish to travel to Lebda —Leptis Magna—which lies about seventy miles eastward, on the verge of the Greater Syrtis, and Mr. Hay promised to obtain for me a letter of recommendation to the Käids, or to commanders of forts.

In the evening we went to the club, as it is called: a simple billiard room, where native merchants and Europeans generally meet in the evenings, to talk business and gossip. Near this club is the Catholic church, with a school attached.

My first impressions of the city had been disappointing, as regards costumes, bazaars, and buildings. Leo Africanus—a Moor, born in Barbary and brought up as a Christian in Granada—the quaint and unintentionally humorous geographer of the sixteenth century, says the houses and bazaars of Tripoli are handsome, compared with those of Tunis. They have sadly altered for the worse since Leo's time, or those of Tunis have vastly improved. The first few days after my arrival were spent in prowling about the bazaars, and through the city in various directions.

Mr. Osman Warrington, son of the former consul-general here, called, and most kindly offered me his services. He was vice-consul at Misrâtah, farther east than Lebda, on the coast, and the journey to Lebda was very familiar to him. The vice-consulate at Misrâtah was to be given up, and removed to Homs, a rising little port within sight of the ruins of Lebda. Osman Warrington was then building, with many difficulties, a house at Homs: which, poor fellow, he hardly lived to enter. He recommended to me a Maltese servant named Giovanni, and kindly brought from the castle the letter of the Pasha of Tripoli. I am indebted for its translation to a gentleman who has done me several similar favours.

With respect and honour we allow it to be known, by the present, to those who are invested with power, honour, and dignity here and elsewhere, that the honourable person called Monsieur Rae, from England, accompanied with letters and documents of introductions, as also by the acquaintance and dignity of the honourable British consul of the Pashalik of Tripoli: and who has now our will and recommendation, to all those dignitaries, &c., during his sojourn and while travelling in this realm: to assist and help him in all his wishes and desires during his stay and travels. The said gentleman has obtained this our Free Will, to show, with our grant and favour, that he may go and return back (there and here) with safety. Delivered on this day, 11th of the month Safar, 1294 of the Hejra.

By order of the Divan Dawlet of this realm,
Potentate
MOUSTAPHA.

Mr. England's servants prepared and purchased necessaries for me—meat, potted fish, bread, salad, eggs, wine, coffee, &c., &c., for seven days—and dates, walnuts, and oranges for fourteen days. They sought out mules, and a muleteer, who, with his boy, was to take charge of the animals. An indolent dreamy young Maltese—Annibale by name—who, like Giovanni, spoke only Italian and Arabic, and who was assistant apothecary by profession, was also recommended as indispensable to a journey of this kind: apparently because idling on a mule's back, with a gun in his hand, was an occupation which afforded him especial satisfaction. As a guide, a muleteer, a sportsman, or a humorist, Annibale was a failure: and I have often asked myself since, what special purpose in this journey, or in the journey of life generally, Annibale fulfilled. He seemed to do nothing, to know nothing, to expect nothing: in fact he was a kind of Maltese Nihilist.

An active day's work, which included all the packing for the morrow, made a good night's rest welcome: and I was awakened soon after daybreak. Going down stairs, I found Giovanni and Annibale, with two Arabs, in a state of high excitement, loading our worldly effects upon the mules. After one or two false starts, we ambled away through the empty streets of Tripoli.

CHAPTER IV.

Set out from Tripoli—Among the Palms—The Dellou—Tadjoura—The Desert—Ras al Hamra—We reach Djefâra—Reception—Accommodation—The Kaïd—The Plagues of Barbary—Taphra—A Rencontre—Sidi Abd el Atti—Syrian Landscape—Weir—Country of the Bedouins—Ruins—Homs.

THE sun was just rising as we emerged on to the seashore, and we cantered along the fresh breezy beach to the palm groves. Looking back, we could see the cream-coloured city of Tripoli glittering in the early rays of the sun. The wind blew freshly from the land, and broke the surf which met it into showers of vapour. Dozens of fishermen's boats with white lateen sails skimmed swiftly to and fro, like swallows fly-catching. Sand blew from the beach into the sea: the white-robed Arabs on their way into the city drew their barracans closely round them.

We passed through the Wednesday's market-place, and entered a sandy way between rows of high mud walls—moulded, as though of concrete, in huge cubical blocks. Within the walls were gardens with delicious green grass: here and there stood a little white tomb or marabout, and beside it the dusty grey trunk and transparent tender leaves of the fig tree. The thin delicate branches of the pomegranate bore red sprouting leaves: poppies of brilliant scarlet stood among the grass: the prickly pear, with its great uncouth trunk and its prickly developments, formed a hedge: the leafless almond trees were covered with pink blossom: the olives were graceful and tall as cork trees. Above and round us towered into the clear pale sky the noble palm trees, through which we were to ride for miles. This forest of palms is the finest on all the North African coast. Every now and then the gusty wind came sweeping through the palms, which hissed and rustled overhead.

Four miles from Tripoli we passed the *Soukh el Djemma*, the site of the Friday's market: with the invariable marabout, over which fluttered a little green and yellow flag. The Arabs were busy irrigating. Their apparatus, which takes the place of the Egyptian *shadouf* or *sakiyeh*, is the *sinieh*. Two uprights of stone, or sun-dried brick, standing a yard and a half apart, support a pulley and axle. At the lower end of a cord which runs over this into the well, is the *dellou*, a half round leather bag or vessel, with an iron rim, and with a leather spout depending from its centre like an elephant's proboscis. The *dellou* is let down into the water and filled: the bullock at the other end of the cord begins to draw, and the *dellou* rises: the proboscis, having a cord attached to its end, is drawn up in advance by an Arab. When both reach the pulley, the end of the spout is released, and the water gushes out into a reservoir. An inclined plane is excavated in the ground, down which the bullock marches, his weight assisting in raising the *dellou* and water. How does he get back? asked a young lady to whom this was being explained. He turns round and walks back up the incline. In every garden or enclosure we heard the melancholy creak of the axle and the gush of the water. It was life to the thirsty soil.

The villages of Tadjoûra we reached after two hours' ride, a straggling collection of little white houses and gardens. There was towards the centre an old mosque, rather of Christian appearance. After three hours the country became barer: we lost the gardens and walls, but there were still palms waving in the wind. To our left we passed a small lake or Salina, from which the Tripolines get salt. We emerged on to the open desert. The sun beat fiercely down from a blue sky upon the yellow sand.

I was full of regret at not having gone by sea: the wind was strongly in our favour, and, as we trudged for hours through the desert in the hot sun, I grew sadder and sadder. Hour after hour we passed through the melancholy waste, having to our right, beyond the pale sand, the distant range of the Gharian, and to our left the heavy surge on the seashore. The wind drove the fine sand in sheets, till we seemed to be riding in a river of sand streaming along with us. Some Arabs with camels joined us—one poor man being bound for Imsellâtah, only fifteen miles from Lebda: and having to travel all night to arrive in time for the market in the morning. We passed in the afternoon the Wadi Roumel, a small stream winding down among tall reeds into the sea, where it soon vanished. Above it was Ras al Hamra, Red Point—the Amarœa upon the river Oinoladon, of the Phœnicians—where, on abruptly rising ground, stood a marabout. Among the green reeds and rushes stood three palms, the first we had seen since leaving the forest at Tadjoura.

On we went, through the soft yielding sand, our mules sinking to their knees, and at times stumbling heavily. We came, towards five in the afternoon, to a second Wadi, El Msîd, with a larger stream than the Roumel. We had ridden since daybreak with only one halt: and, being rather exhausted, threw ourselves down on the ground, while the poor mules had a few mouthfuls of brushwood. Riding on again we saw two or three white *siniehs*, and some palms growing apparently out of the desert sand. Traversing a partially cultivated district, and turning our backs upon the sea, after half an hour we espied in front of us a low white quadranglar building, the Castle of Djefâra.

A few Arabs and blacks were loitering in front of it. The sun had just set, and the dusk was coming quickly on. The Bedouins, whose low brown tents we saw a few hundred yards away, were bringing their herds of goats and kids homewards as we rode under a low archway into the fort. Parts of it were quite ruinous. We were taken to the Kaïd's principal room—a small miserable outbuilding in the courtyard. At one end, on a little brick platform raised half a foot from the floor, and covered with a mat, sat the Kaïd and his secretary : one or two officials squatted near them. I handed the Pasha's letter to the Kaïd ; he looked at it upside down, and the novel form of the fine large handwriting evidently pleased him. He passed it on to his secretary, who spelled through it, the Kaïd smiling and bowing to me as its contents were related to him. He had given up to me the seat of honour, and seemed so glad to see people, that he lighted a cigarette and prepared to spend the evening with us, making me various complimentary speeches. I told Giovanni to make my excuses to him, and to say that I was very tired after our long journey, while I endeavoured to impart to my face a grateful and joyous expression.

When we had bowed the Kaïd out, the Arabs unloaded the mules, our saddle-bags and hampers were brought into the hut, and Giovanni and the good-natured

Nihilist prepared dinner. It was a piercing cold night, and the Kaïd's people brought us a small three-cornered clay pot, full of charcoal. The door, too, had lost one of its planks, and therefore one-third of its width. The Maltese rolled off to sleep on the floor: in spite of my better judgment I adopted the Kaïd's straw pillow, and lay down on the brick platform with a thin straw mat alone under me. In a quarter of an hour I was overrun by a needy and indefatigable swarm of fleas. After two hours' misery I was falling asleep, when the mules outside our door took fright, reared, plunged, and the castle resounded with unearthly braying. They ceased at last and my chances improved, when my attention was directed to a curious scratching and scuttling about the matting and baskets. A colony of rats had emerged from a hole in the corner of the hut, and with angry little squeaks were eating their way into our esparto paniers. At times they varied their recreation by cantering joyfully over my body and those of the sleeping Maltese. Looking out of doors, the castle walls were white as snow in the moonlight, one or two brilliant stars glittered in the cloudless sky, and I could hear—two miles away—the magnificent roar of the sea. I longed desperately for sleep, and it seemed to be coming, when two cocks suddenly awoke, and, imagining the moonlight was the day, began to crow vigorously in turns—the success of one stimulating the other. It

THE CASTLE OF DJEFÂRA.

was now three in the morning. Awakened and encouraged by the cocks, a pair of owls set themselves to screech and hoot, the mules tuned up again, the rats frolicked about, and the fleas sallied out in numbers like ants. At last, in spite of them all, I fell asleep.

It was half-past three, and we were to be on our way to Lebda at six. We awoke then, and after a cup of coffee and a mouthful of bread, rode away from Djefâra. This interesting spot is all that remains to mark the neighbourhood of Pliny's Taphra, Ptolemy's Garapha Portus, Scylax's Gaphara, lying—as all those authors agree—about midway from Leptis Magna to New Tripoli. By the Greek geographers it was known as Oinospora, lying nearer to the coast than the Castle of Djefâra, and having once a double, but very exposed, anchorage at the point now known as Ras el Djefâra.

We passed over a better track, in places much covered with sand. We were two miles from the sea: on our right, among the Gharian hills, were many Bedouin encampments. On either side of our path we passed the low brown tents in dozens, their sunburnt owners tending their herds of goats or ewes, and watching over their poor sparse crops of wheat and barley. After sunrise it grew very hot.

An Arab met us, hurrying towards Tripoli. He was an intimate friend of our Arab mule-proprietor, and their greeting was long and affectionate. How are you? Well, how are you? Thank God! how are you? Goodness gracious! how are you? God bless you! how are you? When each was satisfied how the other was, the stranger told us he was carrying to Tripoli the news of a savage murder. A Maltese blacksmith living at Homs had a young Maltese assistant. This youth appeared to have concerted with the blacksmith's wife the unfortunate man's murder. Early this morning she admitted him to the house, when, falling upon the sleeping blacksmith, he stabbed him repeatedly. The wife then sprinkled sand upon the floor in a vain attempt to cover the blood, gave the murderer a change of clothes, and he returned to his lodgings. In the morning the soldiers knocked at his door and took him to the Castle of Homs, where he remained chained hand and foot.

We passed the dry watercourses of the Wadi Turbat and the Wadi Bijibâra, and rode along as before. Towards noon we met a party of seventy Turkish soldiers, trooping along, poor fellows, on foot, and having their baggage carried by camels. In the midst, on a camel, was a high scarlet palanquin carrying the lady of the officer. The old boy himself, in his shirt-sleeves, and looking as if he had not shaved for a week, rode at the end of the procession on a large donkey. After a short halt at mid-day, in sight of the famous marabout of Sidi Abd el Atti and its palm woods—near to which the English traveller Captain Smyth found traces of a Troglodyte village, and of tesselated pavement—we pushed on.

The Gharian range had been gradually approaching the coast, and we came among the high ground. The country grew remarkably like the Holy Land—round stony hills and grey rocks with brushwood, and rich sheltered patches of cultivation in the valleys. We wound up among the hills, and came early in the afternoon to the ruins of a weir which ran across the end of a valley and ended against the face of a cliff. There was no water now. In some of the valleys we entered were delicious gardens. In the rich red soil stood sprouting pomegranates, fig trees with tender young leaves, and almond trees in full blossom. We were in the Djebel Tarhûna, part of the Gharian range. We passed hundreds of Bedouins' tents, flat and dark, with palisades of matting to shelter them. Dogs would come tearing out open-mouthed as we passed, and the little Bedouin children would run away, scared at our looks. Ruined towers stood on the hills: the country is strewn with ruins. To our right, thirteen miles inland, lay Imsellâtah.

All day we had had but occasional glimpses of the sea, but in the afternoon we came in full sight of it, and could see—some miles away down by the shore—the dark shapeless masses of the masonry of Lebda. Near the promontory of Hermes lay the little white Arab town of Homs or *Khommos*—Chickpeas, though I don't know how the town got that name. It contains now perhaps twelve hundred inhabitants, and is acquiring yearly more importance from the development of the esparto trade. Building is going on, and the little place is rapidly expanding. I have said that the vice-consulate of Misrâtah is to be transferred hither. I cannot help thinking that Leptis Magna extended as far as these hills: ruins of considerable buildings cover them thickly, more than would indicate the mere outskirts of a city. The great Leptis, too—the birthplace of an Emperor, an ally of Rome, possessed of splendid temples and public buildings, renowned for its wealth, yielding tribute at the rate of one talent a day to the Imperial Treasury—could not have been comprehended, as is believed, within the space of ten thousand square yards.

CHAPTER V.

Received at the Castle—The Kaïd—Murderers—Our Quarters—Ride to Lebda—Débris—Columns—Heat—Wadi Lebda—Group of Ruins—Temples—Severus—The Evil Eye—Triple Arch—Depredations—*Lepide*—Its Origin and History—A Legend of Leptis—The Gulf of Syrtis Major.

WE rode down into Homs after the sun had set. We had come in two days from Tripoli: the journey is often made one of four days, generally of three. We rode up to one of the two whitewashed castles or forts, that where the Kaïd resided, and dismounted. There were officers, soldiers, and officials idling about, and we said we had come upon a short visit. As this did not awaken any sudden cordiality, we said we had a letter from the Pasha to the Kaïd, whom we wished to see. They said the Kaïd had joined his family for the evening, and hinted that he must not be disturbed. We asked them not to put themselves out of the way, as we should go to the other fort and stay with the Kaimakam commanding the soldiers. This alarmed them, and they begged us not to go away, as it would distress the Kaïd very much. Some of them hastened off to inform his Excellency, and we were promptly ushered through the courtyard, up an outer staircase of stone, into a large handsome room, with a cushioned divân at one end.

Very soon the Kaïd appeared, an astute-looking Turk in spectacles, who expressed himself very cordially and hospitably. He sent at once to prepare a room for me in a house overlooking the sea, and his servants brought coffee and cigarettes. We had a long chat, he speaking Turkish: and Giovanni, who was a fluent interpreter, and expressed himself excellently, rendering his words into Italian for me. He assured me it gave him profound pleasure to receive me, and trusted I would not fail to express any wish I might have. He added that it would grieve him beyond belief if I did not remain at Homs for at least a week. I said that his friendliness quite reminded me of home, and that I should remain as long as possible his guest. He spoke of the tragedy of the morning: the victim had been buried as we were entering Homs. There were twelve or fourteen murderers, he told me, under his charge: several under sentence of death, and he only awaited confirmation of their sentence from Constantinople. The Kaïd himself was formerly Governor of Pera.

We went downstairs, and, as we spoke to the officials in the gateway, we heard the clank of chains, and saw

beside us a dozen Arabs chained two-and-two, trooping in from building work down by the beach, and guarded by a few armed soldiers. Many had evil-looking faces, and stared at us defiantly. They were the murderers: some of them would complete their sentence in a few weeks by swinging from a rope in the Castle yard. Poor wretches, the look of death was already in their faces. Twelve murderers chained together: it was not a pleasant sight, and there was something very horrid in the jangle of their chains. We found a bare room, made comfortable by divâns and soft quilts, from the Kaïd's own rooms, prepared for us. It was an upper storey, and the roof below us formed a terrace looking over the sea.

Very early in the morning we were under way, on the mules, for the ruins of Leptis, two miles distant. We reached a solitary standing monument: a tall slender panelled and pilastered erection, with the lower portion remaining of the pyramid which once formed its apex. It had been split from summit to base, and the half facing landwards had fallen away, and lay among other strewn fragments on the ground. The sea front was still tolerably perfect. It was a delicious morning, and the ripple on the Mediterranean broke musically on the white beach as we took a photograph of the monument. Close behind it, near a strip of palms, was the grave of the murdered Maltese.

We rambled on through sand-drifts, and over ground covered with fragments of stone, pottery, marble, particles of mosaic, angles of pediments, broken frusta, and chips of acanthus and of shafts. We could not resist wasting half-an-hour in groping among them, finding polished marble tiles, pieces of opal glass, and copper coins: the ground simply teems with them. I sent the Nihilist to a Bedouin *doûar* among the palms to borrow or steal a spade or pickaxe: but the Bedouins would not lend anything to such an irresponsible looking stranger, and he returned shrugging his shoulders and saying, *Non c'è*. In my disappointment I delivered myself ot a bitter smile which I had been maturing, and called him an Italian word. As we advanced, the accumulations of sand became wider and deeper, extremities of columns and angles of buildings protruded, mournfully calling attention to their helpless state. A buried city, however, is a greater satisfaction to the mind than a vanished city.

I confess I was greatly disappointed with what I had seen so far: nothing was in sight but a few grovelling remains among rolling sand-hills, white and quivering in the sun's glare. I thought the whole place was a fraud, and said morosely that I had been sent on a fool's errand. I told Giovanni, who tried to amuse me by conversation, that he was tedious: and Annibale, who said nothing, that he had barely escaped being an imbecile. When I thought of the sleepy stubborn mules, the two days' ride, the fearful night at Djefâra, and contemplated the repetition of them, I gave way to disgust.

We went down to the beach and photographed, for want of anything better, three prostrate columns of considerable diameter. They were of beautiful cipolline, or pale green and white streaked marble, and had a little history of their own. Early in the century the Pasha of Tripoli presented to the British Government forty of the Lebda columns. The *Weymouth* was sent to embark them, and transported to England thirty-seven fine shafts, which were placed in the court of the British Museum. In the year 1824 they were transferred by order of George IV. to Windsor. The hatchways of the *Weymouth* would not admit the three cipolline shafts, and they were abandoned. Farther down by the beach were numerous others, also prepared for shipment by the late consul-general and his son. They are becoming rapidly disintegrated. Above these, on a sand-hill—no doubt accumulated round the wall of the original building—stood the only remnant of it, a melancholy crooked column: left, perhaps, facing the sea in order to serve as a landmark. Beneath it lay, among heaps of sand and fragments, the half of a female form in white marble. We trudged up farther inland, finding two white and beautifully-chiselled capitals lying on the sand.

The baking heat of the sun—it was approaching mid-day—drove us to the inadequate shelter of a few marble blocks. We had become sulky and discouraged, but dates and walnuts restored our cheerfulness. On the hill above us were a party of negroes carrying baskets to and fro. We shouted to them, asking for water, and they directed us eastward beyond some rising ground: and here we found a small clear stream, running nearly due northwards, over a sandy and rather slimy bed, down into the sea. At its mouth, once the Cothon or dock of Leptis, were masses of heavy masonry: and visible below the clear green water were remains of two moles. On the east bank were traces of a dock for smaller craft, though the Cothon could not have accommodated very large vessels. These masses of stonework are being slowly buried by the alluvial deposit of the stream, now called Wadi Lebda. The painstaking Dr. Barth made an examination of the site of Lebda, during his wanderings along the Mediterranean coast, and his book is worthy of translation from the German. It is of course printed in the small Gothic type so painful and tiring to the eyes: and responsible, I am satisfied, for the frequency of spectacles and weakened eyesight among Germans.

Across the river lay numerous ruins of the aqueduct, which once carried to Lebda the waters of the Ciniphus, flowing from the spurs of the Gharian known to

Etched by Edwin Edwards.   RUINS ON THE RIVER OF LEPTIS.   From a Photograph by the Author.

the ancients as the Hills of the Graces. Near them were some large reservoirs and numerous baths, adjacent to a circus—once ornamented with obelisks and columns: and above them were the vestiges of a theatre.

Looking up the river, and on its left or western bank, was an encouraging sight—an extensive and picturesque group of ruins, walls, doorways, a fort or temple, a Roman arch, and other miscellaneous objects, which must have been once a prominent feature in Leptis the White. We strolled up the wet hard sand by the river, and coming within range we photographed the group of buildings, reflected in a clear pool where a mass of masonry had dammed a portion of the stream. Two or three negroes came down from their work to drink in the river. Wallah! they said, as they saw the camera, but they thought poorly of it when they saw no result. They even laughed mockingly at Annibale, as he dozed in the shadow of a wall, and hinted that he was a Kafir.

We climbed up through the sinking sand, and over blocks of fallen masonry, marble pediments, and walls, to the middle of the group of buildings. On the brink of the river stood the corner of a building—rectangular without and circular within—two storeys in height still. The exterior was of cemented rubble, having at intervals a few courses of flat red bricks: the interior was faced with carefully hewn stone. There were traces of stairs, but they were too ruinous for climbing with agility in the hot sun. From this ran northward along the top of the river bank a straight wall, having brick and rubble masonry without and hewn stone within. Great heaps of the white facing lay in long rows, with cornices, jambs, pediments, and slabs. Masses of the concrete had fallen into the river bed. At the south end of the crescent-shaped wall was a fracture, from which had fallen into the river a huge block, weighing perhaps a hundred tons, solid and cohesive just as it had fallen.

From the angle of the semicircular wall ran at right angles a gateway, with a round arch of considerable size. It is still complete, but threatens to yield before long. The sill is visible, worn with foot and hoof marks. This was the entrance to the temple: of which the western wall contained two handsome doorways, also complete, though the white stone was honeycombed and crumbling: and within the enclosure ran a line of white cubical pedestals which supported the inner columns of the temple. At the farther end of the west wall a triple doorway, two-thirds buried, led into an inner temple, which was almost full of drift sand. A few battered and shivered cipolline columns stood here. The Moslems had smashed all of them that they could reach: indeed the sand has to be thanked for burying what must be rich traces of this city. Here the warlike

Severus, familiar in our English history, began his days in the year of Christ 146, ending them at York Eboracum has now the advantage over Leptis. In the angle of the temple court the sand had piled itself up to the height of the spring of the round arch.

We went on to the open space to the southward. On either side of the river the ground is covered with walls, masonry, vaultings, cisterns, fallen cornices, and fragments of every size and shape, lying in sand and brushwood. We came to a fine triple arch or city gate, relatively free from drift sand. We strolled on towards the fringe of palms, beyond which lies the open plain. We came to a Bedouin *doûar*, squatting among the palms: and while I photographed the scene, the inhabitants fearing, poor people, the evil eye with its brass rim directed upon them, took refuge in the tents. Yelping dogs flew at us, and we could hardly persuade the Bedouins to give us a bowl of milk. It was sour when we got it, and undrinkable: but the Bedouins considered themselves underpaid by the piastre Giovanni gave them for it. We came back to a small picturesque arch, once perhaps a suburban gateway, looking to the south: then again past the triple arch to the central group of ruins.

Although of the period when Roman art was on its decline, the public buildings of Leptis are admitted to have been of great magnificence. Indeed, from the remains which have been found of granite and marble monoliths, no cost can have been spared in its construction. The statuary seems to have been of the worst taste, and the ornamentation florid and profuse. Amphoræ, pateræ, intaglios, Carthaginian medals, and coins of Severus, Julia mother of Caracalla, and Alexander Severus, have been found here. The temple, its court and inner shrine, the vacant pedestals and melancholy pile of white and yellow marbles, suggested scenes very different. There is something especially sad and lonely about the ruins of Lebda. So fair a city is now so complete a wreck.

We ascended the hill, and found on its crest a gang of fifteen or twenty negroes, with a Maltese overseer, hard at work excavating. They had come upon the site of a temple, of which the noble red granite columns still stood erect under the sand. They had excavated a huge hole, and length by length the columns were being removed, and placed ready for transport to Homs. This disgraceful traffic is destroying what remains of Lebda's glories. Maltese and low Mediterranean traders in Homs are growing rich upon the sale of columns. They have been doing this since the beginning of the century; and unless some one interferes, future travellers will have to seek for ruins of Leptis in the olive-mills of Tripoli, Sfax, Susa, and the other Barbary ports. Invaluable as olive-crushers, the

shafts are being shipped wholesale for sale to the oil-merchants. One Maltese, who came penniless to Homs, has now a shop of his own and is doing well. We gave the poor hard-worked Africans a piece of money each, though it went to my heart to see what they were about.

Leo Africanus says—'*Of the towne of Lepide* : This ancient towne, founded by the Romans, and enuironed with most high and strong walles, hath twise been sacked by the Mahumetans, and of the stones and ruins thereof was Tripolis afterwards built.' Leo seldom made a mistake, and it requires much more than the drifting of sand to account for the disappearance of great buildings and their materials: but Leptis was not destroyed till the seventh century, and Tripoli was built before Aurelian's time. Leo should have said 'rebuilt.' Unlike Palmyra, where the temples and palaces still lie piecemeal on the ground, and need only the work of man to restore them, Leptis lies within easy reach of the sea, and her materials have vanished bodily.

Leptis, afterwards called Magna from its wealth and importance, was founded, as I have said, at an early period by the indefatigable Sidonians: and next to Carthage and its neighbour Utica, it was regarded as the chief among their foreign settlements. Surviving the first Carthage, it flourished under the protection and government of Rome. The Leptians, though retaining their Phœnician laws and customs, had, from constant intercourse and alliance with the Numidians or Berbers, adopted their language, and retained it in the time of Sallust and the Jugurthine wars. During this period Leptis, being threatened with civil disturbances and attacked by the Numidians, sent deputies to the Consul Metellus, who commanded in Africa, praying for a garrison. The city having been true to Rome from the commencement of the Numidian wars, Metellus sent four cohorts of Ligurians, and relieved the city.

During the Vandal occupation of Barbary, the fortifications of Leptis seem to have been dismantled: to be restored in the days of Justinian, who required it as a strategical point. Once Leptis was closely invested by a Berber tribe, known to the Romans as Levatæ. Eighty of the Lewâteh were admitted to Sergius the Prefect's presence, to complain of certain wrongs. One of the petitioners, in his eagerness seizing the robe of Sergius, was slain by an officer, and this was the signal for the massacre of the remainder of the deputation. After one bloody and successful sally, Sergius was again shut up here, and so hardly pressed that he had to abandon the city and retire along the seacoast to Carthage.

There is a picturesque legend in connection with this city over whose ruins we are brooding. When Cyrene and Carthage were in their glory, the vast sandy waste separating them having no river or mountain they could regard as a boundary, long and bloody disputes took place. Tired of these, the rival powers agreed that from each capital should set out simultaneously certain deputies : the spot where the respective deputies should meet should be the boundary thereafter.

Two brothers—Philæni—set out from Carthage, and, travelling swiftly, outstripped the more dilatory Cyrenians, encountering them on the shores of Leptis. Enraged, and fearing the vengeance of their countrymen, the Cyrenians began to pick a quarrel, and declared they would 'fix' the Carthaginians, who must have started before their appointed time. They gave them the option of withdrawing to the spot the Cyrenians desired as boundary, or of being buried alive where they stood. The disinterested Philæni, for the welfare and glory of their fatherland, chose the latter alternative, and were interred, living, somewhere in the neighbourhood of these ruins. Here the Carthaginians erected altars, and instituted at Carthage religious solemnities in their honour. We were on the point of shedding a tear to the memory of the Philæni, when we referred to our chart, and discovered that the Cyrenians must have travelled from seventy to eighty miles more than the Carthaginians.

In the tide of Mohammedanism which swept along this coast, the walls and temples of Leptis were demolished, and the city was wiped out from the page of history.

The famous gulf upon whose skirts we are, extending hence to Ptolemaïta in the Cyrenaïca, nearly four hundred miles, is said by the ancients to have acquired its name from the frequent dragging or shifting of its bed. When the winds blow violently, the sea rolls with a prodigious swell, and mud, sand, and stones of vast size are forced along by the rapidity of the current. Even half a century ago the Great Gulf of Syrtis retained its evil reputation. Mariners pass, said Della Cella, with a sort of horror before this gulf, whose annals from the remotest ages abound with shipwreck and disaster.

Misrâtah is the last town towards the desert of the Syrtis, and three hundred miles distant from Benghasi, the Cyrenian Berenice. Caravans still go from Misrâtah to Fezzân and Wadâi. In the time of Leo Africanus Misrâtah was the boundary of the independent kingdom of Barca. Couriers used, till the introduction of steamers to the Mediterranean, to traverse this region, from Tripoli to Cairo, in from twenty-five to thirty days. The journey through Fezzân, the ancient Phazania, the country of the Garamantes, was familiar to the ancients, and used by them in conveyance of precious stones &c. from Egypt and Arabia to Europe. All the way to the frontier of Egypt are traces of prosperity and civilisation long since dissipated. These culminate in the noble ruins of Libya Pentapolis.

CHAPTER VI.

Return to Hŏms—A Deputation—The Kaïd's Hospitality—Copper Coins—The Dead City—Start for Tripoli—Wearisome Journey—The Gharian—A Wedding—Djefâra in the Twilight—The Owl-slayer—Continue Journey—Great Heat—The Mecca Caravan—A Bargain—Tadjoûra—The Hermitage—Frederick Warrington—The Times of the Beys—The Harbour—Mussulman Fanaticism—The Bazaars.

THE hot sun was declining over the town of Homs as we turned our backs on the ruins of Lebda. Very wearily we mounted the poor patient half-baked mules, and trudged homewards. So exhausted were we, that one circumstance alone could have exhilarated and cheered us. That circumstance occurred. Giovanni's mule took a header into a quagmire, and tossed his rider into the midst of it.

We found some lemons in Homs, and prepared great quantities of lemonade. After a large dinner, prepared by the Maltese, I devoured dates and walnuts. After this I thought well to send a message of thanks to the Kaïd.

I chose Giovanni as the deputation, and sent my card, with Rae Effendi's compliments to the governor of Homs. Giovanni was to assure the Kaïd that I should long remember his hospitality and the interest of my journey to Lebda; that I should take an early opportunity of acquainting the Pasha of Tripoli with both; and that I hoped one day to have the honour and the happiness of receiving the Kaïd in England. Giovanni was to add that fatigue alone prevented my thanking the Kaïd in person. Giovanni was to ask too, with delicacy—seeing we were not lodged in the Castle itself—whether I was to consider myself as the Kaïd's guest.

After this carefully-framed message, it will seem repugnant to belief that Giovanni should have actually started for the audience in his shirt-sleeves. The cry with which I called Annibale's attention to it galvanised that youth into agility, and he had overtaken and brought back Giovanni in a twinkling. I asked Giovanni what opinion the Kaïd could entertain of an expedition of which the chief dragoman presented himself in the audience-chamber of the Castle without his coat, and how he could be expected to receive any future expedition with consideration. I told Giovanni that the coat was almost invariably worn at audiences in the best circles, and he seemed moved.

In half an hour Giovanni returned, accompanied by an officer, whom the polite Kaïd had sent to bring me an expression of his friendly regard. I was to consider myself as strictly his guest : he was gratified to hear I was pleased with Lebda, and ashamed not to have been able to entertain me more suitably.

Later in the evening, as I was strolling on the terrace or house-top, the officer returned, bearing an envelope which contained the Kaïd's card, Réfi Gouverneur de Pera, and his photograph, in exchange for which he asked that I would be so uncommonly kind as to send him mine from England. He wished to know how many soldiers I should like, to escort me to Tripoli : but I thanked him, and said I required none. Poor Kaïd ! it was a change from Pera to Homs.

By-and-by a native of Homs appeared with a few Roman copper coins, which he wished me to buy. These abound in the ruins of Barbary; and so plentiful are they, that here and in Misrâtah they pass current in the bazaars for their equivalent copper value. My visitor refused for half-a-dozen of the coins, a *mahboob* and a half, for which I afterwards bought a hundred and twenty similar coins in Kairwân.

It was a glorious night. The sky overhead was like a cupola of deep blue steel set with diamonds, resting with a silver rim upon the sea. The restless surge fringed the sea with white, and the white sand gleamed in the starlight. A mile away lay the melancholy buildings of the dead city.

We were up two hours before dawn, and lost no time

in having everything packed on the mules. The air was raw, and a chill breeze came up from the sea, as we rode past the Castle and its silent watchmen. I was glad of a long-hooded coat, and even of the exercise necessary for stimulating my mule.

I will not describe the length and loneliness of that weary journey, the apathy and stupidity of Annibale and the two Arabs, the prosy self-commendations of Giovanni, the sleepiness and stubbornness of the mules. How many times I shouted to Annibale, in what startling language I denounced his laziness, in what terms I described his inevitable decline and fall, I will not weary the reader by repeating. Passing acres of ruins among the mountains, we emerged on to the tedious plain, remote from the sea, and having glimpses of it only at intervals.

In the afternoon, as we travelled along, we heard the frequent reports of guns, and presently came in sight of a concourse of people. The sounds had aroused expectations of a battle, a skirmish, or even an execution: but the affair proved to be a mere wedding. When Annibale heard the joyful shouts, the firing of the guns, the galloping of horses, and could see the Bedouin bride in a brilliant red dress, he was eager to join the crowd. But I told him, in severe Italian, that we were making this journey for strictly intellectual purposes, and not to go fooling about at weddings. I was sorry afterwards not to have gone, taken the bride's portrait, and proposed the health of the groomsman.

We were sad all the way to Djefâra, which we reached an hour before sunset. The needy-looking Kaïd greeted me with a cordial *marhâba*—welcome—and after a cup of coffee, at which he and his officers, three tall fine-looking Arabs, assisted, we sallied forth to take a picture of this forlorn and lonely Castle. They squatted on the ground in front of an angle of the wall: a few loafers, who were the only remaining inhabitants of the Castle, stood round : and, in the light of the rapidly-sinking sun, we took a photograph of the spot. We retired to the Castle—the Kaïd giving up to me his small room, as before. Being very tired, and wishing to make an early start for Tripoli, I went to bed shortly after sunset.

My toilet, before retiring, which had to be performed with a bucket and cold water from the well, excited the greatest interest. The tooth-brushes were chiefly admired.

While thus engaged, I heard the report of a gun, and Annibale appeared, highly excited, carrying a dying owl. I reproached him, and so dwelt upon the evil fortune certain to accompany the assassination of an owl, that Annibale began to look upon himself as doomed to misfortune, like the Ancient Mariner after he had murdered the albatross. When Annibale awoke in the night from time to time, and heard the mournful squawk of the widower owl, which haunted the Castle yard, he did not feel at his ease. I stole a march on the rats, mules, owl, fleas, and cocks: and, once asleep, defied their efforts.

Awaking much refreshed, an hour after midnight, we arose, breakfasted, and in the chilly moonlight rode away from the Castle of Djefâra. We rode for some hours before the day appeared, and got a famous start before the heat. It was fortunate, for the sun was overpowering. When we rested on the sand for lunch, without so much as the shelter of a dwarf palm, it was sickening and almost unendurable. No breath of air from sea or plain or the cloudless sky came to our relief. We were glad to get into motion again: even the exertion of urging on the mules was a welcome change.

Soon we met the Mecca caravan, just returned from the Haj by sea to Tripoli. Many of the pilgrims were on camels, mixed up with quilts, pots, pans, and vessels of water from the sacred well of Zemzem. Many of them were white-bearded and fat, chiefs of tribes in Fezzân, full of arrogance and bigotry after their journey, and regarding the Roumi on his mule with especial displeasure and contempt. Some muttered curses as the camels swayed past us—others growled, *Kafir*! One man on foot, towards the end of the caravan, hissed

Khanzir! I had some thought of sending the Nihilist to recall the whole caravan, that they might apologise.

We made our second halt on the welcome arrival at the skirts of the palm forest of Tadjoûra. I think we should have made a third, if the dates and walnuts had not given out.

Giovanni had had a hard bargain with an Arab of Tadjoûra, who had caught two big fish at a spot on the lonely coast, and had accompanied us for two or three miles on our way towards his home. It had been reduced to a question of half a piastre between them, and rather than yield, the Arab went off a quarter of a mile in advance. Giovanni was much disappointed when I told them to call him back, as I would pay the half piastre. He was not even satisfied when I paid for the two fish altogether, and made him a present of them. He felt that I had spoiled a good bargain, and that the Tadjoûran had got the better of him.

We entered the palms, and rode quietly for hours, the mules being very tired and able to go but slowly. The *siniehs*, and their creaking pulleys, the long lines of mud wall, the fig trees and pomegranates, the Arab huts, and occasional marabouts, seemed like high civilisation and like getting home.

At one in the afternoon, when within two miles of Tripoli, two horsemen met us. Osman Warrington and a young lad, well mounted and armed, were on their way down to Homs, to bring back with an escort the Maltese murderer, for preliminary examination in Tripoli. Osman Warrington told me his brother would much appreciate a visit from me: so taking Giovanni with me, and sending the others on to the city, I turned off through the palm woods towards the seashore, and reached Mr. Warrington's house—the Hermitage. It is a curious rambling house, built of wood and plaster, looking on to the seashore out of a picturesque garden of palms, lemons, oranges, and pomegranates. A little black boy with bright eyes and glittering teeth went to summon Mr. Warrington, who shortly appeared.

A tall man, with white hair and pleasant voice— son of the well-known consul-general here — born in the Regency, and familiar with every part of it, Frederick Warrington had been the foster-father of African exploration from this point, and had gained the esteem of every traveller who had come to the Regency to penetrate into the interior. Rohlfs, Richardson, Vogel, Lyon, Beechey, Overweg, Barth— he knew them all, and had accompanied many of them far on their way.

Tripoli has been with German travellers the favourite starting point for inner Africa, and some of them have shown noble examples of courage and perseverance. Frederick, as every one in Tripoli calls him, showed me the portraits of many of them. Several never returned. He would have accompanied the unfortunate Miss Tinne, but disapproved of the tempting nature of the equipage. There were costly horses, maidservants handsomely dressed, and iron tanks slung on camels to carry water. Ah! said the Bedouins, there are the treasure chests of the Roumi princess. Had Frederick Warrington been escorting her, her life might have been safe. Respected by the Arabs, his presence would protect the traveller where other safeguards might not: and many a Tripoli Arab's oath is By Frederick.

He gave me a long history of his recollections of Tripoli and the interior: his travels, the caravans, the life at Ghadâmes and at Murzoûk, capital of Fezzân, at each of which places he was vice-consul: the old days of his boyhood, when Consul Warrington ruled the Bey of Tripoli: the splendours of Yussuf Pasha's Court, the fiery old man's eccentricities, his grand receptions of the foreign consuls: the decline of his influence, civil dissensions, and finally Tripoli's absorption into the Ottoman dominions. In Fezzân, and especially near Murzoûk, the palm forests are most extensive. One can ride through them for days together, and for many a week dates used to be the only diet.

A Turkish bath was a very agreeable finale to the

journey, and I emerged from it refreshed, but feeling rather as the American traveller felt, like a disembodied spirit. We went to stroll on the beach. Passing the citadel, we saw the benevolent Moustapha Pasha issuing forth in his carriage to take the air. Soldiers were drawn up in two ranks, and saluted as he passed. When Yussuf Pasha used to go forth from the Castle, he had a body-guard of seven hundred blacks.

One morning early we went out to fish in the harbour. We landed on the extremity of the reef, and fished up lovely spiked sea-eggs, while the gentle surge washed over the rocks. The white-walled city and palms looked picturesque under the bright blue sky. Across the harbour we could hear the music of a body of Turkish troops, exercising on the beach under the Castle.

We found an Arab, who had just hauled into his boat a long object coated with shells and gravel conglomerate. It was a mediæval arquebuse, weighing probably a hundredweight. We landed on a small jetty now being constructed in an exposed inconvenient spot, and which should have been placed under the shelter of the Castle walls. We paddled out farther along the shore, and landed close to a ruined earthwork, towards the Sultanas' Domes, the tombs of the ladies of the last Beys. We entered the palm groves, and took several photographs of those stately trees of which the eye never wearies.

After lunch Mr. Hay called. I described to him the appropriations which were going on at Lebda, and he said readily that he would bring the matter before the Pasha. An order would be given which probably would never be carried out, and the matter would be forgotten directly. I suggested that the Government were the losers, and that the Kaïd of Homs, if he were authorised to fine anyone pilfering from the ruins, would keep a vigilant eye upon them. Mr. Hay promised to see the Pasha.

The murder at Homs had shocked the Europeans in Tripoli. Thanks to the vigilance and harassing to which suspicious characters are subjected on arriving in the Regency, they seldom settle : and crime is, taking everything into consideration, rather rare. A story had reached Tripoli of the murder of an Italian by a Maltese in Tunis, of an apprehended outbreak of Mussulman fanaticism, and of unusual precautions urged upon Christian residents in Tunis.

Mr. Hay promised to endeavour to get permission for me to visit the mosques of Tripoli, but he was a little doubtful of success.

Accompanied by an obliging Maltese clerk, who, like an enormous number of his countrymen, was quite innocent of the English language, I daily repaired to the barbers' shops to negotiate for the old inlaid hand-mirrors. The adhesiveness of their owners to them compared favourably with that of a Russian peasant to his household gods. Each barber too, before selling, was waiting to see what his neighbour got for his mirror.

One of my chief friends in the bazaars was a Moorish barber of Sfax—with the manners of an Abencerrage, and the handsomest man in Tripoli. His smile was charming and his expressions of regard were most courteous. He regretted, he said, a thousand times over, that he could not sell me one of his mirrors, which had belonged to his father: and he was so pleasant that it would have been rudeness to refer to the subject again. He wore a rosebud under his snowy turban, a grey pointed beard, dark blue cloth dress, an embroidered sash, and had handsome brown legs. Another friend was a merchant who sold traysfull of *rahatlakoom*, having walnuts concealed in it: and he thought so highly of my capacity for this, that he begged me to go to his house and see how he made it.

I knew the contents of every little drawer and cabinet in the silversmiths' bazaar. Sitting in one shop, the neighbours would bring me what they had to show. Nearly all the silver-work was sold by the weight—which we could have verified by the *Muhhtasib*, or public weigher of the bazaar—and a trifle was added for the workmanship. All the silver bore the fine old silver mark, and was unmistakably pure. All manner of things were brought—amulets, bracelets, very massive and handsome, earrings large enough for necklaces, loaded with pendants: many of them having as a pendant the *khmissa*, or outspread hand, to avert the evil eye. The upper rim of the ear is pierced to carry these: one of the pendants is often attached to the hair or cap to relieve the ear : but the ears of many of the women are torn and frilled round the edges. And yet we attribute to women a want of fortitude. These and other earrings—if women were aware of it—are the next most becoming thing to wearing no earrings at all.

Gold, silver, and copper coins used to be brought me. Some of the copper ones would have been dear if they had been of silver. I got a little coin of Carthage, of yellow gold, bearing the horse and palm tree. This piece of money had about the diameter of a lead pencil, and would have been very easy to lose.

A little Arabic is a valuable possession in these dealings with the crafty Oriental: it establishes in his mind that you have been among his kindred before, and have learned cunning through adversity. It is impossible for him to ascertain how much you don't know, and he gives you often credit for more than you deserve. Arabic, however, like French, is not learnt in a day. How long have you spent in learning French? said a French gentleman to an English one. Only one day, said the Englishman. Ah! said the Frenchman politely, 'tis not enough.

CHAPTER VII.

The Pasha's Gardens—Ostriches—John Leo on the Naturall Historie of Barbarie—Tombs and Coins—Giovanni incorruptible—The Triumphal Arch of Aurelian—Roman Numerals—Prayers for Rain—Offering to the God of Rain—Alteration of Plans—Cyrene in Prospect—The Cyrenaïca.

ONE evening before dinner we drove out past the Sultanas' Domes, to the Pasha's Gardens in the Meshîah. They were very productive and picturesque—full of lemon trees, oranges, palms, and all kinds of vegetables. In one part of them was the Pasha's private menagerie. This consisted of a bull—a magnificent creature—from Bornôu, in the country of the Blacks: several dainty little gazelles: certain odd-looking beasts resembling, as far as I can recollect, a goat, a Thibet Yak, and a Brahmin bull. Finally, a number of ostriches were ranging about. These are brought in great numbers from the interior, and were formerly kept here in stables and farmed for the sake of their feathers. The long painful journey, however, injured the poor creatures' feathers, and they are now plucked in the interior and the feathers brought by caravan.

One camel, I was informed, could carry as much as ten thousand pounds' worth of fine white feathers.

The ostrich, far from resenting the spoiling of his feathers, is multiplying in the regions of Fezzân, Wadâi, and Tomboûkto, and seems to thrive upon it. He is a singular bird, having eccentric tastes. These ostriches made incessant and furious pecks at a ring on my companion's finger. They seemed fascinated and unable to resist it. I gave them pieces of newspaper, which delighted them. They thought they had never tasted anything so nice, for they came again and again, disputing who should get the best pieces. We tried the chief ostrich with a piastre—a showy-looking coin—and the ostrich made three attempts to swallow it. Some scruple seemed to actuate him, and we found eventually that the piastre was of imitation silver.

It has been related to me that an elderly gentleman with a bald head once entered a zoological garden. It was a warm afternoon, and the old gentleman lay down upon a bench to sleep. Presently he was awakened by a feeling of warmth in the head. An ostrich had come along, and mistaking the bald head for an egg, had settled down upon it, intending to hatch it. The old gentleman screamed for help, and eventually the ostrich, disappointed and regretful, was led back to his stall by a keeper. A gentleman once went and furtively contributed some money to an ostrich. After doing so his conscience smote him, and he went back guiltily day after day in dread of seeing the ostrich a body : but the bird continued as lively and voracious as ever. An ostrich has digested as many as twenty copper coins at a time.

The gazelle, which abounds in the interior, is hunted with dogs. The gazelle takes great leaps and easily distances the dogs; but becoming exhausted, especially in heavy sand, is overtaken and caught. The young are brought in great numbers to Tripoli. The gazelle at Mr. England's, who, with his neighbour the little kid, sometimes fraternises with me, and at another time trembles from head to foot, is an orphan gazelle brought from Ghadâmes.

Near the gazelles was a lonely camel, who put out his head and roared like a lion.

I cannot, while on the subject of African beasts, refrain from the pleasure of repeating a little natural history from that wonderful and droll old geographer, Leo Africanus. It is from the Ninth Booke of the Historie of Africa, wherein he entreateth of the principall Riuers and of the strange liuing Creatures of the same Countrey.

Of the Camel.—Camels are gentle and domesticall beasts, and are found in Africa in great numbers, especially in the Deserts of Libya, Numidia, and Barbaria. When the King of Tombuto is desirous to sende any message of importance vnto the Numidian Merchants with great celeritie, his post or messenger riding vpon one of these Camels will runne from Tombuto to Darha, being nine hundred miles distant, in the space of eight daies at the farthest.

Of the beast called Adimmain. — It is a tame beast, being shaped like a ramme and of the stature of an asse, and hauing long and dangle eares. I myselfe vpon a time, being merily disposed, rode a quarter of a mile vpon the backe of one of these beasts.

Of the Elephant. — This wittie beast keepeth in the woods, and is found in great numbers in the forrests of the land of Negros. If the Elephant intendeth to hurt any man, he casteth him on the groũd with his long snout or trunk, and neuer ceaseth trampling vpon him till he be dead.

Of the beast called Dabuh.—This beast in bignes and shape resembleth a woolfe—sauing that his legges and feet are like to the legges and feete of a man. It is not hurtfull vnto any other beast, but will rake the carcases of men out of their graues, and will deuoure them: being otherwise an abiect and silly creature. The hunters being acquainted with his denne, come before it singing and playing vpon a drum: by which melodie being allured foorth, his legs are enwrapped in a strong rope, and so he is drawne out and slaine.

Of the creature called Dub.—This creature, living also in the deserts, resembleth in shape a lizzard: sauing that in length it containeth a cubite and in bredth fower fingers. Being flaied and rosted it tasteth somewhat like a frogge. Being hunted, if it chanceth to thrust its head into a hole, it can by no force be drawne out except the hole be digged wider by the hunters.

Of the Guaral.—This beast is like vnto the former, and hath poison both in the head and taile, which two parts being cut off, the Arabians will eate it, notwithstanding it be of a deformed shape and vgly colour, in which respects I loathed alwaies to eate the flesh thereof.

Somewhat we will here say of the strange birdes and fowles of Africa, and first of the *Ostriche*. This fowle liueth in dry deserts and layeth to the number of ten or twelue egges in the sandes: which, being about the bignes of great bullets, waigh fifteene pounds apiece. But the Ostriche is of so weake a memorie that shee presently forgetteth the place where her egges were laide, and afterward the same or some other Ostriche-henne finding the saide egges by chance, hatcheth and fostereth them as if they were certainly her owne. The chickens are no sooner crept out of the shell, but they prowle vp and downe the deserts for their foode. The Ostriche is a silly and deafe creature, feeding vpon anything which it findeth, be it hard and indigestible as yron.

Of the Camelion.—The Camelion, being of the shape and bignes of a Lizzard, is a deformed crooked and leane creature, hauing a long and slender tayle like a mouse, and being of a slowe pace. It is nourished by the element of ayer and the sunbeames, at the rising whereof it gapeth and turneth itselfe vp and downe. It changeth the colour according to the varietie of places where it commeth, being sometimes blacke and sometimes greene.

Of the fowle called Nesir.—This is the greatest fowle in all Africa, and exceedeth a Crane in bignes. This bird liueth a long time, and myselfe have seene many of them unfeathered by reason of extreme old age: wherefore, having cast all their feathers, they returne vnto their nest as if they were newly hatched, and are there nourished by the yoonger birds of the same kinde.'

The Arabic writer El Khazwini says: There is in certain of the Islands a bird of enormous size called *Rukh*, that feedeth its young ones with elephants. This is something like a bird, and makes us feel sorry for Leo's *Nesir*.

We went to call on Mr. Warrington, who kindly gave me some old Roman pottery, found in a tomb ten feet underground, in his garden—two clay lamps, two lachrymatories, and a little saucer. It must be hard to express the deep and solid satisfaction of being the possessor of an unopened mound or early burial-place. I can think of no greater worldly enjoyment than going in the twilight to gloat over it—picturing jars of glass or pottery, golden spoons, or arrow-heads—reluctant to break the spell of fifteen or twenty centuries, the charm of the unknown. Mr. Warrington gave me a number of copper coins, some found in the tomb and others which had been brought to him by the Arabs. In the tomb were two glass urns of large size and very perfect.

We drove back in the dusk, having to use much caution to avoid great holes dug by former inhabitants as granaries, and which in places stretched half across the road. Arriving at the house, we found Giovanni in high altercation with the old Arab muleteer who had accompanied us to Lebda. The Arab had postponed asking for payment in the hope of inducing Giovanni to join him, by a promise of half the spoil, in an attempt upon my pocket. The old Maltese, having his conscience superior to indirect suggestions, denounced him to me, so that the Arab very nearly lost his backsheesh.

I went out early to photograph the eastern face of the Roman Arch, which stands in sight of our windows, and within a few paces of the Consulate. I mounted on the flat roof of a foudoûk opposite.

This triumphal arch—one of the most ornate and florid pieces of work the Romans ever constructed—stands in a narrow street between the Consulate and the Marina, facing nearly east and west. It is constructed of pure white marble, uncemented. The arches are built up with wood and plaster, and the keeper of a low wine-shop has established himself in front of it. The interior serves as a cellar for the storage of liquors.

It is, very roughly speaking, a square, and was originally a cube: a portion of it being embedded in the ground, its proportions are interfered with. The eastern front is much defaced: the northern face completely built in. Of the western, only the upper right hand corner and a small portion of the arch are visible. Here is some beautiful carving, the figure of Victory erect in a chariot drawn by a pair of she-leopards. The figure and chariot are mutilated. Above, on the architrave, is a clear Latin inscription in large characters:—

> IMP. CÆS. AVRELIO. ANTONIN. AVG. PP. ET.
> IMP. CÆS. L. AVRELIO. VERO. ARMENIACO. AVG.
> SER. S. ORFITVS. PROCCOS. CVM. VTTEDIO.
> MARCELLO. LEG. SVO. DEDICAVIT. C.
> CALPVRNIVS. CELSVS. CVRATOR. MVNERIS
> PVB. MVNERARIVS. IIVIR. Q. Q. FLAMEN
> PERPETVVS. ARCṼ. MARMORE. SOLIDO. FECIT.

To the Emperor Cæsar Aurelius Antoninus Augustus Father of his Country, and to the Emperor Cæsar Lucius Aurelius Verus Armeniacus Augustus, Servius

Scipio Orfitus Proconsul, with Uttedius (?) Marcellus, his Lieutenant, dedicated: Caius Calpurnius Celsus, manager of the public games, Curator, Quinquennial Duumvir, and Flamen of Quirinus for life, made the arch in solid marble.

Marcus Aurelius did not need this monument to his memory: his fine memoir of his adopted father is monument enough. The joint Emperors Aurelius and Verus reigned in the latter half of the second century.

There was formerly upon the arch a Punic inscription. It was, however, detached, sent to England, and presented by H.M. the Queen to the British Museum. Gesenius says: Exstat etiam titulus Punicus in arcu triumphali Tripolitano, quem ætate Septimii Severi, ipsique anno P. Christum N. 203, vindicatum ivimus.

At each angle of the building is a recess which once contained a statue, destroyed long since by the Moslems, being contrary to their religion. The interiors of the recesses are of plain hewn marble: the lintels and jambs beautifully moulded and carved. The marble has taken stains of grey and yellow: the carvings and mouldings throughout, where not defaced and worn, are extremely delicate and clear.

The interior is a square, minus the recesses mentioned above. In the centre is a dome of marble, formed without cement: each block panelled deeply, with decorated borders, and having in the centre of each panel a rose in relief. The four spaces round the dome are likewise panelled and ornamented. There is but little injury done to the interior: and if cleared out and cleaned, and the plaster partitions removed, it would be a most picturesque and interesting monument.

In Colonel Playfair's Footsteps of Bruce there is an elaborate and graphic description of this arch, illustrated by a beautiful Indian ink drawing.

The western face could not be photographed until early in the afternoon: and Peppo was posted to watch from the windows, and instructed to rush suddenly out and inform me directly the sunlight fell upon the leopards.

The Latin character and numerals are both clear and handsome: but it has often struck me that to multiply or divide, in the latter, must have been a severe trial. The reader may amuse himself by dividing MDCCCLXXVII by LXXVII, and see how he likes it.

It was market-day, and half the population were out at the Soukh buying provisions.

I dined in the evening with Mr. Hay and his family, and spent a most agreeable evening. Mrs. Hay showed me presents from native chiefs: beautiful work from the country of the Blacks, rugs in blue and white, parchment boxes stained in red patterns, baskets woven of palm leaves and coloured cloth by negro women, leopard skins, &c.

I was awakened one morning by the chanting of children: and throwing the windows open, I found a band of them, headed by an old tangle-bearded Arab, swarming down the narrow alley. They were praying for rain, and moving in procession all through the city. The Moors regard the prayers of children as more acceptable to the Divinity than those of their elders. The heat was very great, the wells were becoming exhausted, and unless rain should come soon, many poor Arabs would be half-ruined. The Pasha himself, I was told—barefooted and bareheaded—went to the mosque, and afterwards down to the beach to throw stones into the sea.

We went down to the shore. At a well of brackish water a number of Arabs were engaged, raising water by a *sinieh* into a tank, whence other men drew casks full and loaded them on camels. These were taken down to the water's edge and emptied into the sea. A gutter, too, was cut in the beach, to let the overflow water run into the sea. *Zapati* were watching that no one touched or used the water which was being offered to God. This melancholy superstition is observed during a failure of rain.

My plans had a sudden dislocation this morning. A steamer's smoke was descried on the horizon, away beyond the reef. She steamed into the harbour and cast anchor. In another hour intelligence came that she was the Maltese steamer *Allegra*, sailing hence in a few days for Benghasi. This would be an excellent opportunity of visiting Cyrene. Since the land telegraph through Barca to Egypt became defunct, communications are very infrequent with Benghasi. From Benghasi the *Allegra* was to sail to Malta, and I should thence reach Tunis. I decided to adopt this route. Dr. Camilleri, who had spent a considerable time in Cyrene, encouraged me, and helped me to form plans.

The plains of Barca and the peninsula of the Cyrenaïca are very extensive and beautiful, perhaps richer in vegetation than any country bordering upon the Mediterranean: and the climate is one of the finest in the world. The country is well watered: olives, dates, caroubs, cedars, arbutus, cypress, fig, myrtle, and evergreens grow luxuriantly. The ruins of the Pentapolis are very grand. The harbour is insecure, and the system of pilotage does not improve the access. The late pilot was a shopkeeper. Poor Cyrene! Failure of crops, famine, cattle plague, extortions of ten years, have brought her very low indeed. The sponge fishery alone seems to prosper of all this unlucky province's industries. As late as 1872, the slave trade existed to an enormous extent.

In the year 265 of the Hejreh, when El Abbas, grandson of Touloun, revolted against his father Ahmed, Sultan of Egypt, he seized upon the Cyrenaïca, the city of Leptis, and attacked Tripoli without success.

CHAPTER VIII.

Evening Ride—Esparto Grass—Black Families—An Ingrate—The *Allegra*—Usury, Caravans, and the Slave Trade—The Pashalik of Tripoli—Resources—Fall of the Leaf—Charity—Arab Home—Outer Bazaars—Love Charms—The Sheikh el Biled.

The vice-consul called to-day to say that no arrangement had yet been made for my visiting the mosques, and Frederick Warrington called later upon the same subject. He was in hopes of getting permission in a day or two, but it was a matter of arrangement both with the Castle and the Mufti.

We went out for a ramble. Mr. Warrington got a donkey for me, and we went to find his horse, a fine grey Barb, which was put up outside the Castle gate. In a yard which was crowded with esparto bales, was a rude screw press, in which the bales were being compressed. A screw descends upon the esparto from a platform above. The screw is driven round by half-a-dozen negroes, stamping and shouting in chorus. When the last turn is given, iron bands round the bales are riveted together, and the bale is rolled out into the yard. The hardness of these bales is astonishing. Hydraulic pressure was tried for packing them, but it was found to injure the fibre.

Esparto grass, which was known to the Tyrian colonists and Romans, resembles the beautiful feather grass of Southern Europe. Long used in the Spanish navy for cordage, and in Spain for the manufacture of baskets, shoes, and mats—most of the London Hansom cabs use them—it was first imported into England in 1862. In 1868 more than 500,000*l.* in value came into this country. Tunisia and Tripoli have taken it up, and it bids fair to replace some of the decayed industries of those Regencies. It is the best known material, next to rags and cotton, for the manufacture of paper. The first newspaper printed on paper manufactured from it was the *Akhbar* of Algiers. Homs is the chief and most convenient point for its shipment from this Regency. It grows in illimitable quantities in the Gharian range, and the only cost is that of pulling it up and transport. Who knows, Homs may yet revive or reflect some of Lebda's vanished prosperity.

The American consul in Tripoli has adopted the practice of protection of natives. Of course any Moor is glad to escape certain taxes, and to claim the interest of a powerful foreign government. As Mr. Warrington told me, if the English consul were to begin, he would have three thousand protégés in a week. To us the protection system seemed only to entail trouble and responsibility: but the American consul may have been right, and we incapable of understanding the lofty considerations contained in his head. The English are respected by Arabs of the interior: many of them have asked Frederick Warrington whether England means to take possession of the country.

Mr. Warrington recommended me not to go to Kairwân in the present uncomfortable state of feeling between Mohammedans and Christians. Some Tunisian Moors in the bazaar confirmed this advice. Within two months, as is well known, the ill feeling culminated. The French and German consuls in Salonica were assassinated: the populace marched through the town with drawn swords: the holy standard was hoisted. General panic existed in Constantinople. Softas and low class Mussulmen were purchasing arms and bidding Christians prepare for imminent death. The presence of European squadrons alone served to allay the fanatical excitement, and possibly to avert a Holy War. (I quote from the *Times*.)

Outside the garden wall was a miniature village of two or three black families, dependent upon Mr. Warrington. Their huts, resembling bee-hives, are most charmingly constructed. A bamboo framework, umbrella-like, crossed by horizontal rods, like degrees of longitude and latitude on a half globe, are covered with palm-leaf matting. The whole effect is snug and picturesque. The little black servant came out with us, and was pleased to see the impression the hives made upon us, for one of these was the home of Mahmoud's parents, and the two little india-rubber babies rolling about in one tent were own brother and sister to Mahmoud. The women were weaving beautiful boxes and dish-covers, of cane and palm leaf and little rags of red and black cloth. Mr. Warrington sent me a message a year after this. 'He begs of me to tell you that Mahmoud, the little black boy, kisses your hand and says Inshallah—please God—you will always have health and plenty of money.'

Mr. Warrington described these blacks as honest, faithful, and affectionate, excelling in good qualities the Arabs, who are generally strangers to gratitude. When Mr. Warrington returned from Fezzân he brought with him an Arab boy, whom he had cared for and adopted, but who turned out a thorough ingrate.

In the evening a young Maltese, son of the agent for the *Allegra*, came in to play cards. This steamer is reported to be the slowest steamer in the world. Some say she can steam four knots, some five with a fair breeze, but these are the more sanguine and reckless in statement. When I asked what the *Allegra* could do with a head wind, there was an awkward silence, which disquieted me when I thought of the voyage across the treacherous Gulf of Sidra. It is said that the look-out on this Skimmer of the Seas is kept over the stern, to warn off vessels coming up behind. The Maltese youth was engaged with his father in caravan ventures, pawnbroking, money-lending, and fleecing generally among the Arabs.

Usury here is an excellent mode of turning an honest piastre. The usurers get thirty, and even at times sixty per cent. interest on good security, though the maximum rate authorised by law is twelve per cent. In the year 1869 a bank was established under Government auspices, upon the condition of twelve and a half per cent., but one cannot wonder that it was not a success.

Salvatore's ventures in the caravan trade resulted sometimes in nothing, sometimes in a return of a thousand pounds upon a hundred. A partnership or bond is generally formed with a native, who has some available property in Tripoli affording a security for his good faith, and who accompanies and conducts the affairs of the caravan. Consisting of perhaps fifty or a hundred camels, loaded with goods of European manufacture, the caravan takes its departure for the interior; to be absent for a year, a year and a half, or two years, as the case may be. To Ghadâmes—the ancient Cydamus, one of the cities of the Garamantes—the journey occupies perhaps a fortnight: to Murzoûk, the capital of Fezzân, from thirty to forty days: to Wadâi five months:

to Tomboûkto the best part of a year. Caravans are constantly leaving and arriving at Tripoli.

Tripoli is now the centre of all the caravan trade of northern Africa. Tunis and Algeria have from various causes lost their footing in this lucrative business. Tripoli, too, as I have said before, is geographically situated more conveniently than other countries for the purpose, being connected with the interior by a chain of oases. The great Mecca caravan from Fez no longer traverses Barbary, Barca, and Egypt. In recent years three thousand pilgrims, conducted by a religious chief of Kairwân, with ten or fifteen thousand camels, would encamp for sometimes a month's repose under the walls of Tripoli. The commercial caravans carry coarse European cloths, silks, barracans or Arab wraps, powder, muskets, glass, hardware, beads, toys, looking-glasses, paper, real and false corals, imitation pearls, turbans, amber, porcelain, coffee cups, copper vessels, kaftans, embroidered muslins, handkerchiefs and cotton goods, essence of roses, and spices.

Murzoûk is a great centre of this trade. Hither the European goods are brought and exchanged for those of the interior—gold dust, senna, ostrich feathers, red alum, alkali, ivory, and, till comparatively late years, slaves. This villanous trade died out first in Algeria, next in Tunis, then in Tripoli: Barca's turn is next. Two or three thousand blacks used to be annually exchanged for goods at Murzoûk, which is in direct communication with Wadâi, Bornoû, Cashna, Bogoû, Soccatu, and Tomboûkto. The senna of Fezzân is considered next in quality to that of Sidon, but East Indian is now replacing them both.

The Mecca devotees used to combine their worldly interests with their religious duties, and to bring from Morocco and elsewhere wax, gold dust, feathers, silk and cotton *haïks*, morocco leather, perfumes, kohhl, henna, vermilion pinguent, and drugs. On arriving at Tripoli they would exchange a portion of these for European goods, and on returning after a year or less from the East would oblige the Tripolines with Indian stuffs, pearls, Mecca balsam, musk, aloewood, incense, myrrh, civet, Cashmir shawls, precious stones, coffee, pistachios, naphtha, opium, and other Eastern valuables.

It would be well to define in a few words, in connection with the subject of caravan trade, the geographical position and limits of this Pashalik of the Ottoman Empire. Extending from Cape Razatina on the borders of Tunis, to Port Bomba on the frontier of Egypt, it has a coast line of nearly eight hundred miles. Its extension inward is very irregular, owing to the interruption of the desert: but it comprises the large and wealthy province of Fezzân, the district of Ghadâmes, and may be said to extend, as cultivated territory, two hundred and fifty miles inland. Its population has within half a century been estimated from one million and a half to two millions. Mr. Hay now estimates it at five or six hundred thousand—the urban population being, as a rule, Turkish or Moorish—the rural, Arab or Berber. Fezzân projects southwards into the Great Sahara: Wadâi, the next fertile region, lies to its southwest. In Wadâi, a thousand miles from Tripoli, is the large inland lake, Tchad. I must apologise to the reader for saying so, but I have always had a vague and silly wish, which I cannot account for or excuse, to go to Lake Tchad. Ali Bey writes of a Central Sea: probably meaning Lake Tchad, described to him as lying fifteen days' journey eastward from Tomboûkto—and of which Negro barques took forty-eight days to navigate from shore to shore.

At a distance of from ten to twenty miles from the coast runs the Gharian range of mountains, almost east and west. Farther inland run the Zuâra mountains, separated from the Gharian by a fertile plateau.

The soil along the coast is of great richness, producing tropical and European vegetation freely. Indian wheat grows to the height of a man. Barley yields twice as much as in Europe. In the interior the date tree attains a height of a hundred feet, and the dates are of a fine quality. Cassob, a plant yielding a nutritious grain, grows abundantly. Cotton has been successfully cultivated, as well as the mulberry and the castor, or, as an Egyptian dragoman once called it, the cod-liver oil plant. The lotus tree is said to grow here, the fruit being contained in a pod not unlike that of a tamarind, and tasting when ripe sweet and agreeable, somewhat like gingerbread. Gold is found in veins towards Fezzân, and even on the sands of the seashore.

Early one morning one of my barbers from the bazaars appeared in sad trouble. We were in treaty together for an old mother-of-pearl mirror, profusely carved, and having in the centre a double-headed eagle. So fat and puffy was the body of this bird that we were satisfied it had swallowed the other eagle and appropriated its head. Having been in his family for more than eighty years, the barber had not the heart to part with it: but as I used to go daily and sit in his shop for half-an-hour, he knew he would have to give in at last. It occurred to him that he might save it by getting for me a friend's mirror, equally curious and handsome. In riding with the friend's mirror the donkey fell, and the tip of the frame was broken and lost. This mirror was, as many Moorish mirrors are, of leaf-form: perhaps to signify the transient and fading nature of this life. However, I reassured the barber and bought it, taking advantage of his gratification to secure the double-bodied eagle too.

We went to the office of the *Allegra's* agents to choose

my berth, and to the Usury department to change some circular notes: finding it uncommonly difficult. A fine tall Tripoline Jew, by name Nano, managed this business. Nano Sahib charged me fivepence for every *mahboob* or dollar, which seemed ample.

Tripoli is of all the Mediterranean cities the most difficult place for changing money. In the bazaars it was almost impossible to pay separately for the objects we bought. Anyone who goes there should take a keg of small silver with him from Malta. Not long ago— there was a dead-lock in trade, owing to some foolish prohibition on the import of silver—business was paralysed for a month. A very common coin here is the Maria Theresia dollar.

This day was the Mohammedan Sabbath: the Moors and Turks were in their cleanest linen, and every beggar of Tripoli was in the streets. It is the day of almsgiving among the Arabs. The Jews here are charitable, and, in every commercial transaction, one in every thousand of value is set aside for the poor. This is better than in Archangel, where, if I remember rightly, a tax of two per cent. on the freight of every ship arriving was imposed under the name of Church-money. No one who knows the Russians will ask how much of this money used to go to the Church.

We went to see an Arab Home—founded more than two centuries ago by Osman Pasha, of Constantinople

—for the reception of poor Mussulmans of decent position. It is a cleanly comfortable kind of khân, having small apartments round it. Some of the inmates—whitebearded and feeble, busy reading old books—were rather pleased with our visit. Afterwards we went to a native gambling house, where Arabs and Levantines were drinking raki and brandy, and playing cards and dominoes.

One morning we started on foot for a general circuit of the bazaars and city. Commencing with the woollen and the old slave bazaars, we came to the eastern extremity, where beyond the Bab el Meshîah we found them weighing oil. Men were making rude wire brushes for wool carding: in pottery shops we saw sieve-like pots for *kouskousou*, earthen jars, water bottles, and little money pots. Next came shops with red chiles, blossoms of pomegranates, which are used as an astringent, and pomegranate husks, used in tanning skins: *helba*, a small bitter grain which, when powdered with corn in cakes, has fattening properties: ropes of esparto grass, and native sulphur from the plains of the Syrtis. Sulphur, when mixed with tar, serves as a plaster for camels afflicted with the irritable disease called *djerâb*, which leads them to rub themselves against walls. Bundles of brooms or brushes of palm leaves hung in some shops, with baskets of dead sponges—those drifted up by the sea. Some shops had cotton, nails, gunflints, necklaces, matches, and palm-wood cages all together—looking a little mixed.

We watched them make neat sieves of beechwood and sinew, drums, and *dellous* or leather bags for the *siniehs*. Camels, which had brought up from the harbour great Djerban oil and water jars, were moaning and trumpeting while they were being loaded with lime, as if they had a pain in their stomachs, and nothing would ever do them any more good. This sentencious-looking beast, to gain his private ends, takes a satisfaction in making a fuss about nothing, so that one would almost wish to give him a really good load, worth moaning for.

Above us, towards the Castle, was the cemetery for the better families of Tripoli, with the customary marabout and little white domes. Above the towering Castle wall, rose the buildings and green latticed windows of the Pasha's seraglio. This building has lost all proportion, from the constant additions made to it, in order to contain the members of the successive reigning families: no such individual having lived, under ordinary circumstances, elsewhere than within the Castle precincts.

We found a native quack doctor squatting on the sand, surrounded by simple Arabs, whose fortunes he was telling, while he prescribed for their ailments and sold them amulets and love charms. I wanted to satisfy myself as to my own fortunes, but it would have given offence to the Arab dupes. Close by was the base of a marble column sunk in the ground, where two years ago, I was told, the last murderer was beheaded. They are hanged now, in the Soukh el Halfa, or esparto market, near the beach. We watched a native blacksmith on the sands, heating a sickle blade, while a fish roasted in the red coals beside it. The donkeys are all stationed outside the gate of the Meshîah : they are not allowed, except when carrying travellers, to perambulate the city.

We went to the Bazaar Foûm el Bab, where the saddlers and accoutrement makers were at work. We saw high red Arab boots, leather covers for flint locks, embroidered boots for rich Bedouins, gold embroidery upon parchment, and leopard-skin saddle-cloths.

Across the bazaar were Moorish gunmakers, inlaying the stocks with ivory and silverwork made by the Jews in the city. Arquebuses or blunderbusses, known to the Italians as *tromboni*, and which would admit an egg into their muzzle, hung in most of the shops. Farther on was an Arab café, having native water-colour drawings on the walls, and rows of sherbet syrups in bottles on shelves.

The whole of this fine bazaar belongs, I was informed, to the Sheikh el Biled, who came to Tripoli a poor man, from the islands of Kerkeneh, and became governor of Tripoli. In this capacity he amassed great wealth. Recalled to Constantinople on account of his extortions, he died there, and his brothers are now the richest men in Tripoli, owning much house property in it. Unwilling to intermarry with the Moors of Tripoli, they are said to have bought Circassian slaves and married them.

A row of five old cipolline columns stood near the gate. They once carried poles for the overland telegraph to Egypt, contemplated by the Government; but the Arabs, in their superstition, destroyed portions of the line, and it was never carried more than ten miles out of the city. The telegraph to Malta, which got out of order in 1870, might have been restored, but for the unwillingness of the Government to give a moderate guarantee.

Near a fountain is the corn market: and not far from here are the private mosque and kiosk of the Pasha, who comes here and smokes behind the latticed windows in the summer evenings. Close by is the prison for slight offences: criminals are imprisoned in the Castle. We passed the Artillery Barracks, the end of the silk bazaar, a soldiers' hammâm—a foudoûk for Europeans, then an Arab foudoûk.

We were passing along the seawall. Looking over it on to the harbour were two European consulates, and the comfortable house of Dr. Dickson. Then came the mosque and marabout of Sidi Dragut, the famous old filibuster, who is said to have built the city walls: and who, laying siege to Malta in 1565, met his end by a ball from the guns of the Knights. Women were coming out from the marabout, where they had been praying.

Turning up into the city we pass the Club—close to which are Zapati Barracks and a soldiers' guard-house, and entering an alley one yard in width, reach the Greek church and convent. Then we traverse a Christian bazaar, and emerge among the fruit sellers near the Roman arch.

Looking over the Harbour wall, I was a little startled to see the Blue Peter flying on the *Allegra's* foremast. I was not ready to leave Tripoli, not having seen the mosques and many other things: but I was unwilling to miss the chance of going to Cyrene, and hastened to the house. Peppo was despatched to buy a week's provisions, as the *Allegra* carried nothing for passengers: my luggage was ready, and I was on the point of sending all down to the harbour, when news came that the *Allegra* would not sail before daylight.

CHAPTER IX.

Djemma 'l Basha — Djemma 'l Gordji—Djemma 'l Sheikh Bel Ain—
Djemma 'l Sidi Dragut—Panorama—The Crescent City—Delusions—
Productions and Misfortunes—Voiage of the *Iefus*—The Genowaies.

I HAD begun to fear that the deliberation and procrastination characteristic of Oriental countries would result in my never seeing the interiors of the mosques. The number of visits by Mr. Warrington both to the Castle and to me, the number of journeys to and fro by the Consular dragomans, the negotiations and consultations by the civil and religious authorities, would have been more than sufficient if I had been in treaty for marriage with one of the Pasha's most attractive daughters.

At length I learnt that an afternoon was appointed for my visit: the Mufti had arranged that I was to enter before evening prayer. I should not be able to visit more than one or two, I was told, but I had confidence in Maria Theresia dollars. At the hour fixed, a soldier from the Pasha, bearing a staff of authority, presented himself, with another official, and with one of Mr. Hay's well-dressed dragomans, who carried my little camera on its tripod like some joss or mysterious emblem. These dragomans needed tempering in the furnace of the miseries of human life. Civil to their superiors, they were insolent and rapacious with the lower classes.

The first mosque we came to was that of Hamed Pasha, situated at the south-east end of the city, and surrounded by the bazaars. I removed my boots, and, to the astonishment of many of the bystanders, went in with the soldier. Djemma 'l Hamed Pasha is surrounded most picturesquely with an irregular colonnaded court, which I photographed, while my escort turned back any passers-by. The tiles and white marble columns and Moorish arches give this exterior much grace and lightness. We entered the building, which is a perfect square. Four rows of graceful white streaked marble columns and capitals, from which spring round arches, support the roof, which is vaulted with twenty-five small equal white cupolas. Sunlight entered through grated windows and fell upon the great strips of matting and old Turkish carpets. Railed and latticed galleries run round the prayer chamber. The floor, where not matted, is tiled in zigzags of black, white, and red. Beautiful old Persian tiles in soft colours line the walls to the height of twelve feet. In the space above these runs a great band of fretwork arabesque. Between the cupolas is snowy fretwork in plaster, also in the inimitable Arabesque and Moorish designs.

MOSQUE OF HAMED PASHA.

From the ceiling hang lamps of iron, brass, and old Venetian glass. Venice has for centuries traded with Tripoli, and I have bought in Tripoli old Venetian glass beads which had come back from the interior. Over the central door stands out the broad square canopy-shaped gallery of the choir, supported on four elegant spiral pillars. It is corbelled out on all sides above the pillars, with the carved Moorish stalactite pattern, and is all delicately painted and gilded. The *mihrâb*, or niche, consists of a horse-shoe arch and white marble pilasters, inlaid with black marble. The *membar*, or pulpit, is of inlaid marble, having coloured flower designs, and the sides of the staircase of carved wood. The doors of the mosque, in wood, delicately carved outwardly, are painted within. The whole building is an airy, bright, and graceful example of Saracenic architecture. Yussuf Pasha—the richest, cruellest, and most energetic of the Pashas of Tripoli, who died old and blind—lies, with the male members of his family, buried here.

Hard by the British consulate stands Djemma 'l Gordji, the most beautiful of the Tripoli mosques. Its prayer chamber is the counterpart of that I have just described. Beautiful Turkish carpets cover the floor. The exterior colonnade in the white marble court is most picturesque. Its inner wall has lovely Persian tiles up to a height of ten feet. The doors, of plain wood, stand in frames of coloured marbles. The roof of the colonnade is picturesquely coloured within, the little rafters showing, and painted red.

The mosque of Sheikh Bel Ain is entered from the Turkish bazaar. Its proportions are similar to those of the other two, but it is much disfigured in its details. Nine old and massive columns, very probably from Lebda, but coarsely painted in imitation of marble, and having their acanthus capitals smeared yellow, support the sixteen even cupolas of the roof. The walls are whitewashed, the *membar* is vulgarly painted with red roses and crescents. Low galleries stand under the arches: there is a little *kubbeh*, entered from the prayer chamber. The mosque is very old, and, with the examples of the other mosques, it is hard to understand the reason for vulgarising this building. The outer doors, decorated with roses in ironwork, are most beautifully and elaborately carved.

The mosque of Sidi Dragut—the oldest, I am told, in Tripoli—lies down by the harbour side. The grim old corsair himself, who made the flag of Tripoli the terror of the Central Sea, lies sleeping here. The mosque is of the form of a headless cross, having a row of four columns running down each side of the prayer chamber. They are rudely painted to represent blue veined marble: indeed the whole of the decorations of this mosque are tasteless to deformity.

We ascended, by a winding stone staircase, to the upper gallery of the high minar of Djemma 'l Gordji. At our feet lay the historical and interesting city. To the north ran a curved point, containing the old fort and ruins of the Spanish battery, and ending in a reef of dark rocks with the white surf sweeping over them. A dense black fog lay on the horizon, the sea was dull: the air, close and oppressive, seemed to indicate bad weather at hand. The little fleet of sandals, speronares, and boats, clustered snugly in the harbour; farther out lay the Malta steamers and the war ships, among twenty sailing vessels.

It was a city without a gable—an irregular surface of white and creamy roofs—one could traverse the city on its housetops. We had glimpses of brightly-coloured interiors, colonnades, and green lattices. Snowy groups of cupolas and the half-dozen minarets showed the positions of the mosques, and at the far south-eastern extremity towered the irregular storeys and battlements of the Castle. A single tall palm, the South palm, rose from the Jews' quarter. Many attempts have been made to abolish this palm, but it is marked on charts for the use of vessels making the harbour, and the authorities will not have it touched. Doves and pigeons flew quietly about us, and the hum came up from the streets. Beyond the Castle stretched the white curve of the harbour beach, towards the Sultanas'

Domes. The landscape ends in the palm forest of Tadjoûra. Behind the white crescent city westward stretch black rocks: the barren shore dwindles away into nothing: a noble grove of palms rises beyond the walls, and beyond the palms stretches the rose-coloured desert of sand, away to the faint range of the Gharian mountains.

Leo Africanus writes: The inhabitants of this region affirme that the city of Tripoli it selfe was situate in times past more to the northe, but by reason of the continuall inundations of the sea, it was built and remooued by little and little southward. For proofe whereof there stand as yet ruines of houses drowned in certain places of the sea.

This must be taken under reserve, for the depths indicated in the chart beyond the reef are from five to ten fathoms. Such misplaced convictions are not confined to Barbary. We have found it difficult in our own country to persuade persons that their lands were situate in times past under the sea, and that their ancestors must have been a race of mariners and fishermen.

The abundance of dates in Tripoli is a comfort to the Arabs, providing them with a cheap and wholesome diet: but for those they sell they get next to nothing, the price being at times as low as a halfpenny a pound. Horses are good, though scarce: the cattle and sheep are poor. The wool is coarse: much of it is woven at Misrâtah into carpets and barracans, in striped colours. Of these there were sent to the Cyrenaïca alone, in one year, sixty thousand pounds' worth.

The foreign trade of Tripoli is carried on chiefly by steamers, of which two were trading during my visit between this port and Malta. Occasional steamers call on their way from the East—generally to complete their cargo by loading esparto at Homs. Small coasting vessels sail eastward to Homs, Misrâtah, and the ports of the Cyrenaïca: and westward to the Lesser Syrtis and Tunis. Formerly Tunisian steamers traded here, but they were, as Mr. Hay says, deficient in steam power, and imperfectly navigated.

In 1871 the drought half ruined the Arabs. Of their cattle, once a profitable and considerable item of export, owing to the small meat consumption by the natives, two-thirds died. The same fearful proportion of camels and horses perished, or were slaughtered, and sheep became nearly extinct. The crops almost failed. The import of necessaries of life amounted to half a million sterling. The subsequent years were brighter for the Regency, crops improved, esparto was obtained in larger quantities, and caravans were richer and larger. The existing drought caused serious anxiety to the Tripolines.

The government officials squeeze the poor Arabs

cruelly. I have been told that assessors will rate an Arab's crops at four times their value; and make him pay on that. Indeed, the Arab has sometimes to pay beyond the whole revenue from his crop. Kaïds and others, who are unrestricted, amass much wealth.

In Hakluyt's old Black-letter Collection of Voiages and Travels, is an account of a voyage made to Tripolis in Barbarie, in the yeere 1583, with a ship called the *Iefus*. The commodities of that place, says the chronicler, are sweete oiles. The king there is a merchant. The rather willing to preferre himselfe before his commons, he requested the factors of the said ship to traffique with him, and promised them that if they would take his oyles at his owne price, they should pay no manner of custome: and they tooke of him certain tunnes of oyle. Afterwards, perceiving that they might haue farre better cheape, notwithstanding the custome free, they desired the king to licence them to take the oyles at the pleasure of his commons: for that his price did exceede theirs: whereunto the king would not agree, but was rather contented to abate his price: insomuch that the factors bought all their oyles of the king custome free, and so laded the same aboord. Eventually some dispute arose, the captain of the *Iefus* was hanged, twenty-six Englishmen were cast into prison, of whom eleven died: —the ship and merchandise, worth seven thousand ducats, were confiscated: and the unfortunate survivors of the crew were only released after a vigorous but polite representation to the Sultan Mourad, by her Majesty Queen Elizabeth.

Leo tells a good story of the Tripolines' capacity for business. Tripolis was surprized and sacked by a Genouese fleete of twenty sailes. Whereof the King of Fez, then Ruler of Tripoli, being advertized, gave the Genowaies fiftie thousand ducates, vpon consideration that he might enioy the towne in peace. But the Genoueses hauing surrendred the towne, perceiued after their departure that most part of their ducates were counterfait.

These glorious days have passed, but Tripoli may take courage: she has children not unworthy of her traditions.

CHAPTER X.

The Jews' Quarter—The Place of Stoning—The Dyers—An Austere Sentry—Bab el Djedîd—Jewish Reception—The Synagogue—The Murderer—The Dutch Consul—The Black Village—In the Palm Groves—Orange Garden—Essence Distilling—Fruit and Blossom—The Castle—A Roman Lady—Boûba—The *Circe*—The Last of Tripoli.

WE went to the Jews' quarter one Saturday morning. A poor shabby alley led to it. We came to a square of waste ground, a dirty ill-drained area. It had a melancholy interest, for many a poor Jewess, who had been unfaithful to her husband, was stoned to death here. Banishment, of late years, has taken the place of stoning. We passed a school, shops of mat weavers, overtook a caravan just starting for the interior, and watched the barracan makers in the weavers' quarter. In a corn mill a blindfolded camel was trudging round, an apparatus ringing a bell at intervals to mislead him. We came, behind the Jewish quarter, to the curriers' quarter. Here were great jars of red dye, with which the stainers were busy. The goatskin, stretched across a pole, is violently tugged at, and polished with a coarse pad. The skin, after being soaked for twenty or thirty days in cold water and the powder of small dried figs, is stripped of its hair and boiled in the cochineal stain. In a basin hollowed out of a beautiful old capital, two Arabs were pounding coarse salt, brought from the salt mere beyond Tadjoûra.

We were passing along under the fortifications, and mounting the rampart to obtain a commanding view, were warned off by a Turkish sentry. We pretended not to understand him, and tried to explain that we considered the fortifications some of the most handsome and efficient that we knew, and that the whitewash did him much credit: but he was a poor practical minded fatalist, and told us to be off at once. We traversed the worst quarter of the city, and went out by the Bab el Djedîd. The angles of the wall were defended by heavy bastions. Under the walls the once broad moat was a sheet of black mud. The Jewish cemetery was close by, looking over the sea. Within the gate El Djedîd stood a small revenue building: above it grew a gigantic plant resembling the coriander. The leaves and blossoms are used for poultices, and the seed for food, in the country of the Blacks.

We went to visit the brother of Nano Sahib, in a pretty and picturesque dwelling of the Jewish-Moorish type. We were very hospitably entertained with brandy and sweetmeats, of which, understanding it was good breeding to do so, we ate large quantities. We passed along the Har el Kebîr, the chief street of the Jews' quarter, and entered the synagogue. Such a disorderly, noisy, irreverent congregation, with its forest of dark blue turbans, I have never seen. One of the rabbis read from the Hebrew Scriptures, while conversation was animated and general. At the door we asked a young boy for a light for a cigar. It is the Sabbath, he said, turning away. We were within a short distance of the Consulate, when we noticed a large crowd near it. Getting among the people, we presently saw Osman Warrington, armed, ride up to the Consulate gateway. Behind him, escorted by two soldiers, came a camel, on which sat a youth chained hand and foot, apparently eighteen or twenty years old, with a small cat-like face and a hunted look. It was the murderer from Homs. After him came other soldiers, with two children riding in front of them, and escorting a mule which bore a miserable, emaciated, frightened creature, carrying a child in her arms. This was the wife of the murdered man. They were assisted to alight, led into the courtyard of the Consulate, and the gate was closed.

Having one day occasion for some money, I was recommended to go to the Dutch consul. I found a dark individual seated at his desk, and said I had been directed to him in the belief that he would be glad to change some English circular notes for me. Looking at me with the expression of a mud turtle who thinks it is possible he may be taken advantage of, and turned over on his back, the Dutch consul asked to see the notes, and examined them carefully. Suppose the notes should be counterfeit, the stranger a deceiver, who had travelled to Tripoli in order to profit by his, the Dutch consul's, simplicity. He eyed me vigilantly, and I began to enjoy it. Had I any letter of introduction from the bank? he asked. I had been on the point of handing it to him, but said I was not at the moment in a position to present it. Had I any friends in Tripoli? I could hardly say that I had. Had I any means of showing how I came by the notes? I said it would be difficult. Having aroused the Dutch consul's worst suspicions, I asked for the notes, told him that I had the bank's letter, had brought introductions to Tripoli, was a man of immense means, and wished him good morning. The Dutch consul ground his teeth as the crisp bank notes and the golden commission vanished, and began to think that to be suspicious was not always to be wise.

Nano Sahib took the notes cheerfully, though he charged rather cheerfully too: and I should not recommend any traveller to go to Tripoli in order to profit by exchanging his letters of credit. So scarce is small change, that the miserable copper and zinc piastres, half and quarter piastres, are at a great premium here. On gold or on silver dollars the traveller loses fifteen or twenty per cent. in order to fill his pockets with the debased coinage of Constantinople.

One fine sunny afternoon—although almost every morning and afternoon here were fine and sunny—we mounted our donkeys and rode over to the Black village, which squats on a sloping sandbank near the palm woods. It was a perfect village from the heart of Africa. Three or four hundred *Dzrîba*, or palm and bamboo beehive huts, like those adjoining the Hermitage, were huddled together. Some were surrounded with screens of palm mats, and prickly pear bushes stood at intervals between them. We entered the wigwam of the chief man of the village, very neatly constructed, and having furniture simple in the extreme. A few earthen vessels, mats, and a mud stove were the whole of it. We walked from hut to hut. Some of the negroes, and, I am sorry to say, negresses, were sprawling about, drunk with *buha*, or *bokha*: a kind of cheap spirit distilled, chiefly by the Jews, from fermented dates, green figs, or raisins. *Leghma* is another temptation to the lower classes here. Poetically it is called the Tears of the Date. It is the sap of the date palm: an unproductive tree is decapitated, a cavity is made in the head of the trunk, and here the sap collects. When fresh it resembles the milk of the cocoa-nut, and is pleasant enough. It soon becomes sharp, not unlike cider or kvass, and is intoxicating. Herodotus says Cambyses sent to Ethiopia by the hands of the Ichthyophagi, a vessel of palm tree wine. It is also said to have been used by the Cave-Dwellers of Arabia. I had always regarded the Troglodytes as a quiet deserving race, subsisting chiefly upon roots or snails, and water: had it been used by the Ichthyophagi I should have wondered less.

A negro murdered another here last evening: indeed these poor Ethiopians seem sunken in vices to which, in their native land, they were strangers: and their moral condition reflects but little credit upon their neighbours in the city. I was told that occasionally a negro murderer is decapitated at an hour's notice, to make an example.

We rode off through the palms between high mud walls. We could hear the voices of children in an Arab school. A negro was enjoying the fiendish and heart-rending noises he was producing from a rude bagpipe. The juicy sprouts of the fig trees, increasing daily as it seemed, stretched above the walls. Solemn palms stood in carpets of brilliant poppies, and the air was thick with the sweet scents of fruit blossoms and creeping plants. Arabs, barefooted, and slung by a girth of palm fibre, were climbing the palms to remove the fibrous growth and dead branches from the crests. We pulled up at a garden.

In the court, near a deep well lined with maiden-hair fern, were four black women in white barracans,

wearing coral and silver earrings. Near them were two
or three tattooed children, with necklets of orange
blossoms. One woman was spinning wool, the others
were distilling orange flower water. In a round-headed
bell-shaped copper retort, placed over a rude stove, the
orange blossoms, having been exposed on a mat to the
sun for an hour or two, were being boiled. From the
head of the retort ran a long tapering spout or tube,
which passed through a large earthen vessel filled with
cold water. The orange flower vapour passing through
the cold tube is condensed, and falls in liquid into bottles
placed at the mouth. A moderate-sized bottle of
orange flower water costs here four or five shillings.

These flower waters are much used for sweetmeats
and sherbets. Barbary is a paradise for essences. The
blossoms of jasmine, acacia, quince, narcissus, aloe,
lemon, rose, scented poplar, orange, geranium, tuberose,
thymes, mint, and *sambak*, or double jasmine of
Arabia, are distilled in great quantities: and the essence
bazaars are most fragrant. The method of distilling
rose attar is similar to that described above. A damp
spring is more favourable for the rose blossoms than a
dry one. They contain more essence the less quickly
they develop. A stony, sandy ground is the best for
them, and under favourable conditions 5,000 lbæ. of rose
leaves will produce 1 lb. of oil. In a dry season the
yield will be only half as much. The best attar is worth

Edw:Rae.77

nearly 1*l*. the ounce. If a bottle of good oil is put in water of the temperature of 63° to 68° Fahr. it will freeze. Poor oil will not freeze at 52°. Idris oil is much used in the adulteration of this attractive and costly essence.

In an inner court of the garden we found five ostriches, brought, poor things, from Fezzân only ten days ago, and still very shy. Their legs were chafed and sore from the cords which had bound them. The fruits of Tripoli have long been famous for their fine flavour, and we ranged about among mulberry trees, and orange trees laden with blossom and oranges of all shapes and kinds. Some had coarse rind like Mandarins: some were blood oranges, said to be the result of grafting the orange on the pomegranate. No evidence of this is in the trees, however: it may have been in some earlier stage of development. It was rather late in the season, the skins of many were thin and dry, and every tenth orange I ate would be dry and woolly. The rest were perfect. We cantered home, bearing huge branches of orange and lemon blossom which scented the whole house.

In the evening we went to the Castle, a rectangular building about two hundred yards square, with bastions. We mounted the broad approach and came to the Treasury, where sentries stood with fixed bayonets. Thence to the printing office whence the newspaper *Trablus* is issued. Entering a court, we found the Mint of

Yussuf Pasha, the Court of Justice of the Beys—
Tripoli has always been regarded as prompt in justice—
the Government Pharmacy, and the establishment of
the chief of the Treasury. Here were arches and
fragments of columns. We went to the prison, where
we found fifty or sixty criminals condemned for murder,
in a barred and grated chamber. Some of them
advanced to mock us, and several shook their fists at us.
One tall, bold-faced man approached the grating with a
joke : he had murdered the keeper of a gambling-house
at Benghasi.

One day Mr. Saïd called, bringing with him a servant, who carried the marble head of a Roman lady to
show to me. It was white and smoothly chiselled—the
hair and features were as clear as when cut. The hair
was twisted up in a picturesque coil at the top of the
head. Mr. Saïd had lately bought for one shilling and
sixpence a Roman jar, three feet and a half in height,
and very perfect and fine in form. It had been disin-
terred in the neighbourhood. The *Allegra*, it trans-
pired, had come to Tripoli with a view to transporting
the lately appointed Pasha to Benghasi. Her conduct
during the last few days excited my constant uneasiness:
one morning the Blue Peter would be flying and I would
hasten to pack. In the course of an hour I would learn
she was not to sail till next day. In the evening the
departure flag would be flying again. This went on for

days. It seemed the Pasha would not agree to the terms demanded for his conveyance, and the signal of departure was a playful mode of inducing him to give in. I awoke one morning to find the *Allegra* disappearing on the horizon on her way to Malta. So much for my journey to Cyrene.

One evening a little Jew came in, as we were drinking tea and orange flower water, to announce his imminent marriage. He had paid fifteen *mahboubs* for his wife, and seemed to think he had done a clever thing. He did not even know his wife's name, but understood she was known as Boûba. On the last Sunday I spent in Tripoli I went to the Church of England service at the Consulate. Nearly all the English residents were there, but they barely numbered a dozen. Afterwards I went to the service at the Catholic church, an ordinary plastered building with votive pictures, where many Maltese were assembled.

The *Circe* had arrived, and was to sail, weather permitting, for Malta in the evening: but as the weather was stormy and threatening, the barometer was falling, and heavy seas were rolling over the reef, while every vessel in the harbour rocked uneasily at her moorings: it was contemplated to postpone the steamer's sailing. I went to Mr. Saïd, to prevail upon him to send the *Circe* to sea, and the good-natured little man wrote the order to get up steam.

In the afternoon a message came from the *Circe* to ask me to go on board. At the landing-place were my kind and considerate host, with Mr. Warrington and other gentlemen, and I was sorry to wish them good-bye. The anchor was got up, and in a threatening evening the little steamer *Circe* made her way out of Tripoli harbour.

The houses, walls, Castle, and palms faded out of sight, and as night fell, the *Circe* was pitching into the heavy waves of the open sea.

CHAPTER XI.

Malta—Cape Bon—Tunny Fishery—Goletta—Perruquier—The City of Verdure—Preparations for Kairwân—Sketch of Tunis—Purchases in the Bazaars—Scenes in the City—Rosebuds and Orange Blossoms—Adopt a Young Moor—Braham the Silversmith—The Bardo—The Great Aqueduct.

ALL that night and all next day we rolled quickly. Sagramo! groaned a Maltese, sick of the rough voyage. Men for the land and fish for the sea! Towards nightfall we saw the flashing light of Delimara. We entered the harbour of Valetta at nine in the evening, and slept on board the *Circe*. The Tunis steamer was lying alongside of us, waiting for cargo and fine weather.

I remained several days in Malta. Mackintosh, of the *Junon*, dined with me one evening, and I was shocked to hear of the death of our fellow-passenger Cholmeley, who died two or three days after our arrival here. At length the obliging agents of the Tunis steamer sent to tell me that she was ready for sea. As the sunset gun was fired from St. Angelo, we steamed out of Malta harbour.

Two or three months after this I had a letter from

Captain Kirkpatrick, telling me the sequel of the Maltese murder at Homs. The woman, who gave evidence against her companion in guilt, was released, and the young man was condemned to twenty years' imprisonment. 'A Maltese jury,' the captain added, 'can hardly be prevailed upon to punish murder by death: it is not considered a capital offence.' Each nationality has its peculiar sentiments. A French gentleman was brought before the Correctional Police in Paris, for giving little boys money to strew orange peel and make slides on the pavement in front of his house. The case was dismissed when the gentleman explained that he was expecting his mother-in-law to dinner.

In wind and mist next day we passed three steamers, making but little headway. Off Lampedusa we came among numerous whales and porpoises, and a lonely turtle who looked seasick and upset. It was very cold and cheerless—rough squalls came incessantly. Towards evening we were abreast of Cape Bon, and its flashing red and white light. When the wind is in the south-east, the captain told me, very sudden gusts come down from the mountains of the Dakkhul: the glass falls, and the wind will shift abruptly to the north-west. So the apparent absurdity of Virgil's tempest, in which Æneas's ships were attacked by Eurus the east-south-east, Notus the south, Africus the west-south-west, Aquilo the north-north-east, and eventually Zephyrus the west, winds, at once, is only one of the many examples of the poet's faithful observance of the facts of nature:

> *The East, the West together there, the Afric that doth hold*
> *A heart fulfilled of stormy rain, huge billows shoreward rolled.*
> *Therewith came clamour of the men and whistling through the shrouds,*
> *And heaven and day all suddenly were swallowed by the clouds,*
> *Away from eyes of Teucrian men; night on the ocean lies,*
> *Pole thunders unto Pole, and still with wildfire glare the skies,*
> *And all things hold the face of death before the seamen's eyes.*

We passed the uninhabited islands of Zembra and Zembrotto to seaward, rounded Ras el Ferthass, and entered the Gulf of Tunis. At Sidi Dâoud are rich tunny fisheries. The survivors of the poor tunny caught here in May, are caught at Cape Passaro in August and September. Last year the sea destroyed the fishing nets and tackle, to the great satisfaction of the tunny. There are two other Tunisian tonnâras—one ten miles east of Bizerta and one near Monastir—both abandoned, however, since 1853. The Carthaginian prawns are historic and famous, having been sent in old times to Imperial banquets at Rome. They measured six or seven inches in length. The mullets of the Lake of Tunis, says old Dr. Shaw, are esteemed the largest and sweetest on the coast of Barbary.

We were at anchor off the little white seaport, Goletta, in the morning. The landing was much less disorderly than formerly. The place was smarter, and seemed to be looking up in the world, after its vicissitudes. Once a deep and capacious harbour, in which the fleet of Belisarius rode when he made his triumphal demonstration before Tunis, the lake had so dwindled away by the time of Barbarossa, that when he attacked Goletta its garrison retired across the lake to Tunis. Recaptured by the Christian armies and given to the Spaniards in 1535, Goletta, after a most brave defence, was regained by the Ottomans, who massacred all but three hundred of the garrison.

At the small inn of Goletta, waiting for the train, I got into conversation with the landlady's son, a youth of French parentage, Tunisian birth, and of evident intelligence. His name resembled Perruquier more than any name I remember, and that name will do very well for him. Perruquier had an excellent face for a lie: I recognised that his family must be of great antiquity—in fact, dating from the Age of Bronze. This pleased me, and I engaged Perruquier as dragoman. He had served, so he told me, in the Mobile Guards during the siege of Paris, and shared their sacrifices and glories. This gentleman proved a smart and useful servant, though he endeavoured consistently to get to windward of me in money transactions: and so bold and subtle were his schemes that much ingenuity was needed to defeat them. Perruquier had all the instincts of the filibuster: he was fond of napoleons: he could not regard them without a certain melancholy longing. Unlike the much-abused Catiline, who was *alieni appetens, sui profusus*: Perruquier was greedy with his own property, lavish with what belonged to me.

Beside the lake stood a large herd of camels, while gulls and flamingoes were busy fishing. The western breeze shook the old olives to our right hand, and rippled the waters of the lake. We could see Tunis, the City of Verdure—a mass of picturesque cream-coloured buildings and minarets, surmounted by the Kasbah— sloping gently up a background of purple and green. No smoke rose to soil or obscure the city. Round it stretched the mountains which make of the Gulf of Tunis so lovely a panorama. In the lake stood a small island containing a fort, which that famous soldier and author Cervantes defended against the Turks in 1573. It was a falling off to enter Tunis by rail, instead of through a postern gate at dead of night, escorted by a dozen irregular soldiers with lanterns.

There were few guests at the hotel. One was a short gentleman, who seemed unconscious that nature had provided him with two ears and one mouth, in order that he might hear much but say little. In the visitors' book I found the name of Comte Pepper, Engleterre, and wondered which of our leading families he represented, and where he had learnt French. The consul-general advised me not to go to Kairwân, except under Government protection, and promised to do his best to get me a letter and escort from the Bey. It had hardly been my wish to go thus: but when we cannot have what we like, it is well to like what we have. Mr. Wood himself went to the Bardo, and his dragomen were constantly going to and fro during my stay in Tunis. A Sicilian pastrycook, a few days before, had shot a judge attached to the Italian consulate, and afterwards destroyed himself. The judge was dangerously wounded, but likely to recover.

We went to the bazaars, which, though not so rich as those of Cairo, Constantinople, or Damascus, are more picturesque and charming. The population seemed scantier, and the life less animated than four years ago. The shops are not open till nine or ten, closing soon after half-past two: the Tunisians go early to bed, to repose from the fatigue of doing little all day.

I will make no excuse for giving a brief sketch of Tunis and its capital, in order that the reader may make a passing comparison between this and the neighbouring Regency of Tripoli.

Tunis, the leading Barbary state, lies midway between Gibraltar and Egypt, on the high road of Eastern commerce, and has large internal resources. Having a coast line of four hundred miles, it comprises perhaps forty thousand square miles of territory, and practically represents the two Roman provinces of Zeugitana and Byzacium. It is possessed of eleven harbours, once invaluable for corsairs and the slave trade. It has two considerable rivers, the Medjerdah and Wad el Kebîr: three large lakes, those of Bizerta, Tunis, and Sidi el Hâni. Its population, once estimated at seventeen millions, and again in the eighteenth century at five millions, has, through the plagues of 1785 and 1829, and the famine and typhus of 1867, dwindled away to a million and a half. It is said to have contained in the days of the early Christian Church one hundred and thirty-two episcopal sees.

The southern district, the Djerîd, or Country of Dates, contains sixty thousand inhabitants, two millions of date palms, vast groves of orange, lemon, fig, apricot, peach, and pomegranate trees, with rich tracts of cereals, vegetables, melons, &c. &c. There are mines of lead at Djebel Resass and at Zaghwân, both known to the Romans: but the Beys, fearing the cupidity of Christians, till late years discountenanced any development of the country's resources. The public credit of Tunis, since the establishment of a financial commission, has been good. Railways, telegraphs, a bank, and other steps towards improvement have been encouraged.

The history can be sketched in a few words: it cannot be dissociated from that of Carthage. First came the establishment, five centuries before the Christian era, of the Phœnician colony on the heights of Cape Carthage: the development of a splendid city: its intercourse with the known world and explorations into the unknown: its military glories and rivalry with Rome, its fall and destruction, while our ancestors were still sporting among the oak trees in skins and paint. Then its restoration as a Roman city, and its second rise to splendour: its conquest by Genseric's Vandals in the fifth century after Christ: its recovery by Belisarius for the Byzantine Emperors in the following century: and its final destruction by the Saracens under Okhbah, founder of Kairwân.

These last invaders, not having maritime capabilities, rather than revive Carthage, thought well to establish their capital at Tunis, farther from the sea: and eventually, not feeling secure there, at Kairwân. After centuries of vicissitudes, disputed by Turks and Christians, taken by the famous pirate Redbeard—the elder of the Barbarossa brothers—in 1531: Tunis was captured by Charles V., and again taken by the fleet of Sultan Selim after a brilliant defence. Impatient of control from the Ottoman capital, the Tunisian Moors declared themselves a Republic one and indivisible, and elected their own Beys. They then entered upon an active course of maritime requisitions, which made the Barbary flag unpopular in the Mediterranean. The present government rather resembles that of Egypt, the Beylik being hereditary.

The stately and populous city of Tunis, as Leo calls it, has five large and many small mosques, eight-and-twenty baths, eighty public fountains, a hundred and ninety-three caravanserais, two hundred and forty coffee shops, sixteen barracks, Moorish and European hospitals, two libraries, containing twelve thousand MSS., the remnant of seventy-two thousand destroyed by the Spaniards —Cervantes' comrades in the Abdallah Palace early in the sixteenth century. Its chief manufactures are linen and woollen cloths, embroidery, morocco leather, burnouses, horse accoutrements, silk shawls, silk and gold and silver tissues, jewellery, wearing apparel, woollen rugs, *haïks*, and mats. The fez, or *sheshiya*, famous throughout the Levant, is made in large quantities: although from the manufacture in France and Trieste of cheaper ones, the export has fallen off. The Romans brought water, fifty-two miles, from Zaghwân and Ain Djugâr, by an aqueduct, in some places a hundred feet high: the present government in 1859 did very much the same, partly utilising the old aqueduct.

We became the largest possessors in Tunis of Arab dresses, attar of roses, pearls, amber beads, engraved stones, old silver work and gold work, Oriental china, old blue and white tiles, mosaics, coins, musical instruments, pottery, *hasheesh, rahatlakoom*, old brass lamps, silk and wool materials, Tripoli and Benghasi rugs, little old essence cabinets carved and inlaid, and old hand mirrors. What in the world we should do with them when we got them home we did not know. The Tunis gold coinage is good: the copper is bulky, giving much satisfaction in the receiving, less in the carrying, and least in repaying it. So much goes to make a piastre, that the traveller's spirits droop and he becomes discouraged.

We made a point of bargaining firmly with the merchants. On one occasion, having positively refused to give more than eighteen piastres for an old silver amulet, and the Jew having refused to take less than nineteen, we were at a dead lock. Anxious to give way, but to save the principle, I took a napoleon, and, pointing to the Emperor's head, said, *Shoûf, Samaniyatashar!* Eighteen! Then to the reverse, *Tasatashar!* Nineteen! *Maléh!* said the silversmith, Good! Spinning the coin, it fell in my hand head upwards, but I called out, *Tasatashar!* and the Arab bounded into the air, clapping his hands, and ran about the bazaars telling everyone how fortune had given him the advantage over a Roumi

The wanderer in Tunis will traverse narrow winding alleys with irregular white buildings: through fine old arabesqued Moorish arches are glimpses of cool bright courts, with waving trees and trickling water. Suddenly he will emerge into the brilliant bazaars. Series of vaulted roofs are supported on light graceful arches, all white, and springing from delicate, brightly coloured pillars: the little shops are recessed on either side. The costumes of Tunisians, Moors, Tripolines, Djerbans, Algerians, Fezzians, Arabs from the Djerîd and the desert, blacks and infidels of all nations, are indescribably picturesque. The Tunisians' costumes are almost invariably in perfect taste. The silk *djubbas* were of deep red and apple-green, or deep blue and golden yellow, the vests and jackets pale rose coloured, or of delicate blues, greens, and yellows, in silk, cotton, and wool. It is a constant picture, always varying and always charming. Here is a regular Moor, with a cinnamon face, a snowy turban, a rosebud above his ear, a deep blue embroidered jacket, waistcoat, and drawers, white stockings, and yellow shoes. The next man to him is in slaty blue and pink, the next a negro in a blue cloak lined with brown fur. Women pass in white woollen *haïks*, holding out in front of their faces red, black, and blue silk scarfs.

Strolling from one bazaar to another, the traveller will be more pleased as he goes on: past beautiful angles of Moorish buildings, mosques, arches, and colonnades: past caravanserais, where vines or fig trees throw cool shadows on the camels feeding in the court, while the dark-faced white-robed Bedouins lounge among them. Thence perhaps to the silk bazaars, where lovely flox silk hangs in great bunches, suggesting wonderful embroidery. Then to the merchants of carpets, shawls, and stuffs, and through zigzag streets beyond the bazaars, with the beautiful blue sky over-head, and where solitary palms stand up from courts and gardens. Lovely minarets abound, square, arabesqued and tiled, others thin and graceful, with delicate little galleries: domes covered with old green tiles, like dragon's scales: inviting cafés, with splendid studies of Arabs. The traveller will decorate his coat with sweet musk-roses, his lips with the golden tinge of orange juice, and he will drink numerous cups of coffee as he squats on little square sugarcane stools.

The evening sky melts from turquoise into golden, and thence into the rosy colour of a flamingo's breast. The abundance of flowers in the bazaars is charming. Small bouquets of rosebuds and orange blossoms, stuck on slips of wood, are in almost everybody's hand, and cost one caroub. There are four caroubs in a penny. A bouquet is very generally worn over the ear, just beneath the turban.

We often went in the evenings to ramble about and watch the phases of Oriental life—sometimes to an Arab concert, or a Jewish concert, or a *hasheesh* establishment, where *hashashîn* were smoking away their senses. From this word comes 'assassin,' its present sense being curiously diverted from the original. One is a person who occupies himself in killing himself, the other in killing other people. On one of these occasions our guide's lantern light fell on a little bundle of clothes and rags, huddled up under an archway. It was a miserable starving little Arab. We had him brought to the hotel, and he stayed a week or so there before we left Tunis. He would probably not have lived long, poor little creature, and food could hardly be given to him at first.

He became attached to us, and apparently grateful. He became distressed when the time for our departure came nearer, and begged to be allowed to come to England. The landlord assured him it was impossible, and told him that no Mussulman could go to England, which was a Christian country. Ali, who was not over eight years old, went one day to the hotel kitchen, and after persuading the cook, received some ham and a little wine. Then he went straight to the landlord. Now, he said, I am no longer a Mussulman: I can go with the English gentlemen. He would steal into our bedroom and raise our hands to his lips, then seat himself on the floor watching us with tears in his eyes. Eventually a kind and charitable American lady, then living in Tunis, prevailed upon us to give her charge of Ali.

A year after our return to England we wrote, asking if it were time to send more money for the boy's wants. His kind mistress sent the following reply:

'I regret exceedingly I have no good news to communicate to you regarding the little Arab boy you took under your protection. After your departure I sent for the child, bought several suits of clothes, shoes, stockings, &c., and kept him with me in Tunis, fearing that, in the very delicate state of health I found him in, he might be neglected at my farm. He was taken ill, and for three weeks I had the doctor every day. I nursed him most faithfully: he recovered, and a month after he ran away. He was found, completely devoid of clothing, at the Bardo. I dressed him again, and again he ran away, selling his clothes. Three times he did the same thing, and at last my researches were in vain. At last a Spanish lady here told me she had found a poor child, and had taken it in to feed and clothe it. The child was the same, and after a few weeks he left her also, taking with him several articles besides his clothing. Twice he did the same, and not being able to be found the last time, we suppose he has left the town. I regret extremely that your action has met with so much ingratitude.'

We had grown friendly with one of the leading Jews among the silversmiths, Braham by name. We used to sit in his shop while we bought souvenirs from his neighbours, and one day he begged us to do him the uncommon honour of visiting him at his house. Here he regaled us with eau-de-vie, and sweetmeats made of almonds and honey. Our farewell to Braham was picturesque. We exchanged many complimentary speeches. We promised to think frequently of him when we should have returned to our native land, while he assured us that the recollection of our personal beauty and amiability should be for ever engraven on his heart. We said that the hours spent in his shop were amongst the pleasantest we had passed in Tunis: and he declared that we were the only Christians he had ever really loved. We said his upright dealing had given us a very high impression of the character of Tunisian goldsmiths: and he said all his regret was that he had not been able to make even better bargains for us. We left the good old man with tears rolling down his cheeks, and next day returning for a final visit to the bazaars, we detected him in the act of plundering us in the matter of some pearls.

I remembered Braham, and went to his shop. Another tenant was there. Poor Braham—had he defrauded his last English traveller? I asked for him, and learnt he was in the bazaars. In two minutes I saw Braham pushing through the crowd: he recognised me at a glance. I am thankful to God for your return, he said: which I believe he was. But where is the other gentleman? he said in the same breath—remembering how rich the other was. I shook my head. What has become of him? he asked Perruquier. I said I would rather not say. Has misfortune befallen him? I lowered my voice and said—Married.

We went twice to the Bey's Palace of the Bardo, driving under the city wall, along a road bordered by acacias with sweet clusters of white blossoms. All this side of the city wall is in a state of neat repair, and armed with modern artillery. On one occasion, four years ago, in preparing for the visit of a foreign prince, the workmen were set to whitewash the walls, and the guileless Arabs whitewashed the guns too. We passed the high modern aqueduct and reached the palace fortress. At each angle were heavy bastions armed with fine brass guns, and defended by the Bey's Zouaves, his best troops. Crossing a drawbridge, we drove under many archways and entered a square court. Mounting to a second court, colonnaded and lined with lovely tiles and the green lattices of the women's apartments, we reached a fine broad marble staircase with handsome balustrades in the Moorish style. We traversed the whole of this very beautiful building, which resembles the Alcazar Palace at Seville. Its interior details are much disfigured by European decoration.

We drove out, past gardens and orange groves, fields of barley, cypress trees, aged olives growing in a dry and exhausted-looking wilderness, and past the Manouba, a suburban village. Beyond this the road divides, one branch running to Bezha, the other viâ Kef into Algeria. The latter is a journey of five days on horseback, but a courier travelling quickly can do it in three days and a half. We reached the great Roman aqueduct, built to bring the waters of Ain Djugâr to Carthage. I have a silver coin, showing the stream on its way, and a lion bearing Severus, hurrying along, delighted to bring the news to Carthage. A great stretch of forty-six arches of the aqueduct stands out of the plain, very complete still. The piers are of mud blocks founded upon white hewn blocks of stone. The fine round arches are faced with stone: the conduit itself is in cement. These ruins of a magnificent work stood amid thistles, wild marigolds, prickly pear, and fig trees. Bees were humming about, and a flight of forty hawks, having their nests in the clay arches, hovered overhead.

We returned by the Carthage Gate to Tunis and drove past what was now, and ordinarily, a grass market, where hooded Arabs were bargaining for fodder, but what was lately a place of execution. Three weeks ago an Arab who had plundered General Khaireddîn's house, was led for two or three hours through the streets —the officers with him crying that all who did the same should be treated alike—then brought here and hanged.

CHAPTER XII.

Bakkoush—His Antecedents, Career, Characteristics, and Accomplishments—Old Times—Mosaics—Stroll through the City—Panorama—The Diamond Market—Sanctuaries—The Mosque of the Olive Tree—Departure from Tunis.

We made four years ago in Tunis the acquaintance of a remarkable man—a deaf mute—Bakkoush by name, and buffoon to the Bey. He entered the hotel one day, and remained to dinner. He was a tall man in a fez, with a heavy black moustache, and eyes that moved like lightning, that nothing escaped, and which served him well in the place of his two lost senses. He was known in all classes of Tunisian society, and all manner of stories—true or untrue—were told about him. Some said he had been a collector from his youth upwards. On one occasion, having inadvertently collected something belonging to his neighbour, he was brought before the Bey. During the inquiry the deaf mute entertained his Highness by mimicking any minister or official who turned his back, and eventually made signs that he wished for a pinch from the Bey's snuffbox. The Bey, to humour him, handed him the box, which Bakkoush returned. In a few minutes, feeling for his box, the Bey found it had vanished. Bakkoush had picked his Highness's pocket, and the Bey was so much amused that he had patronised him ever since.

His gestures and mumbling sounds were unmistakeable—he positively talked. His facility for expressing himself and for assuming the expression of others was startling. Nothing escaped his penetrating eye, and still less his sense of humour. A whisper behind one's hand put him on the alert at once, and it was useless to refuse to repeat by signs what had been said. The tricks he played with cards or upon us were incredibly clever. He was a born conjuror: it was inconceivable how he stole one's watch, pencil, or money, and transferred them to a neighbour, and what versatility and subtleties of expression his face assumed. In the same instant a diabolical contortion would pass into a jovial, rollicking smile. A German Baron with a fat simple face sat near us at table, staring at the mute. In the midst of some description or mimicry, Bakkoush—who took in the company at a glance—suddenly stopped, and pointed to the Baron's fat countenance staring in open-mouthed astonishment. It was so irresistibly comic that the whole room roared, while the Baron grew crimson. None of us was safe to turn his head, for his faintest peculiarity was in a second reproduced in Bakkoush's face.

His mode of life and means of subsistence were a puzzle. He would get a present, of some garment let us say, and upon that he would live for days and gain money. He would take that garment, perhaps, to a man who had a cabinet—no matter what—and the marvellous fellow would satisfy the man with the cabinet that the garment was worth the cabinet and a little money: and make the exchange. The cabinet he would take to a man with an engraved ring, and persuade him that it would be a profitable thing to give the ring and a little money for the cabinet. And so on. He was a real genius. He was known at all the consulates. Spy, robber, and worse names were bestowed upon him, but none were established. He would certainly have made a magnificent spy or freebooter, from the opportunities his faculties of amusement gave him. He had been sent to Constantinople to accompany the Tunisian tribute, and must have entertained the Commander of the Faithful.

This singular being took a fancy to my friend and myself: would daily bring old engraved stones and offer them to us as souvenirs, and when we were leaving, Bakkoush spent an hour and a half upon his knees helping us to pack our boxes of curiosities. When we wished him good-bye, he told us by gestures that he would carry the recollection of us in his innermost heart while he existed. I asked for him when I returned to Tunis: no one knew where he was: some said he was out of favour with the Bey, others that the late chief minister had sent him on some private mission to Europe: at all events, he had disappeared from Tunis.

We were cheered at the hotel by the arrival of more guests, passengers by the French mail steamer. Among them were Colonel Playfair, the popular and hospitable consul-general at Algiers, and his genial travelling companion, the Earl of Kingston. They were interested to hear I had come from Tripoli, having photographed the Roman ruins, in quest of which they now came to Tunisia.

While we were at dinner a little Italian fiddler came in, and in a heedless inconsiderate moment I gave him two piastres. In a quarter of an hour another musician arrived, and a gentleman promised me we should have a bad time of it, for they abounded in Tunis. Time was, when Tunis had a gigantic organ-grinder brought over in an Italian steamer, whose strength and ferocity drove all the other musicians away. In a foolish moment the authorities of Tunis banished him. I resolved to inquire for this organ-grinder on my way through Italy, and tempt him by a heavy reward to England, where every leading city would quarrel for him. The question in our country must one day be decided, whether or no it is justifiable to give an organ-grinder poisoned meat.

After dinner one evening I went to a café. Behind the counter was the old landlord of the Hôtel de France, once a good-looking, well-dressed ex-soldier of the French army. Poor old man, how changed now! Keeper of a poor café chantant, his eldest son outlawed from Tunis: his second son, a smart handsome youth, our guide in Tunis and whom we had taken with us to Bona to join the Chasseurs d'Afrique in Algeria, had struck his officer and been shot at Constantine: his daughters had abandoned him: his wife was with him still, but looking twenty years older. They remembered me, and talked hopefully of being able to take another hotel. Poor old couple. I fear they never will.

Our company at their old hotel had been a little mixed: Bakkoush, whose antecedents were unknown: a Sicilian gentleman who left his country to escape his creditors: a Sard who had given a husband an excuse for shooting his wife, and who escaped to Tunis: an old German chemist, who afterwards wrote a book of his travels in which he handsomely referred to us as his so angenehmen englischen Reisegefährten, and so on.

One day Mr. Wood showed me the finest examples I had seen of mosaic from Roman Carthage. A lion grinning, of almost life size, and a fine female head. The consul-general seems to be the right man in the right place here: his ability and personal influence have contributed materially to the steady advance of the Tunis government in the path of civilisation. Old and oppressive restrictions towards Europeans have been removed, concessions have been made, and freedom of all kinds encouraged. Real property can be held safely by Europeans, and the consul-general has set the example by buying some property near the railway station. Indeed, Tunis is showing an example which her suzerain the Sublime Porte, if wise in its generation, would endeavour to follow.

We will take one final stroll through the city. Beyond the silversmiths', lies the picturesque bazaar of the saddlers and leatherworkers, where the white-robed Bedouins come to buy high red boots, holsters, &c. In one or two shops were chiefs' hats, with vast brims and crowns and covered with ostrich feathers. A mulberry tree with tender green foliage stood in the centre of this bazaar. We went out behind the Kasbah. Near the gate sat a row of respectable negro women, twenty or thirty in number, selling bread.

We sat by the great fountain of the waters of Zaghwân and Ain Djugâr, surrounded by a pretty garden full of wallflowers, roses, geraniums, strawberries, violets, and bananas, and looking over the snowy city's roofs and palms. Beyond were the olive-clad hills, the lovely panorama of the lake, the gulf, the sea, and the purple lead mountain—Djebel Resass. To our right lay the holy mount of Sidi Bel Hassan, having a cemetery, and a maraboût whither childless women go to pray.

We returned to the city, and, passing through the woollen and stuff bazaars and the wool market, reached the chief entrance of the Kasbah. That once fine old building is disfigured by restoration and new plaster, in the worst style of art. It contains accommodation for four thousand soldiers. Its mosque has a beautiful minaret, with arches in black and white marble and tile work. In front of the Kasbah is the place of execution, a Europeanised open space. A few weeks ago five Arabs were hanged here for carrying off a woman. Below this is the fez, or *sheshiya* bazaar. This trade is almost a monopoly of rich Moors. A thick and closely-woven woollen skullcap is soaked, swollen, and dyed: having been scraped with thistle brushes, combed, and hammered, it resolves itself into one of those compact shotproof red head dresses. The weaving is done in the country, most of the dyeing at Toburba, on the river Medjerdah.

The stuff bazaars of the Jews were closed and securely padlocked, it being Saturday. This recalls Hammerfest, where the warehouses and stores are full of valuable walrus ivory, whalebone, seal oil, skins, and furs of all sorts, and where the doors are carefully locked too. Only the keys are hung up on a nail outside. Dishonesty is almost unknown to the poor Laplanders and Norwegians.

We went one day to buy some Arab paper. The

merchant was an aged man with a long white beard. He had long outlived the term of mortal life, being apparently about a hundred and eighteen years old: and when he asked us twenty piastres for the paper, we said one to another that it would be unworthy to offer him less. When we gave him the money the old man refused it and wanted his paper back. We wept as we reminded him that he had only asked so much, and said we trusted he would let the paper go. It was the first time in his long, long life that he had received what he had asked. He was quite upset, and as we went away the fine old boy shed tears because he had not asked more.

The mosque of Abdallah—a beautiful tiled and marble building—once used as a Spanish church, stands in the bazaar. It has a stately hexagonal minaret. Indeed, the Tunis minarets are models of grace and variety. In the quiet street of the Bey's mosque were a few shoemakers, and some boys indolently spinning silk. The little mosque itself has a green tiled roof, plaster fretwork in the eaves, Moorish arches, and marble pillars stained by time and splashed with whitewash. It has marble slabs inscribed with Arabic text: the minaret and its gallery, panelled in tiles, stand out into a blue sky.

Not far from the Bey's town residence—whither he rarely comes except in Ramadhan—is the diamond market, where those stones are hawked about from eleven o'clock till noon on all days except Saturdays. Men hurry about here with *haïks*, shawls, and carpets for sale, and soft transparent stuffs made in Djerba and the Djerîd. Here is the centre of the Tunis bazaars, the scene of almost daily auctions, and a spot where an idler can spend hours simply watching Oriental life and picturesqueness in their purest and most graceful form. This grace is inherited by these descendants of the Moors of Spain, who attained a culture and refinement reached by no other Moslem race. Narrow streaks of sunlight stream through the wooden peaked roofs—falling on the columns and their white capitals, on Moorish arches or marble fountains, on old arabesque tablets—on women in black masks and bundles of clothes—Jews in blue turbans—green-turbaned scherîfs—on brown *haïks* from the Djerîd, Bedouins in white hoods and burnouses—negroes with baskets—on embroidered cloth dresses of delicious harmony and softness—apricot, lemon, and pale blue, black embroidered with red, straw colour, and pink *abbas*, blue and brown striped *cashabiyeh* from the Sahel. We wander through this masquerade to cafés where groups of Arabs smoke and sip coffee on matted seats, watching bamboo birdcages, wonderful pictures of Tunis, Stamboul, and Algiers, by native artists, and gold fish in glass bowls.

We stroll on, and watch them spinning silk, white,

yellow, red, and all manner of colours. Here comes a donkey laden with oranges and lemons. At one caroub each! sings the Moor: oranges! very sweet and full of water! one caroub each! We traverse the grocers' bazaar, where the groceries stand in brightly-coloured Djerba pottery. In a pipe manufacturer's shop are ostrich eggs and leopard skins, left no doubt in exchange by some Arab of the interior. Then through the copper bazaars, where all manner of red copper pots and vessels hung. We went on towards the Jew quarter, reached the decaying mosque of Sidi Mahhras, once but no longer a sanctuary. We were shown one or two of these in Tunis, into which if a criminal or refugee escaped, no pursuers could follow him. All they could do was to brick him up.

Towards the centre of the bazaars stands the fine Mosque of the Olive Tree, Djemma 'l Zitûna: we would pass one or other of its entrances a dozen times in a day. We had glimpses into the marble courtyard, arcaded with white pillars brought by Hamoûda Pasha from Carthage and other ruined cities. For a Christian or Jew to enter this mosque in open daylight would be almost certain death. If he escaped the armed sentries who guard its doors, he would be torn to pieces, or stabbed, or knocked on the head, by the shopkeepers, scherîfs, or saints who haunt the bazaars. Consequently I very rarely entered the Mosque of the Olive

Tree—indeed I do not remember entering it at all. The essence bazaars were favourites of mine: the atmosphere was rendered fragrant by ambergris, attar of rose, and twenty other essences. The whole heart of this city is a moving panorama of freshness and picturesqueness of which one never tires. It is probably a picture of what Cordova and Granada were.

I spent the evening with Colonel Playfair and Lord Kingston, who, like myself, were about to start on their travels. The light-hearted nobleman had a very elaborate and perfect photographic apparatus, with which he meant to illustrate their journey on Bruce's footsteps. An hour before Perruquier and I had to start for the Goletta, the Bey's letter arrived. This was all I needed, and we travelled down to Goletta, embarking the same afternoon on the Rubattino steamer *Corsica*. She was a fast seaworthy little boat, having a comfortable saloon, and, for ladies, who are not of much account in these latitudes, a cabin over the screw and round the rudder-post, where the sounds of both could be heard to great advantage. The wind began to rise, and the green waters of the Gulf of Tunis grew crested and rough.

Perruquier had blossomed into blue serge garments and high-heeled boots, and looked so imposing that I felt quite abashed to ask in his presence for second-class accommodation for him. He sauntered about the poop, and laid the foundation of deadly sickness by smoking many cigarettes. He means to spend some months in Paris this year, he tells me, to régler quelques petites affaires which originated in a former visit to that gay and festive city.

CHAPTER XIII.

Sail for the East Coast—Susa—Bazaars—The Sahel—Adrumetum—
The Port of Kairwân—The Revolution—Monastir—Leptis Parva—
Ras di Mas—Mehdia—The Patriarke of Cairaoan—Salectum.

THE *Corsica* put to sea at four o'clock. The sun set, and the young moon came out. We passed Ras Addar or Cape Bon, the promontory of Hermes of the ancients, rounded Ras el Mustapha, where stands Kalibia, close to which the Numidian King Massinissa was killed: and entered the Gulf of Hammamet, passing at early morn the little town of that name. A strong breeze blew from the land, and, while filling our sails, raised no waves, so that we were scudding with sail and steam over a smooth sea. Then the engines were slowed and stopped, and the anchor went down off Susa.

It is a Moorish town sloping up a moderate hill, white in the glittering rays of the morning sun, which it stands facing: of a compact trapezium form, fortified with a heavy wall, and surmounted by a castle. All its buildings are contained within the walls. Only scattered roofs and domes appear in the low wooded country to the left, which ends in a grove of palms. To the right the land is equally low, but more bare and stony, and it runs up due north-west to the picturesque range and peak of Zaghwân. One considerable ship lay at anchor near a schooner, several white lateen sails skimmed about in the fresh breeze: this was the existing shipping of Susa.

We went on shore, passing an Arab boat on its way to the steamer. Too small to contain half-a-dozen barrels of olive oil, the proprietor had attached them in a string to the boat's stern, with one empty barrel as a safeguard or float, and was towing them with much satisfaction. We believe we recollect olive oil with a strange taste to it. This Arab will be trying his system one day with barrels of wine.

A boatman took me to the vice-consulate. Mr. Dupuis, our vice-consul, whom it was unfair to disturb at seven in the morning, was most kind. He sent to the Castle to ascertain that the governor of Susa had received instructions from the prime minister about my escort to Kairwân, and promised to have the Ispahis ready for me on my return from Sfax. Mrs. Dupuis also insisted very kindly that I should remain at the vice-consulate on my way to and from Kairwân.

I went to the Kasbah—a high walled fort with dwellings within it, which can contain four thousand troops on an emergency. Then we went through the dirty unswept streets of the bazaars. What is that mosque called? we said to an Arab, pointing to a square tiled minaret. It is called a mosque, he said with reserve. We said to another, Have the kindness to tell us the name of that mosque. It is called the mosque, he replied. But it has some name, we said with deference. How does its name concern you, who are Christians? he said abruptly.

Sir, we said with ceremony to a negro, whom we might have bought outright for fifty or sixty piastres: what is the name of this street? It is Hammâm el Bey—the street of the Bey's Bath, he answered civilly. That is because the mosque is in it, we said. No, he said, how can that be? But it bears the name of the mosque, we explained. Not at all, the negro said: the mosque is called Natreddîn. The people of Susa have a reputation for fanaticism: no doubt they have some of the prejudices of their neighbours of Kairwân.

We ascended by a series of dirty alleys again to the Kasbah, and went out to the grass market behind the town. Returning by the open quarter of the blacksmiths and carpenters, we came to the bazaars proper—cool, dark, and vaulted, and very picturesque. The shopkeepers seemed goodnatured. The customary silk and woollen goods were for sale, with groceries and essences. Here and there were capitals and pedestals degraded to the purpose of stepping-stones. We left the covered bazaar, which runs in a continuous line, with small side bazaars to right and left: passed a foudoûk, a hammâm with firewood heaped on the roof, and racks for drying the linen: noticed the cane baskets of the form of great coffee-pots, used in fishing here: then went out by the Water Gate and returned to the wooden landing-place.

The mosque of Natreddîn, or that of the Faithful, is one of the oldest, but not the largest, in Susa. The Djemma 'l Kebîr, or Great Mosque, is down by the northern Water Gate: it has a low minaret, not seen from the sea. Portions of the building are very old. Susa contains probably eight thousand inhabitants: of these many are Christians and Jews. Some of the foreign merchants are wealthy, and the trade is considerable.

The principal exports of Susa are olive oil, esparto grass, wool, and soap made from olive oil. Pottery comes from Nabel or Nablus, and sometimes a small quantity of wax from Zaghwân. The esparto grass was first shipped from Susa to any extent by an English firm well known in all the Barbary states, Perry Bury & Co.

The Sahel, or east coast province of the Regency, of which Susa is the chief port, is, from its position, of considerable commercial consequence. Its three districts are Susa, Monastir, and Mehdia. It measures about ninety-five miles in length and twenty in width.

Susa is on good grounds identified with the Adrumetum, which first, of these Eastern ports, offered Julius Cæsar any serious resistance. That remarkable man landed here a small force of three thousand foot and a hundred and fifty horse, and riding himself round the walls, reconnoitred the city. After this he set to work to forage in the neighbourhood, and establish his camp.

After the establishment of the Aghlab dynasty in Barbary and the building of Kairwân, Susa was made its port, and from this insignificant little harbour set sail the armadas destined to conquer Sicily and Rome. When civil war took place between the rivals for supreme power, the Beys of Kairwân, supported by the Sahel towns and harbours, overcame the Deys of the capital.

It is said the Arabs of the Sahel can bring thirty-five thousand horsemen into the field, but I doubt it. The province has been heavily punished within the last ten years. After the abortive revolution, General Zarruk encamped under the walls of Susa, and imposed upon the Sahel towns 600,000*l.* indemnity. Wasted as the inhabitants and their means had been in seven previous years by famine, pestilence, and short crops, they were unable to pay: and had to raise money at usurious rates to meet the demands upon them. The gates of Susa are scrupulously closed soon after sunset, and have been so ever since Doria surprised the town in 1539.

The harbour of Susa is the worst on the coast, ships being liable to be blown from their anchorage. Gusts of the Tramontana and north-east wind whirl a strong current round Cape Bon between Malta and the Barbary coast: and ships caught here must either go to sea, or run for the shallows of the Syrtis. There is no inn at Susa; a Greek has a sort of restaurant and one or two available rooms : nor are there many attractions for travellers beyond boating, shooting, and riding. Rent and living are very high in Susa: the journey by land to Tunis occupies two days.

Tunis, like all other countries of consideration, has had a revolution. It lasted for six months, and the authorities seemed for a time paralysed. However, foreign ships of war appeared in the various ports, and frightened the inhabitants into submission. They were afterwards mulcted handsomely, Susa being called upon for its proportion of the 600,000*l.* I have mentioned. The little town of Mehdia, for example, had to contribute 75,000*l.*, to encourage the others. All arms, down to knives of a hand's length, were taken away, and the majesty of the government was reasserted.

The exports and imports of Susa and the other seaports are collected by the Commission of Ceded Revenues, established first in 1867 for the purpose of assuring and simplifying the payment of interest upon the government loan. This Commission—chiefly composed of representatives of European states—hand over yearly to the government a fixed sum, for expenses of administration, army, marine, and other requirements: to be increased in case of urgent need, at the discretion of the Commission, by a similar amount. In addition to this income, the governors of districts levy from the population what they think fit, so the government does not do badly. Each male, fit to work, pays a yearly tax of forty-five piastres.

The gunpowder monopoly is a strange one. The manufacture or sale of gunpowder by private individuals is forbidden, the government manufactures none itself, importation of it is forbidden, and yet it is to be bought in every quarter of Tunis, and guns are blazing away at quail and snipe in every marsh. This is one of those things that they manage better in Tunis.

We steamed out of the bay, and in an hour we were abreast of the picturesque walled town of Monastir, the Ruspina of Cæsar. The Castle rises prettily from the walls, which are light in colour, and above them are just visible the white flat roofs, a few minarets, a few palms, and a large white dome. The town lies back from the white sandy beach: we have to pass outside of three small outlying islands. There are numerous square marabouts and tombs, on this side of the town. It is said the people of Mehdia used to send their dead by sea for burial here.

The harbour is bad, but perhaps the best on this coast. Only one vessel lay in the roads, and the little place or port whence the oil and produce of Monastir are shipped, lies at half an hour's distance from the town, and is defended by a fort. Beyond the town are gardens and olive woods stretching close down to the shore, and interspersed with palm trees and prickly pear. The *Corsica* lay one third of a mile from the beach, and her stay was too short to allow of going up to the town. We still see Zaghwân—the highest peak of Tunisia, four thousand and seventy-eight feet high —but faintly in the warm haze.

The inhabitants, numbering probably eight thousand, are not noted for politeness, and there is a proverb on the coast here, Let him who has no dog, put a Monastiri before his door. The lion-voiced Monastiri, however, has not a heart of oak, for, give him a blow, and he immediately begins to pay you compliments. The Arabic here is said to be of a very indifferent kind.

We see, in an hour after leaving Monastir, low islands known to navigators as the Conigliera Islands, because swarming with rabbits. The islands are low, sandy, and covered with brushwood: behind them lie the remains of Leptis Parva. The roads of Monastir afford no shelter from the N.E. or E. winds: but behind these islands, though the anchorage is not first-rate, vessels can lie in moderate security. All the way from Monastir to Leptis run olive woods. Leptis Parva was a considerable colony of the Phœnicians. The name Leptis means—so Barth says—port, but I know of no such word in Greek or Latin. The Arabic name of the village lying twenty minutes southwards, Lemta or Lemba, probably originated in the Phœnician name, and helps to identify the spot. The name of the Greater Leptis has been corrupted not very differently into Lebda.

'The ancient town of Monastir,' says Leo, ' built by the Romans vpon the Mediterran Sea, is enuironed with most impregnable and stately walles, and containeth very faire buildings: but the inhabitants thereof are most miserable and beggerly people, and weare shooes made of sea-rushes. Most of them are either weauers or fishers. Their fare is barlie bread, and a kinde of foode mingled with oil. The territorie adiacent aboundeth with oranges, peares, figs, pomegranates, and oliues: sauing that it is continually wasted by the inuasion of the enemie.'

As we approached the passage between the islands, the steamer's engines were slowed. Otto piedi! shouted the leadsman. Adagio! shouted the captain. Sette piedi! Stop! roared the skipper, and we glided over the white sand shining through the green water. Nove piedi! and we went on at full speed. The breeze fell, and cinders from the funnel came floating down on us, so we had the awning put up.

A Moorish gentleman of Sfax came aft every now and then to chat with us. A stout, goodnatured old boy, who looked as if we were welcome, for all he cared, to enter all the mosques of Barbary. We were soon abreast of Ras di Mas, the Thapsus of Julius Cæsar, a point whence the coast runs directly south. Cæsar himself did not penetrate farther south than this: he contented himself with defeating Juba I. here. I have a silver coin of Juba. He wears a head-dress like that of a Laplander, and looks as if he would be easily defeated. There are here remains of a great mole, an amphitheatre, a fine reservoir of Roman work, built in stone and cement, and numerous cisterns, which the water fills one after the other, after the principle of Solomon's Pools. Monsieur Daun, a French civil engineer, sent to explore by poor Napoleon III., found many antiques here: marbles, lamps, coins of J. Cæsar, stone balls for catapults, urns containing ashes, water vessels, statues, et cetera.

An hour's steaming brought us off the narrow promontory beyond which stands El Medea—Mehdia—all that remains of the Roman town of Afrikia or Africa. We rounded the point, and anchored on the south side of the town. The walls of Mehdia, originally of Roman construction, faced with stone and of rubble within, are very ruinous. The promontory is bare of all but a castle and marabout: the town lies inland within it, and stretches across its neck from shore to shore.

There are six thousand inhabitants, of whom maybe three hundred and fifty are Christians. Five vessels lay in the roads, which are exposed to the south and easterly winds: and the *Corsica* had anchored at a quarter of a mile from the beach. Her stay was very short. We had time to distinguish the great mosque —once a barrack for Roman legionaries—of which the square minaret rises within the town, and the blank white wall extends down to the water's edge. In the interior of the mosque, I was told, were numerous inscriptions, Arabic and Roman. The natives, not knowing what spell or evil import these latter might possess, have effaced all within reach. Christians as usual are not admitted.

Leo says : ' El Mehdia, founded by *Mahdi*, the first patriacke of Cairoan vpon the Mediterran Sea, and fortified with strong wals towers and gates, hath a most noble haven belonging thereto. *Mahdi*, when he first came vnto this region, fained himself in an unknowne habite to be descended of the linage of *Mahumet*, whereby growing into great fauor of the people, he was by their assistance made prince of Cairoan, and was called El Mahdi Califa. Afterwards tyrannising over the people, and perceiuing some to conspire against him, he erected this toune of Mahdia, to the ende that he might there finde safe refuge when neede required.

'At length one Beiezida, a Mahumetan prelate, came vnto Cairoan: but Mahdi fledde vnto his newe toune, where with thirtie saile of ships sent him by a Mahumetan prince of Cordoua, he so valiantly encountered the enemie that Beiezid and his sonne were both slaine. Afterwards returning to Cairoan, he grew in league and amitie with the citizens, and so the government remained vnto his posteritie for many yeeres.'

Shaw does not believe Leo's account. He rightly thinks Mehdi only rebuilt the town: certain details of architecture in it being too polite and regular for Arabic origin.

Half a day's journey distant from Mehdia—twenty-seven miles—stands the beautiful amphitheatre of Tysdrus, now known as El Djem. It is still very perfect. A short way south of Mehdia are the remains of Salectum: it is disputed whether Hannibal embarked from Mehdia—Turris Hannibalis—or from Salectum. At Kasr Alal, towards Monastir, are numerous families of silk weavers.

CHAPTER XIV.

The Barbary Coast—The Khassîr—Kerkeneh—The Flying Camp—Djerba—The Lotos Eaters—Skull Pyramid—Gulf of Kabes—Palus Tritonis.

WE ramble out again over the blue water, having merely awaited a couple of boats which took off some boxes and two passengers. The wind is still fresh, and delightfully in our favour, satisfying even the steward, a big dark Italian, who sings sonorously in fair weather, and curses in rough, till our flesh creeps.

We get all our canvas up, and steam away at the rate of nine knots down this pleasant coast of Barbary. There is a telegraphic line running from Tunis through Birloubuîta, Susa, Monastir, and Mehdia, to Sfax. A French company, under the auspices of the Tunis government, are the entrepreneurs. They received the concession of the land and houses necessary for their purpose from the government, who in return have free use of the wires. There are, in all, four hundred miles of telegraph lines in the Regency. In two hours we came in sight of the village El Khadijah and Burdj el Shebba, a tall tower of lighthouse form—and easily convertible into one—raised in honour of a holy woman who was buried here. They stand on the promontory of Ras Kapoudiah. Shaw says: Capoudia is the Caput Vada of antiquity. It is a low narrow Strip of land, which stretcheth Itself a great Way into the Sea, and upon the Point of It there is a highe Watch Tower, with traces of severall Ruins that might formerly belong to the City built here by Justinian.

After dinner we had lost the low coast: nothing was in sight but the sea and the setting sun. Sitting chatting on deck with three Moors, I received from a native of Djerba, the Island of the Lotos Eaters, by name Sidi Suleiman Ibn Zukkri, an invitation to stay with him in Djerba, where he promised to entertain me with *kouskousou, assida,* eggs, coffee, and mutton. This Lotos Eater was much pleased when I guessed his age to be thirty-three years and a quarter. He had no exact idea himself, indeed the Moors here can give no idea in years of their age: they have to refer to some circumstance or other. For instance, one will say, I was born in the year when the first steamer came to Sfax: another, I was born in the year of the cholera, or of the revolution. My friend of Djerba, Solomon son of Zachariah, was so satisfied at having an estimate of his exact age, that he will go about quoting it hereafter, and anyone who asks him in the next five years his age, will learn that he is just thirty-three years and a quarter.

Another Lotos Eater, a friend of Sidi Suleiman, gave me a cordial welcome to his house in the hills: he would take me to see ruins, enrich me with ancient copper coinage, his house should be my house, and his servants my servants. Wallah!

It grew dark: the young moon, the evening star, Arcturus, and the noble Sirius shone in the dark blue heavens, and there was a solitary falling star. Then we went at half-speed. Two fathoms! One and a half! then we touched ground. The screw was reversed, and we backed off. Very soon we cast anchor in the shallow sea.

We were off the vast banks of the Kerkeneh, the Khassîr, or Shallows—the calm sea of the dreamy Lotos Eaters. This was a very snug corner of the world for them to find. Within a radius of forty miles round the Islands of Kerkeneh to the north and the Isle of Djerba to the south, lies the Khassîr—the smaller Gulf of Sidra or Lesser Syrtis (Σύρτις, a shoal), otherwise known as the Gulf of Kabes. The Lesser Syrtis may be said to extend all the way to Kapoudîah, since from this point to Djerba there is a succession of little flat islands, banks of sand, and small depths of water. Sheltered northward by the banks of Kerkeneh, westward by the mainland, southward by Djerba, and seaward by their own shallowness, these tranquil waters are convulsed by no storms. On them the

North wind has but little effect, it cannot beat them up into great waves: and here the sandals, *loúds*, *karabs*, and *shabecques* come to shelter in the winter months, flocking like swallows from the stormy coast of Tripoli. Here is a region for yachting, a refuge for victims to hydrophobia, for those who dread the bitter sea.

It is strange to be lying at anchor in the open sea. We are not many hours from Sfax, but the channel between Kerkeneh and the mainland is very narrow, and at night navigation is impossible, except for small vessels, so we must wait for daylight. Virgil wrote of Tunis harbour as follows, but he might have sung of Sfax instead:

> *Within a long recess there lies a bay:*
> *An island shades it from the rolling sea,*
> *And forms a port secure for ships to ride,*
> *Broke by the jutting land on either side.*
> *No haulsers need to bind the vessels here,*
> *Nor bearded anchors, for no storms they fear.*

The Kerkeneh Islands are the Cercina and Cercinitis of the Romans, whither Cæsar sent Crispus with vessels to get grain for the troops. The Tunisian government has for ages employed a body of troops to bring grist to the mill, in the shape of taxes from the outlying provinces. This flying camp has always been commanded by the heir to the throne, who is consequently known as the Bey of the Camp. As much as a hundred thousand pounds used to be netted by this expedition, in cattle, money, and valuables: but since the establishment of better local government, the expedition does not travel yearly: the governor of Kairwân only proceeds to some of the chief towns of the Djerîd. I met an aide-de-camp of Ali Bey, who commanded the last important expedition some years ago. Two thousand troops and a number of Arab horsemen formed the expedition. It would push on from spot to spot, merely spending time enough for the Bey to administer justice or apportion and collect the taxes. The journey through the Djerîd occupied two or three months, some trouble and delay arising from the decamping of many of the Arab tribes at the Bey's approach.

On this occasion several foreigners accompanied Ali Bey, taking the opportunity of botanising, searching for ruins, antiques, coins, game, &c. Arrived at Kairwân on its journey south, the army encamped for three days on the plain: the Bey entered the city to pray at the Great Mosque, and then the troops marched through, entering by the Tunis Gate, and leaving by the Gate of Skins. Assessors accompanied the Bey, to determine the value of tribute offered in the shape of oxen, camels, sheep, corn, olives, or dates. Fowls, or gazelles, which abound in the Djerîd, were not regarded as acceptable. Lions would roar round the camp at night—exasperated, the noble beasts, by the smell of good cooking: for the cuisine of an Eastern prince and his household is a lavish one. Ostriches were often seen, but not often taken.

On her previous voyage the *Corsica* had sailed to Djerba, and it was a disappointment to be unable to go on thither. To be so near to the Insula Lotophagorum and to turn back, seemed a misfortune. This interesting island, once known as Meninx, Lotophagitis, or Insula Lotophagorum, fifty miles or five hours distant from Sfax by steamer, forms the southern extremity of this gulf. It is separated from the mainland by a mile or two of shallow sands, almost traversable on foot. The coast round the island is so shallow that the *Corsica*, drawing not more than eight feet of water, has to lie out in the open roads three miles from the shore. The wind is often high, but the sea never, and the anchorage is safe and good enough. Djerba has no ports, towns, or even considerable villages, so widely are its habitations dispersed.

The Lotos Eaters number probably about twenty thousand. The island has the aspect of a beautiful garden, the fig trees are as large as walnut trees, the pomegranate shrubs attain the size of ordinary trees, apricots abound: the olive grows in extraordinary luxuriance, and seventeen date trees are sometimes known to spring from one root. This is something like an island, and was an earthly paradise for the lazy Lotos Eaters.

> *A land where all things always seemed the same,*
> *And round about the keel with faces pale—*
> *Dark faces pale against that rosy flame—*
> *The mild-eyed, melancholy Lotos Eaters came.*
> *They sat them down upon the yellow sand,*
> *Between the sun and moon upon the shore;*
> *And sweet it was to dream of Fatherland,*
> *Of wife and child, and slave—but evermore*
> *Most weary seemed the sea, weary the oar,*
> *Weary the wandering fields of barren foam.*
> *Then some one said—We will return no more.*
> *And all at once they sang—Our island home*
> *Is far beyond the wave, we will no longer roam.*

The modern Lotos Eaters—when I say modern, I don't want to offend the Djerbans, who are only in the year 1292 of the Hejreh, and nearly six centuries behind us—have shaken off such traditions and are an industrious, thriving people. They manufacture pottery, soap, stuffs in great quantities: they have extensive fisheries and sponge fisheries, and they turn the richness of the island to the best advantage. The stuffs of silk and wool can be bought very cheaply: the wool is peculiarly fine and suitable for shawls, which are beautifully wrought. For twenty-five piastres or twelve shillings, a very beautiful coverlet or a burnous can be bought. The mules of Djerba, which I have already said are excellent, are much used in carriages of native Tunisian gentry. They endure both heat and cold, and have in a great measure superseded the famous Barb horse. The wants of the French army contribute to drain Tunis of horses. Great quantities of Djerban stuffs, of wool and silk, are sent to the East. The islanders are good-natured and hospitable, like the Arabs of the Djerîd. Towards the Tripoli frontier, however, on the mainland behind Djerba, they are of a different character, untrustworthy and treacherous. The Djerbans are enterprising; being established as merchants in Tripoli, Alexandria, Constantinople, and throughout the East.

While Ferdinand the Catholic was besieging Malaga, there appeared a wild fanatic or dervish, Abraham of Djerba, who, after a desperate and partly successful effort to relieve the city, was taken prisoner. Attempting to assassinate the King and Queen, he was put to death, and his body flung from a catapult into the city, where he was interred and honoured as a patriot and a saint.

It is barely twenty-eight years since there stood upon the northern shore of Djerba, on the western side of the Castle of Es Soukh and marked upon the charts, a whitewashed tower, twenty feet in height, originally a pyramid, and composed of skulls. Skulls of the Spanish soldiers of Alvar de Sande, who were surprised and massacred here by the Turkish fleet. But few escaped in ships to Sicily. There were bones of men and buttons of soldiers' dresses to be found near, and birds had built their nests in the hollows of the skulls.

It would be ungracious to turn our backs upon the Gulf of Kabes without a word as to the spot whence it takes one of its names. It was known as Epicus, but Tacape was its chief name, a great emporium of Roman times. It now consists of two villages, the natives of which cultivate date trees and the famous henna plant, whose leaves are dried and powdered for export to the Levant. This is the region of the Troglodytes, famous from the time of Homer downwards. The modern village of Ghabs lies half a mile from the ruins of the old city, and Ionic capitals and fragments of columns are still found here. Tacape may one day recover some of its maritime importance.

Seventy miles inland lies the Sebkha el Laoudîah, meaning the Marsh of Landmarks, from the number of trunks of palms once placed at proper distances to direct caravans in their marches over it. According to one tradition, these trees sprang from date stones left by an army of the Egyptians in one of their invasions of Barbary. In the same way some future Egyptian army may be guided by my line of march, over the desert from Lebda to Tripoli. Only in certain seasons and in places does this lake contain water: it is ordinarily a vast plain of salt. It is the Palus Tritonis or Triton swamp, which it is believed lies below the level of the

Mediterranean and may again be placed in communication with it. Should this be possible, a shallow inland sea, seventy miles in length by twenty in width, might be formed in the heart of the fertile Djerîd : making its chief town, Toozer, Tisurus, a seaport on a small scale : and the laborious transport by camel might give way to traffic by sandals, or smaller boats. The river Akrout, entering the Mediterranean thirty miles north of Ghabs, tradition says, once connected the Palus with the sea, and, unless there have been geological changes, might be made to do so again.

It may be found that an entrance from the river of Ghabs, rising twelve or fourteen miles from the coast, would offer better prospects of success, though the distance for channelling would be greater by one-half, and certain high land intervenes. The environs of Ghabs are rich and beautiful : we are told of vines twining round lordly palms, of rich cornfields among almond trees and lotos.

Temple found here great abundance of the lotos, which he calls Rhamnus Lotus, growing in the neighbourhood of Ghabs and the surrounding villages. Lane calls the lotos *sidr*, and it has been supposed that this name acquired for the Gulf its title of Sidra. Far more likely Sidra is a Moorish corruption of Syrtis. The modern Arabs use the leaves of the *sidr* dried and pulverised, as soap. The bush resembles a blackthorn : the berry was so highly esteemed by the ancients that it was said to be worth forsaking one's country for. I have on various occasions forsaken my country, but generally more with a view to green figs and bananas. The legendary lotos of Egyptian sculpture was a water lily, but it seems to have vanished with the papyrus from the Lower Nile.

CHAPTER XV.

Arrival at Sfax—Gale—A Mistake—A Deaf Mute—The Quarters of Sfax—Mosques—A Caravan of Dates—The Bazaars—Gracefulness of Sfaxins—Environs—The City of Twelve Thousand Gardens—Slave Caravans—Street Auction—Costumes—The Great Mosque—A Tragedy—The Silversmiths—Bakkoush at Home—An Eccentric Dervish—A Modest Marabout—Ruins of Lebda.

WE slipped away from our anchorage just before dawn. The wind had risen, and blew a heavy northerly gale. We dared not try the inner passage, but made our way outside the Sponge Islands, and dropped anchor in the roads of Sfax, three miles out from the shore. The anchorage is good but shallow, and in such weather the captain thought well to keep out. Sfax, El Sfakkus, Asfax, or Asfachus, is said to owe its name to the quantities of water melons, *Fakkus*, abounding in its neighbourhood. It is of origin subsequent to Roman times.

Squalls came at times, with drifting rain: two hours passed, and, though it was still early morning, the prospect of landing seemed remote. Sulking in the cabin, or pacing about on deck in the moist whistling wind, did not kill the time very fast. The insidious Perruquier was sent to the captain to intimate that if a few men could be spared with one of the boats, they should be rewarded with gold. The captain told Perruquier that the sea was heavy enough to swamp a small boat, and that he could not let us have one. We asked some of the Moors what they would do if the steamer sailed for Tunis without landing them. *Maktoûb*, they said, good-naturedly. It is written. When Ali Bey landed in this neighbourhood, his boat was swamped, while the ship rode quietly at anchor.

At length we saw a boat with a small white sail, beating out, and our spirits went up 10°. But when it came alongside, with difficulty, in the fierce wind—pitching as if the four drenched natives would be flung into the sea: when we saw it was half full of water, ballasted with a heavy stone, kept afloat only by constant baling, the rudder attached by a piece of string only—our spirits fell 15°. It was a miserable boat, worth about three *mahboobi* and a half, and it did not seem very sensible to venture on three miles of sea in it, with the same necessity of getting back: but Perruquier and I slipped down a loose rope, three or four Moors followed us, and we shoved off, very nearly capsizing in doing so.

The stone and our weight made the boat so heavy that the waves washed over her sides. We had gone a mile or two, the water came in too fast to bale and rose steadily, gusts came faster than ever; when gradually a sense of satisfaction stole into our spirits. If the boat should capsize or sink, Perruquier and I should get out and walk. We remembered the long shelving shore, and guessed that there would be little more than five or six feet of water, a mile and a half out from the town.

To right and left of the city and its cream-coloured walls—which lie on flat ground close by the water—stretch miles of gardens, with little houses scattered among them. The signal tower of Sfax and the red dome of the Catholic church are the only conspicuous objects standing above the white houses.

A number of people came together to see us land—strangers not being plentiful in Sfax. I had asked a pleasant Italian in the boat if he knew Mr. Cardona of Sfax. Mr. Carton, you mean, he said: he is the English vice-consul: and we went together to the vice-consulate. A tall white-haired man rose as I went in. I have a letter for you, I said, from the captain of the *Circe* steamer. Circe, he said, Circe—I don't know the *Circe*. An English steamer, I explained, which came here just a year ago. I was absent, sir, he said, at that time. I was disappointed to see him throw his acquaintances over so readily, and said I understood he was Mr. Cardona. He laughed. No, I am Mr. Edward Carleton, and very much at your service. Mr. Cardona was a neighbour of his.

We had a long chat over a cup of coffee. I beg your pardon, he said, interrupting himself: here is a poor dumb man I want to speak to. Somebody had come behind my chair. I looked round and rose slowly: the mute started back, then seized my hands and gibbered at me inarticulately. It was our old friend Bakkoush, the Bey's buffoon. The vice-consul was much surprised, and Bakkoush made signs to him that we were old friends. It was four years since we had met: the storms of life had impaired his raiment, and poor Bakkoush was both thinner and seedier. I told him that he was thinner, and he explained that he had been ill. We set out to see the city. Mr. Carleton sent his dragoman, Perruquier came, and Bakkoush would not leave my side.

There are two quarters in Sfax—one within the old walls, for the Mohammedans, and the other without, down by the harbour, for the Christians. The gates of the Moorish city are closed after sunset to Christians. We entered the Arab quarter by an old gate with horseshoe arch, and close by it found the mosque of Sidi Ali Aziz. Within a few yards of it stands that of Sidi el Bahhri— Sidi the Sailor. Can it be the last resting-place of our old friend Sindbad the Sailor? It had marble work delicately carved and arabesqued in text, and a curious brick minaret.

At many angles of the streets and gateways were

columns and capitals of marble brought from Roman ruins. Many doorways were carved in a beautiful pink or salmon-coloured stone of Ghabs, closely resembling marble: in fact a kind of marble. Across the streets at many points were flying arches of horseshoe form. The mosque has a new gateway with minute arabesques in stone and alternate bands of tiles. Almost every doorway had carved jambs and lintels.

We met a caravan just arrived from the Djerîd— the camels laden with dates packed in skins, the Arabs tired and dusty—and arriving, poor fellows, to find the dates they had brought from so far almost unsaleable. Such is the plenty of dates this year that they are barely worth the trouble of picking, or of transporting from the interior. The finest dates of Tunisia, or indeed of Africa—the *deghla*—can be bought in Tunis for thirty five shillings the hundredweight: in the Djerîd for perhaps ten shillings. There are dates in Djerba, known as *bilahh* and as *b'sîr*, but they are far behind the *deghla*. In Morocco is a date also known as *bilahh*. On the flat islands of Kerkeneh there grows a soft dark date, called *ertoûb*, cheap, and not very good.

The Tunisian pound, the *rotal attari*, is just equivalent to our lb. avoirdupois: the *oke* contains two *rotals*, and the *kantar* fifty *okes*. The Tunisian measures for corn, flour, &c. are the *sah*, equal to four and a half imperial pints: the *ouîba*, containing twelve *sah*, and the *kafiss* sixteen *ouîbas*. There is a second scale of weights for precious metals. The coinage begins with the *karoûb* or farthing, which is nominally equivalent to six and a half *bourbe*. The silver *piastre* is worth sixpence: the *bouhamsa* or *mahboob*, half-a-crown. There are ten, twenty-five, fifty, and hundred piastre pieces in gold: of which the most common are the twenty-five piastre pieces, representing just fifteen francs. We can now start fairly, and the reader can accompany Bakkoush and the rest of us into the bazaars without fear of being taken in.

Camels carrying water for sale move about the bazaars of Sfax. The green turbans of the *scherîfs* simply swarm: the Friday's market place, or Soukh el Djemma, was alive with them. The Prophet's family is indeed handsomely represented: more are to be seen here in half an hour than in Cairo or Damascus in a day. They were very inquisitive, the Sfaxins, and Bakkoush was steadily employed in thrusting them aside as they stood gaping at us. Some he pushed with furious gestures, but none seemed to take offence: they all knew the privileged buffoon of the Bey.

In the Turkish bazaar were groceries of all kinds: in the corn market were great esparto baskets full of grain. We came to the Djemma 'l Hammâm, or Mosque of the Baths, and saw the piles of pearwood for burning in the baths: came to the shoe bazaar, where the canary-coloured leather is made into picturesque shoes, passed the harness makers who embroider the red leather: and everywhere a crowd of a dozen or twenty Moors hung on our heels to see what we were about, only dispersing momentarily when Bakkoush turned upon them.

It is a very general and pretty custom among the Sfaxins and many of the Tunisian Moors to carry, under the turban and above the ear, a small bouquet—sometimes a couple of lovely rosebuds, or a rosebud in a ring of orange blossoms. The contrast with the snowy white, straw-coloured silk, or green cotton turban is very telling. There is among the Moors of Tunisia grace both of dress and manner which does not characterise the Egyptians or Syrians, and which recalls their ancestors, the refined Moors of Granada and Cordova. There are no bazaars where such delicacy of taste in dress and colour are to be seen as in Tunis. The people seem tasteful by instinct, and it is a positive treat to sit and watch them. They reflect the polish and good breeding of the Spanish Moors, and are noted for their intelligence. Reading, writing, and the Scriptures are ordinary acquirements among them. The turbans of Sfax are larger than those of the chief Eastern cities, and approach those of the extinct Janissaries of Constantinople.

We saw beautiful mules—those of Sfax and Djerba are considered the best in the Regency. The greyhounds of Sfax are noted. A gentleman here has one, for which the Arabs have offered him forty sheep in exchange.

We watched them make the curious rude pack saddles for camels—generally from wood which had a natural fork. We came to the outer city through an old arched gate, and entered a foudoûk where dyers had established themselves. Here deep crimson and blue stuffs were hanging up to dry: while camels were waiting to transport them to the Djerîd, and devouring grass to pass the time. Bakkoush's raids upon the crowd were capital: mumbling and gesticulating, he fell upon them as if to devour them alive.

We passed the mosque of Djemma 'l Bou Shouîsha,—an aged building, where the whitewash of centuries had so encrusted and accumulated, that it looked as if thickly sugared, or covered with pure white snow. Stalactites of whitewash hung from each brick moulding and projection. Near this were blacksmiths and sickle makers, beating those thin crescent-shaped blades out of glowing iron. The high old city walls have machicolated battlements and square turrets at intervals. Above the forts floated the blood-red flag which is hoisted on the Mohammedan Sabbath.

Near the walls is a village of blacks, similar to that

described near Tripoli, and very African looking. Prowling dogs hang about the traveller's ankles, and he is fortunate who has Bakkoush for an escort. This extraordinary man explained with incredible facility the features of the surrounding country. He drew my attention to the numerous marabouts' tombs—to the great plain extending ever so far to the south—to the Sahara, in fact. He described to me the figs, almonds, peaches, olives, and pistachio nuts with which the environs of Sfax richly abound. How the country for half-a-day's journey round is full of gardens and fruits, till you reach the pasture lands of the Bedouins. This was all in dumb show, but there was no misunderstanding it. Wine is made here from excellent grapes : cucumbers are plentiful, and so are bananas. As to olives, which are taxed by the tree—every third tree being exempt—the district has paid to the Bey's government at the rate of a hundred and sixty thousand piastres a year.

The extent of the gardens of Sfax is immense : there are no less than twelve thousand of them about the city. There is not a really poor man in Sfax : each one has his 'garden' outside the walls, if only containing a fig tree and half-a-dozen olive trees. The man who comes to beg for bread has his country seat, though it may be only a dozen yards square.

Bakkoush told me he had lately returned from

Ghabs or Tacape. *T'kabh,* curiously enough, was about the only sound he could utter. Here he had found, in digging among the ruins, old engraved stones and a beautiful statue of a woman. Bakkoush and I formed plans for an expedition to T'kabh. The Arabs of the country are unspoiled and uncorrupted, being honest, peaceful, and hospitable—coming rarely into contact with the Europeans and coast races.

It is not twenty-seven years since caravans used to arrive in June regularly at Tunis from Tomboûkto, Ghadâmes, Wadai, and the interior, viâ Sfax and Susa, bringing slaves, ivory, gold dust, and ostrich feathers. The English Envoy, however, using his influence with Ahmed Bey, who was himself a humane man, obtained the emancipation of all slaves within reach: and slave-holders were compelled to issue them *teskeras,* or letters of discharge. Mr. Carleton received at one time in his house sixty poor creatures thus released, but left without means of support. Only a few months ago a black slave was brought to Sfax, but he was set free by the governor at the instance of our vice-consul.

As we passed through one of the city gates, we had to make room for a caravan of camels coming from the interior. Every few weeks caravans depart for the towns of Toozr in the Djerîd, Nafta, and Tebessa in Algeria, carrying English manufactures, and returning with dates, blankets, burnouses, wool, wax, &c. From

Ghadâmes they come no longer. Some attribute the change to the impolicy of the Beys, others to the suppression of the slave trade. Within the inner gateway, among the shops of the wool carders, was a lively scene —a street auction. Men were striding to and fro, and crying: Fine shawl for sale! who will buy? Excellent silk, and going for an old song! Boots! Is no one prudent enough to buy of me these admirable boots? A ring! In the name of the Prophet! Of the very purest silver, and beautified with a costly carnelian stone! Offered for six piastres! I seized the merchant by the arm and took the ring, which was old silver of Mecca work. How much? I asked. Six piastres. I told Perruquier to stay and buy it for five piastres. Monsieur can't do that, he said: the auction price is six piastres, and a slight augmentation has to be made. So Perruquier and I bought the ring for six piastres and one karoûb; and it now adorns the scarf of a popular and estimable member of society, who imagines that it is worth at least a golden twenty-five-piastre piece.

We watched them spin the silk and wool for *haïks* and for the *djubba*—a garment of singular picturesqueness, common to the Barbary towns, but I believe originating in Sfax. It is a plain, square-cut loose robe, like the *abbah* of Egypt, but open only at the breast, and there ornamented, as well as round the neck, with silk embroidery.

The material—often in alternate bands of silk and delicate wool—is generally of an indigo blue, faced with amber-coloured embroidery, or of a deep chocolate red faced with green.

The bazaars proper are cool, and vaulted with round arches, while the little shops are recessed in the whitewashed walls.

We came to the Djemma 'l Kebîr—one of the finest mosques in Barbary. It has a great court paved with marble: but, standing in a poor and crowded quarter, it makes no appearance externally. Horseshoe arches of pure white marble contain doors beautifully carved. Its floors are covered with straw-coloured matting. It was the Mohammedan Sabbath. In the huge vaulted prayer chamber—of which the great doors were open on to the street—knelt hundreds of Moors, with white and green turbans, in ranks as even as soldiers. As the Imaum's voice resounded, Oh ye who believe, bless and greet our Lord Mohammed! they fell upon their faces, chanting after him the praise of Allah and their Prophet. Their prostrations were as even as their ranks. The sight was interesting and impressive, but the Moors about us showed some impatience and displeasure, so we sauntered on.

Why has the Englishman come to Sfakkus? Perruquier was asked constantly in the bazaars, and what is he writing in the book? Oh, true believers, Perruquier would say, do not marvel if there arise from his visit a *baboor* in the midst of your city—a swift fire carriage which shall be as the Prophet's carpet to you, and shall transport you to Tunis in a twinkling.

When Perruquier confessed to this story, which went all through the bazaars, I asked him to subdue his natural aptitude for untruth, as I had no wish to come to the country of the Moors as an impostor.

In the vegetable market we saw baskets full of date seed on white stalks, exposed for sale. Beyond this quarter is the fish market, near which stands the prison. There is a small mosque adjoining the prison, so we could not enter. There are but few prisoners now: one is there under singular circumstances. A rich Moor owed a Christian of Sfax three thousand piastres. A poor Jew, clerk to the Christian, went two days ago with a receipt to the Moor's house to ask payment. Come into the house, and I will pay thee, said the Moor: and taking him into the room, he fell upon him with a knife, and stabbed him repeatedly.

On the day of my arrival at Homs, a shocking murder took place: on the day of my return to Tripoli a second: immediately before I reached Tunis another: and on the eve of our arrival at Sfax, a fourth. I hope that nothing unfair will be inferred from these circumstances.

Outside of the bazaars, which are decent enough,

are squalid open streets, below the average in cleanliness of ordinary Moorish towns. We could not move without considerable crowd. Indeed, the Sfaxins are the most appreciative people I have met in Barbary.

We went to the silversmiths' quarter, and sat among them for two hours, securing old enamelled beads, pure silver earrings in beautiful simple work, small silver gilt beads like peas, and great cubic beads like huge dice, gilded and enamelled. The Sfaxins rejoice very much in enamelled ornaments, and we found numerous examples of their work. Bakkoush was a sincere enjoyment: the unfailing clearness of his gestures or glances and the rapidity of his intelligence were a study. A glance at me and a tap upon his pocket meant, There are nimble fingers about, O gentle traveller. The silversmiths would offer me rings, bracelets, or engraved stones, and Bakkoush—who has a perfect genius for antique stones—by a momentary change of expression would approve or condemn them. The vice-consul's dragoman, who was willing and useful in the bargaining, was an imbecile compared with Bakkoush.

Bakkoush had made of old stones a study and a trade, and he was distracted when he told me of the pocketful he had brought from T'kabh: and sold only a week before. Next year we would go together to Djerba and Ghabs, the islands of Serkenis, and the great plain inland, and come back with asses' loads of them.

Any Moor who might be disposed to haggle or waste time was quickly disposed of. Bakkoush, after having it valued by the Amîn of the bazaar, would seize the silver object, thrust my money into the Moor's hand, and push him out of the bazaar—threatening him with loud inarticulate mutterings.

The dragoman had a cast in his eye, and, as we sat bargaining at the entrance of a dark little shop, Bakkoush sat beside him. The dragoman turning his head for an instant, Bakkoush shot a momentary glance at me with a terrific squint. In the same second the expression had vanished, and as the dragoman turned, Bakkoush was rolling up a cigarette with a solemn and impassive face. These flashes of humour and intelligence were irresistibly funny. In one moment Perruquier and his self-sufficiency shone out from the mute's face, in the next came a passing caricature of the silversmith talking to us. At times Bakkoush would take my hand and place it on his heart as a mark of friendship.

By many people in Tunisia this remarkable man is regarded as a clever impostor, as less of a buffoon than a spy, who pretends this infirmity in order to gain access and information in the Bey's interests. That he carries information about, it may be, but nothing could be more unfair than to suspect his muteness to be assumed. Mr. Carleton has known him deaf and dumb for thirty years, and if any fair reader will endeavour to feign dumbness for thirty hours, she will support me in stating that to carry on the imposition for thirty years is beyond the capabilities of our poor weak nature.

I was introduced at Sfax to an elderly dervish of ragged and hairy appearance, who takes an imbecile delight in the English Union Jack. When Mr. Wood came to Sfax many years ago in an English ship of war, the elderly dervish danced wildly about. Has the flag come? Has the flag come? he cried. What flag? said the consul-general. Why, the English flag! cried the elderly dervish, shedding tears of delight: I know no other flag. We have known people who made pets of spiders, wolves, toads, and even of cats: who sentimentalise over a plant, a solitary column, or dote upon old flint implements and hawthorn blue china pots: if this old boy had had a craze for postage stamps, or even for portraits of other people's ancestors, we should only say we have known people equally misguided; but to go silly about a flag, to dance and dream about it, is very original and creditable for a Sfaxin who has not had the artificial advantages of civilisation. It may be guessed that I did not tell this elderly saint that I had laid up in my portmanteau a deep blue silk Union Jack, lest he should cling fondly to me, and oblige me to take him home to England, or to give over the flag to him.

We went to see some conical stacks of esparto grass ready for shipment, which were impervious to rain, and to a cannon-ball. To strike one of them with the foot was like kicking at a wall. We strongly recommend them to armies. By the shore, close under the walls, is a marabout of very modest pretensions. It appears that the saint being what I suppose no other marabout on record has been, bashful and self-depreciatory, declined on his deathbed to have anything more elaborate than this simple white box and dome erected to his memory.

After this we saw down by the water's edge, near some villanous Maltese craft, six lengths of red granite columns. I knew them at once, though a Moorish stonemason had already chiselled over the surface of one. I asked where they had come from. A Maltese captain had brought them from Homs, where he had paid twenty-five piastres for them : and had sold them here for a hundred piastres each. I was assured that some of the harder and finer ones are worth as much as six hundred piastres, but those must be of uncommon length. They are taken, O Marcus Antoninus Pius! into the oil mills, where they are invaluable for crushing the olives, and will wear for generations.

We did not see the pirate who brought them, or I should have committed, or desired Perruquier to commit, an imprudence. Sfax is a city which has itself discreditable antecedents. It is believed to have been constructed from the materials of the famous Thainæ or Thenæ of antiquity, ten miles south-west of Sfax: and so complete was the plundering, that there is hardly a vestige of hewn stone to be found at Thainæ. It was shameful to see the noble shafts with the gloss of eighteen centuries upon them ground and sliced into crushers of the ignoble olive. There are numbers of them in Susa. This accounts for the total disappearance of many a noble ruin throughout Barbary, and will account for the disappearance of many more, unless the authorities are urged in their own interests to prevent it. Near these melancholy ruins of Lebda lay quantities of soft stone, pure white, brought from Mehdia.

We watched them building Arab *loûds*, shallow, long, half-decked boats, much used by the Kerkeni in tunny and sponge fishing. There are on the islands of Kerkeneh upwards of a thousand of these boats. The vice-consul, finding I had brought away no sponges as souvenirs of my visit to Sfax, insisted upon hurrying to his house and bringing me several specimens, three of Jershîsh, one of Serkenis, and one of Djerba. There were on the quay great oil jars, brought from the south side of the Djerîd, where the clay is highly suitable for pottery. These were of a huge size, beautiful in form, and they cost six piastres each.

The heavy rain of last night was a godsend to the

Sfaxins. I trust it was general, and extended to Tripoli where the poor Arabs were praying for it weeks before, and would be half ruined if it failed. I found an English engineer at Sfax, and made his acquaintance under the discreditable circumstances of having opened on the voyage some newspapers directed to him. He was engineer on board the Bey's corvette *El Bashir*.

CHAPTER XVI.

Embark on *Corsica*—Privations—Facts about Sfax—Sail for the North —Sponges of the Lesser Syrtis—The Oulad Azim—Octopi—Sponge Culture and Chicken Manufacture—Mehdia—Sardines—Arab Cemetery—Port of Mehdia—Turris Hannibalis—Relics of El Djem—A Moslem Companion—Monastir—Collectors—Susa.

WE put off to the steamer. Our waterproofs were no longer necessary in the dry cold evening, the wind had fallen, the sun set, and the city looked cold and white. We made friends with a green-turbaned Moor, who lay at his ease in the bottom of the boat, with his head resting affectionately upon an anisette cask. This descendant of the Prophet had one eye and a good-natured face. He had some successful oil works, and was no doubt a heavy importer of ruins. I told him, what had only then occurred to me, that I had not eaten a mouthful for eight hours and a half. The scherîf not only begged me to eat with him on the spot, but to share his food all the way to Susa. I told Perruquier to say that under the circumstances I would say nothing to the Imam about the liqueur butt on which he was reposing. Aniseed grows plentifully in the Regency, both here and near Tunis.

When I appeared in the cabin of the *Corsica*, much reduced by fasting, and told the steward how hungry I was, he began to swear magnificent oaths at society in general, and went out of the cabin with a *sacRRRRRAMENTo* that rolled like thunder. Eight hours and a half! (in a voice like a twenty-four-pounder gun). *Cospetto!* not a mouthful of bread even! *Cento mila maledizioni!* and he strode to the galley and ordered an ample meal to be made ready. Then he came and watched me solicitously, thrusting dishes upon me and murmuring over my hardships.

The city of Sfax with three suburbs contains about thirty-five thousand inhabitants. The Islands of Kerkeneh, eighteen miles away, have a population of twelve thousand. The principal manufactures of the Sfaxins are woollen cloths, blankets, burnouses, &c., which are sent on a large scale to Alexandria and other parts of the East, towels with which they supply the vapour baths for the whole Regency, scarfs for Moorish and Jewish women, yellow slippers for the surrounding Arab tribes. They are excellent dyers.

The Sfaxins are an industrious race. The same individuals are merchants, traders, weavers, husbandmen, fishermen, caravanists, according to occasion. Sfax has an independent governor, under the Prime Minister's sole control, and this simplicity of responsibility contributes to the facility of settling disputes between Europeans and natives. The anchorage of Sfax is the safest in the Regency, from which circumstance the Bey's little flotilla winters here. It is the only place on the coast where there is a tide, which rises about four and a half feet.

Mahhras has had great rain-water cisterns, said to have been built by Ibn Aghlab, Khalif of Kairwân, for whose memory the people of this country have a great esteem and veneration. He was author of many similar beneficent works in various parts of the Winter circuit. At Mahhras some beautiful square marble columns were found by Dr. Shaw, but they have since disappeared. This southern extremity of the district is distant from Sfax about thirty-five miles. Here a French vice-consul has been lately nominated, and English vessels occasionally ship esparto.

The droll old Leo writes: Of the town of Asfachus. It is compassed with most high and strong wals, and was in times past very populous; but nowe it containeth but three or fower hundred families, and but a fewe shops. Oppressed it is both by Arabians and by the King of Tunis. All the inhabitants are either weauers, marriners, or fishermen. They take great store of fishes called by them *spares*, which word signifieth nought in the Arabian and Barbarian, much lesse in the Latine toong. Their apparell is base and some of them traffike in Egypt and Turkie.

We passed the night at anchor in the roads of Sfax, the steam winch rattling up to a late hour. In the morning we were on our way northward: the soft warm sun was shining upon the deck, and the air from the Barbary shore blew deliciously upon us. The coast line to our left was low and hazy. Among the palms stood the marabout of Sidi Mansour—the Victorious. We were heading for the Islands of Kerkeneh, of which the palm trees and fish weirs were visible.

A thin tall Jew was on board, in a black jacket and dress, and with the deep blue cotton turban worn by his race. As he sat by me on deck, he began to talk in excellent Italian. He was on his way to Tunis, to give evidence, poor fellow: for the murdered Jew was his brother.

All along the Tunis coast are sponges, but not sufficiently numerous to repay their collecting. Towards Sidi Mansour are numerous sponges, but of too light a texture to serve for much. To our right, on the banks of Kerkeneh, which extend twenty miles seaward, are small but fine sponges, the best on the coast of Tunis. Unfortunately, the currents are so strong that it is almost impossible to fish for them. A sponge merchant told me that in twenty years he never recollected sponges so dear as now: they cost twice the usual price. To cleanse them, half-a-dozen are attached to a stake in the sea: if the sponges are young, for one night, if old and the crust is hard, for three days, that the current may wash them to and fro. They are then well trodden, and when the Kerkeni has sufficiently lacerated his feet with the gravel and saline incrustations, the sponges are replaced in the water. Eventually the crust is pared off with a knife, and the sponges are stuffed compactly into a sack. The Kerkeneh sponges grow in water from ten to fifteen feet deep, and in parts as clear as crystal: the Benghasi sponges, which are closer and finer, in much greater depths, perhaps fifteen to twenty fathoms. The Kerkeneh fishermen, I was told, spread oil in rings upon the water, that they may see through the little smooth circle down to the bottom. They also use a kind of tube in the form of a telescope, then spear the sponge with harpoons.

There come to Kerkeneh every year from Trapani Sicilian boats: this year eighteen came, together with thirteen Greek boats: two years ago more than a hundred Greek boats came, but they have now gone to Benghasi, where the results are more profitable. I was told that a merchant this year gave nearly twenty-five thousand pounds for the yield of Benghasi sponges.

The Greek sponge fishers have the reputation of the utmost skilfulness in using the harpoon. It is reported that they are in the habit of discharging one harpoon, then a second, striking it on its head and increasing its impetus, then a third to strike the second.

If the reader doubts this, he will probably disbelieve what I shall relate to him on excellent authority. On the coast of Norway the puffin hunters come in search of those astute birds: and, finding a cavern on the face of a cliff containing a puffin family, let down a cord having a hook at its end. The head of the family, imagining the hook is intended for him, lays hold of it, and, as he disappears slowly out of the cavern, the second puffin lays hold of his tail, the third lays hold of the second's tail, and so on, till the whole family, strung like beads, are hauled up to the top of the cliff.[1]

Fifty miles south of Sfax, on the uninhabited island of Serkenis, otherwise known as Kneiss, there grow enormous quantities of sponges, and in the lagoons on the mainland also: but mineral springs in the neighbourhood stain and rust the sponges, and render them good for nothing. At Zwâra Zwâra, a double village midway from Tripoli to Jershîsh, grow black sponges. On the banks of Jershîsh (Zarzis), under the lee of Djerba, are quantities of sponges, and sixty or seventy boats are employed in fishing them. They are superior to those of Djerba and Kerkeneh, and resemble those of Benghasi. Djerba has a considerable trade in sponges. On her last voyage the *Corsica* brought thence three hundred sacks, weighing thirty to forty pounds each. They are cheaper than the Kerkeneh sponges.

[1] *Hartwig's Polar World*, p. 114.

In the winter the Djerban fishers use harpoons; in the summer they dive. They are famous divers: indeed, I was solemnly assured that individuals of a certain village lying eighteen miles from the island, Oulad Azim—Children of Azim—can remain under water for an hour and a half to two hours. This is their profession: they do nothing else. I should think not. In the winter and stormy weather they rest, to avoid injuring their lungs. They descend to depths of twenty or thirty fathoms, and remain there till they collect a net full of sponges, which they uproot by the hand: they pursue the fishes, and catch them in holes among the rocks: indeed, two of them, this spring, entered a cave, whereupon the fishes came in such numbers that the divers could not get out, and were drowned.

If the reader asks whether I believe this, I would ask what is the benefit of travel if we learn nothing but what we know at home. I would refer him to the unimpeachable Perruquier, who was present, and believed every word of the above. He assured me, at the same time, that he had timed with his watch in his hand a diver at Goletta, who remained under water for six minutes. Perruquier gave me his name, to remove any doubt I might have. The old Spanish chronicler, Fray Agapida, says: None but light and inconsiderate minds hastily reject the marvellous. To the thinking mind the whole world is enveloped in mystery.

The Kerkeneh shallows abound with fish. The natives of the seven island villages, a sober and industrious race, catch, in the labyrinths of palm rod palisades, enormous quantities of polypi. All round the smooth and shallow shores of the Syrtis these creatures abound: some of them are of an enormous size. They are capital eating, and the natives devour them greedily: the greater part are shipped to the Levant for use on fast days. The natives string earthen jars together, and lower them into the water. The octopus, thinking he has found a good thing, a home ready made for him, settles down in the jar, sometimes with several others. They are attracted by white substances, and bright stones are placed in the water to beguile them.

At Lésina, in Dalmatia, a Mr. Bucchik has made very interesting experiments in sponge farming. Cutting up a sponge, he attaches the pieces to the interior of a perforated chest, which he lowers into the sea. The sponges begin to grow, they are examined from time to time, and at the end of five or six years are found to attain a considerable size. We regard this experiment with interest and satisfaction, looking forward to a time when everybody will rear his own sponges, and when instead of ferneries or aquaria in our rooms, and mignonette or geraniums in our bedroom windows, we shall be able to watch the growth of the sponge. We do not believe it is yet satisfactorily established whether the sponge is vegetable or animate; and, as we should always as a matter of choice incline to the less probable, we even anticipate the moral culture of the sponge.

We feel that science is fast outstripping the often dilatory and disappointing routine of nature. We cannot disregard, as reflective travellers, the circumstances of chicken manufacture by oven in Egypt, and by steam in Holland: of the culture of mushrooms in cellars, and of mustard and cress in flannel and water: of the universal acclimatisation of species: of the fifty means and contrivances by which seasons are anticipated.

In one year there have been hatched in Egypt eighteen million chickens from twenty-six million eggs. We consider this as peculiarly suggestive and interesting: economical of much valuable time to the mature poultry, who can go on laying as fast as they please, while their proprietor attends to the hatching. It is our belief that some such system of production might be more widely applied: and we look forward to a more certain and perennial state of things, such as may enable us to have snowballing and sledging in the summer, and when roses will blossom in the frost. This would be something like civilisation.

All day we steamed against a head wind. We passed the town of Shebba, then the site of the ancient Salectum, and cast anchor at three in the afternoon off Mehdia.

An Austrian gentleman, who had sailed with us from Tunis, kindly put off to meet me in a boat. We went to the sardine establishment, of which he is manager. It is a private undertaking, and if fairly treated ought to be successful. The operations commence in April, when thirty or forty Sicilian boats come to fish. The year's exports vary from seven to ten thousand barrels of one hundred pounds each. The sardines are rather large, about the size of those we condemn in England as being pilchards or herrings. In the first year five boats came; last year forty-five came. The company, however, having confidingly made advances to certain of the boats, have seen them no more.

The salt they import is subject, I was told, to a duty of ten piastres a ton. In addition to this they have to buy from the government, at a hundred piastres a ton, as many tons of salt as they import: but this salt is valueless, and has only tainted the fish when they have used it. They cannot resell it, for the government has the monopoly of sale. It was handsomely proposed that they might pay eighty piastres a ton without taking the salt, but they preferred to take it and give it away. This seems hard and discouraging.

The obliging Austrian and an Italian gentleman, who had also sailed in the *Corsica*, accompanied me into the town. There is a great Saracenic gateway:

the streets are poor, there are no proper bazaars: the whitewashed houses, save where they have some old shaft or capital imbedded in them, are quite uninteresting: the people and dogs are inquisitive. We went round under the ruined walls to the beach, and behind the mosque found a marble tombstone of a knight of St. John, dated 1563. I was told that there were many of them in the mosque. The coat of arms had the cross of Malta and two dolphins.

We went out of the town to the rocks by the sea, passing through a Mohammedan cemetery, which resembled a rabbit warren more than anything else. The cement and whitewash had crumbled away from many a tomb, leaving skulls, bones, and dust exposed to sight. On the top of the ridge extending seaward there stands an old but remodelled castle: beneath it lies the ancient port of Africa. This is a basin hewn in the rock, measuring about a hundred by fifty yards, into which the sea water still enters to a depth of several feet. The entrance, as broad as a city gate, was defended by masonry and a tower: it is not now practicable, the Spaniards having blown it up when they evacuated Mehdia. If, however, the fallen masonry were removed, and the dock cleared out, at a moderate expense it might still be made to contain half the sandals on the coast of Barbary. There are remains of a secret gate leading from the tower to the water's edge. When the

Spaniards destroyed the place, they massacred, it is said, twelve hundred Mussulmans, and carried nine thousand into slavery.

We went on farther to the brow of the promontory where the citadel, Turris Hannibalis, once stood. Under our feet were dark deep vaults and reservoirs, having small round apertures cut in the rock. These were the cisterns and granaries, and must have been very spacious. The rock echoed hollowly under our feet, and the surf beat dismally upon the point. It is said there is a practicable underground passage running a considerable way inland. That such existed, and once served the Romans as an access to the citadel, is very possible: but whether it would have been practicable for us to get a long way inland through it, we did not stay to inquire. It was cold enough in the twilight on the promontory, with the melancholy sea all round us, without getting let down into the bowels of a cavern, or slipping into some glacial cistern. I offered to help to let anyone else down, and wait till I heard him touch the bottom, but nothing came of it.

It was from this point that that fine soldier Hannibal is said to have embarked for Egypt, after his fortune's star had set. All round the hill were tombs. Many of them had a little cup-shaped hollow on the slab. When the rain falls and fills the cup, the little birds, say the Moors, come to drink; thus the good works of the departed follow him. The dogs yelped hungrily, as we passed through the Arab town, and went to look at some lamps brought from El Djem. One was of red clay, with the figure of Victory driving a four-horsed chariot: the other of grey clay, bearing a stag in the central hollow. Both lamps were well preserved and interesting.

The *Corsica* was not to have sailed until six in the morning; but the excellent skipper agreed at my request to get under way by three o'clock, and at early morning we were off Monastir. A Sfaxin had shared the saloon with me—a well-dressed, pleasantly-mannered Moslem in a green turban, who ate my biscuits and took his coffee with me without restraint. He seemed to be without prejudice, and treated me with much courtesy. The Sfaxins are distinguished, even above the Tunisians, perhaps, for their grace and pleasantness. These Moors, like the Spaniards, will invite you to share their food: will make long and ceremonious inquiries in saluting you. They have all the politeness of the Spanish beggar, who addresses his comrade as Señor y Caballero. A Tunisian private soldier or shopkeeper is always, Sidi Ali, Sidi Mohammed. Another friend of mine on board was a tall Monastiri, very civil and entertaining. There was also the descendant of the Prophet who had come from Sfax, so I was in excellent company.

We had sailed from Mehdia at half-past two. The skipper, Pietro Molinari, had not been to bed at all, and had made the engineer crowd on additional steam. The horses I had telegraphed for to Susa were waiting on the beach at Monastir: but as my luggage was on board, and there were one or two things to do, I sent Perruquier on shore, to follow to Susa by land with the horses, while I stayed on the *Corsica*. My acquaintance of Monastir begged me to go and stay with him for three days—two days—one day—half a day—two hours: he was so civil that I was quite sorry I couldn't go. If the Englishman, he said to Perruquier, could speak a little better Arabic, we should not let him away from the Regency.

In the delicious calm morning we turned out of Monastir roads and steamed to Susa. The *Corsica* is a purely Italian steamer, from the captain to the cooking. The latter was at first difficult to master, but we became cosmopolitan in travelling, and I have only drawn the line at garlic, of which the revolting taste is too rarely absent. This nauseous and abominable herb ought to be exterminated, even at the sacrifice of a religious war upon the garlic-eaters. It is impossible to travel far abroad without recognising that in certain respects England is far behind other countries: for instance, in the habit and facility of eating with the knife. Half-way from Monastir to Malta lie the

Pelagie Islands, Linosa and Lampedusa, almost due east.

One small circumstance on the *Corsica* rather disquieted Perruquier and me. We noticed, but did not name it to anybody, that the electro-plate which came to table was marked Baltischer Lloyd. We did not see what an Italian navigation company ought to have to do with spoons belonging to the Baltic Lloyd. We have always been of opinion that to collect is not to rob, it is to carry out a principle: and, so long as it is confined to chalices, reliquaries, silver ornaments, old books, or embroidery, and such like, that any necessary steps for the purpose are justifiable. We never condemned the First Napoleon's collections from the art galleries of his neighbours, but we wonder that, after Perruquier's unsuccessful defence of Paris, Germany did not ask for some of them back again.

We soon anchored in the roads of Susa, and I landed and went to the vice-consulate, to see if the escort were ready. Mr. and Mrs. Dupuis received me most kindly: their servants ascertained that the soldiers were at my disposal, and we only awaited Perruquier's arrival to start for Kairwân. He was so long that we half fancied he must have fallen into the River Gimmal, which sometimes overflows its banks and interrupts the road from Monastir: but eventually he arrived, condemning the horses as unfit to carry us to Kairwân. The Maltese muleteer who owned them, and bore the classic name of Severio Valentino, was disposed to be unreasonable, but after a little exercise of consular authority he provided better horses. One of Julius Cæsar's generals, Ventidius Bassus, before he joined the army, gained his living by keeping mules and horses for hire.

Mr. Dupuis took me to see some finely sculptured stones lately found in excavating. One block of white marble, probably brought from Italy, contained a fine group. On a chariot with small wheels, bearing on the front of it a Triton blowing his trumpet, stood a consul in his robes, having a bâton in his hand. Behind the chariot sat a half-naked captive, an African, with a broad deep torso and muscular arms: the upper part of the head was missing. The background was smoothly chiselled: indeed, the whole work had been carefully and spiritedly done, and no doubt represented some Roman success in Barbary. Fragments of a horse's flank, a shield and greaves, and a delicately carved cornice had been found in the same place. Such finds are constant here: the Regency teems with traces of its first colonists.

The mounted soldiers who were to be our guards arrived, and I took leave of our hospitable representative. We stopped in the street to let an Arab funeral pass— every man whom it met or passed leaving his occupation according to the Arab custom, and accompanying it to the gate of the city.

CHAPTER XVII.

Of the Great Citie of Cairaoan—Hutmen —Hucba—Muse—Conquest of Andaluzia and Castilia—Site of Kairwân—Decline—Dr. Shaw on Kairwân and its Mosque—Origin of Name—Its Sacredness and Exclusiveness—Plans and Preparations—A Recommendation—Outfit—Disappointment.

Of the Great Citie of Cairaoan.

'THE famous citie of Cairaoan, otherwise called Carven, was founded by *Hucba,* who was sent generall of an armie out of Arabia Deserta, by *Hutmen* the thirde Mahumetan Califa. Hucba persuaded the citizens of Tunis that no armie or garrison ought to remaine in any sea towne, wherefore he built another citie called *Cairaoan.* Vnto which citie the armie marched from Tunis, and in the roome thereof other people were sent to inhabite. From the Mediterran Sea this citie is distant six and thirtie, and from Tunis almost an hundred miles; neither was it built (they say) for any other purpose, but onely that the Arabian armie might securely rest therein with all such spoiles as they woone from the Barbarians and the Numidians. He enuironed it with most impregnable walles, and built therein a sumptuous temple, supported with stately pillers. The dominions of Cairaoan began woonderfully to increase.

'The citie of Cairaoan standeth vpon a sandie and desert plaine, which beareth no trees nor yet any corne at all. Corne is brought thither from Susa, from Monaster, and from Mahdia, all which townes are within the space of forty miles. About twelve miles from Cairaoan standeth a certain mountaine called Gueslet, where some of the Romaines' buildings are still extant: this mountaine aboundeth with springs of water and carobs, which springs runne downe to Cairaoan, where otherwise they should have no water but such as is kept in cesternes. Without the wals of this citie raine water is to be found in certain cesternes onely till the beginning of Iune.

'In sommer time the Arabians vse to resort vnto the plaines adioining vpon this towne, who bring great dearth of corne and water, but exceeding plentie of dates and flesh with them, and that out of Numidia, which region is almost an hundred threescore and ten miles distant. In this citie for certaine yeeres the studie of the Mahumetan lawe mightilie flourished, so that here were the most famous lawyers in all Africa. It was at length destroied, and replanted againe with newe inhabitants, but it coulde neuer attaine vnto the former estate. At this present it is inhabited by none but leather-dressers, who sende their leather vnto the cities of Numidia, and exchange it also for the cloth of Europe. Howbeit they are so continually oppressed by the King of Tunis that now they are brought vnto extreme miserie.'

Dr. Shaw considers that Kairwân occupies the site of the Roman Vicus Augusti, though he gives no clear grounds for saying so. The geographer Thuanus identifies it wrongly with Curubis, Kurba, a maritime village towards the Gulf of Hammamet: but in attributing its first origin to the Mohammedan prince of Barbary, he is nearer to the truth than Dr. Shaw. 'The Calipha,' he says, ' of Africa had his seat of government at Caruan, a city built by Okhbah Ibn Nafi in the Cyrenaïca, after various victories gained over the Arabs : for that the name signifies *Cairo* or *Kahira*—victory.'

There seems to have been some confusion on this point in the mind of Thuanus. For Kairwân is not in the Cyrenaïca, and yet قيروان Käyrawân- more commonly El Krenneh—is the Arabic name for Cyrene.[1] Leo Africanus and Dr. Shaw regard the name Kairwân as identical with كروان *karwân*, caravan—and originally signifying the place where the Arabs had their rendezvous. This word كروان *karawân*, also signifies a crane or stork. Leo writes Cairaouan: Sir Grenville Temple calls the city Kairwân, Kairvân, El Kirwân, لعيروان without suggesting any origin for the name.

[1] Catafago.

Guérin follows Ebn Khaldoun and Nowaïri in writing Caïrouan. Colonel Playfair, an excellent Arabic authority, writes Kerouan كروان: in Tripoli the common pronunciation of the name is Keerwân : while in the city itself, among the educated natives with whom I came in contact, the name was strongly pronounced *Käyrawân*.

It is conceivable that Okhbah the Saracen, who had just overrun the Cyrenaïca—then full of magnificent buildings, which he gave over to destruction or carried away piecemeal — should have given to his new and splendid city a name which would recall the glories of Käyrawân. Of the remains in which Kairwân is still rich, many noble shafts and capitals were transported from Cyrene.

Dr. Shaw says : ' We have several fragments of the ancient architecture at this place, and the Great Mosque is accounted the most magnificent as well as the most sacred in the Barbary States. It is supported by an almost incredible number of granate Pillars. The Inhabitants told me, for a Christian is not permitted to enter the mosques of the Mahometans, that there are no fewer than five Hundred : yet, among the great Variety of Columns and the ancient Materials used in this large and beautiful Structure, I could not be informed of one single Inscription. The Inscriptions likewise which I found in other places of the City were either filled up with Cement or else defaced by the Chissel.'

The city's present character is much what it has been for centuries. Its buildings circumscribed, and still too large for its shrunken population: its trade decaying, and now restricted to some few objects of manufacture, such as carpets and leather articles, and to the supply of the Arabs of the plain, who come to buy or barter for copper utensils, boots, and saddlery. Forty thousand strong, they come to encamp in the plain, of which they and the natives of Kairwân cultivate portions. The population is said to be, of the city fifteen thousand, and of the suburbs five thousand —both, I am satisfied, excessive estimates.

Temple says: 'Kairwân is, as is well known, a sacred or holy town, the present hotbed of all the bigotry of Mohammedanism in Africa. The traveller who wishes to enter within its walls must take upon himself all the risks of the enterprise.'

'Our promenades through the town were managed with the greatest mystery, and the Kaïd at first positively refused to let us walk out, except after sunset. After further difficulties he appointed an officer to attend us, making us promise not to stare about too much, take notes or drawings, or speak in any European language. Disguised in Arab dress, we paraded through the town, observing a dignified silence and a steady solemn pace. More than one walk we were not allowed to take, as I was told that if we were known to be Christians whilst walking about, we might be torn to pieces by the infuriated populace.'

M. Guérin writes in 1860: 'Though Tunis has been for long ages the political capital, Kairwân has always remained in the mind of the masses the religious capital of the country.

'It is the Holy City *par excellence*, where the Crescent reigns undividedly. For twelve centuries no minister of the gospel has entered it.

'Though singularly fallen from its ancient splendour, Kairwân is, after Tunis, one of the most populous towns in the Regency. What above all distinguishes it is the sacred prestige with which it is invested: a character due to its origin, to the sanctity of its chief mosque, the great number of its shrines and tombs, and to the inviolability of its proper ground.

'Situated in nearly the heart of Tunisia, it has never been attacked by Christian troops, as the coast towns have so often been. No Christian has ever had the right, I do not say of establishing himself in it, but even of penetrating thither, except by a quite special favour. Jews have been entirely excluded, so that it has remained virgin to the contact of any Faith but that of its founder Okhbah.

'Hence the sort of holy and mysterious aureole with which the Mussulman religion surrounds it. Caravans which resort thither from all parts of the Regency come to steep themselves in some measure in Islamism: its Great Mosque—whose stones, according to popular tradition, which the Imams keep up among the masses, came miraculously to place themselves in the spots they now occupy—is ceaselessly visited with deep reverence by the adepts of the Koran. The shrines of its saints are equally the object of constant pilgrimage. All this maintains in the mind of the populace a fanaticism which nothing hitherto has succeeded in weakening.

'The Bey himself, when at rare intervals he delivers an *amar* to a Christian, has not the right to impose the infidel's presence upon the inhabitants: his order, absolute elsewhere, is here a simple prayer, a pure letter of recommendation. The Christian who bears it, when he approaches Kairwân, must halt at some distance from its walls, and despatch one of his escort to show the Bey's letter to the governor of the city.

'The governor assembles the council, and if they agree that the stranger recommended by the Bey shall be admitted, an escort is sent out to bring him in: his entry has always perforce a certain solemnity. Even the presence of the governor, who would accompany me wherever I went, did not protect me from all insults.

'I need hardly say that I was unable to enter the mosque: I could barely make the exterior circuit of the quadrilateral which it forms: and even then the sheikhs and shaoushes of my escort urged me to hasten my steps, and not to cast too attentive an eye on this religious monument, one of the most venerated of Islamism, for fear of exciting annoyance and insult among the inhabitants.'

Mr. Wood, the consul-general, in his report for 1875, writes: 'Kairwân is considered so holy a place that no Christians or Jews are allowed within its walls, and a traveller must be accompanied by a government escort for protection.'

The reader will recognise that Kairwân is, or was, a place of consideration and an enjoyable object for a visit, and will make allowance for the interest with which I prepared for the journey. I was anxious to go privately, disguised as an Arab, choosing a familiar dress of Barbary: to stain my face, neck, arms, and ankles: to travel to Susa, and there seek out some native willing to accompany me, tempted by the price of gold. At Susa I should buy or hire a horse to carry myself and bundle, the native accompanying me on foot, and answering all questions put to us. We should contrive to reach the city towards the *mughreb* or sunset, shortly before the gates would close, and enter in the twilight.

On approaching, the native should mount the horse, while I, carrying the bundle, should walk behind or beside him as his servant. Once inside, I should probably feel exceedingly alarmed: we should seek some caravanserai, avoid conversation, and roll ourselves up in a corner to sleep. As there would be a moon at the time, we should rise and make the circuit of the city, entering the Great Mosque for midnight prayer. Very early on the following morning we should sally forth again, muffled, according to the Arab habit, about the face, until the atmosphere should become warm. In the heat of the day, if possible during some market, when the crowd's attention would be distracted, we would traverse the bazaars: I calculated upon their being dark and vaulted.

The chief risk would lie in the infernal inquisitiveness and gossiping of the bazaars, and in the fear that my native might fail in readiness on an emergency. There was a risk, too, in the fanaticism of those religious buffoons, the Maraboûts, who in a sacred city like this were sure to abound. A genuine Maraboût is a kind of irresponsible Kalendar. A Kalendar is a Mohammedan wandering monk, who abandons all to the exercise of his profession. Kairwân, I was also assured, was a spot of refuge for criminals and the escaped rascality of the seaport towns. Six feet of height and grey eyes are not strict characteristics of an African or Asiatic: but the chances would be in my favour, and a little tact and adroitness ought to be enough to keep one out of predicaments.

I prepared a note-book on which to record my

impressions of Kairwân: and went into diligent training for writing in my pocket, in the breast of my coat, or behind my back. I had it carefully ruled with lines in relief, so that I could feel my way along with a pencil between the lines, and, by returning to any given spot on the page, avoid writing twice over the same spot.

To provide further against chances I had obtained from a Persian Mussulman a most friendly recommendation, under the name of Abdul Malek, to Mussulmans in general. The writer's translation ran thus:—

'In the name of the Omnipotent, that we utter his name with zele and fervant lips, Him our Creator, the Compassionate, Bless He be! We the undersigned (then follow the writer's name and description) do declare that the bearer of the present our beloved friend the son of a very distinguished family amongst us— whose name is Mirza Abdul Malek, an accomplished young gentleman of good society and birth belonging to a family of first-water—wishing to visit the Beylik of Tunis and its adjacent towns, etc:—We the said Vekil insisted upon the said gentleman to take with him this our declaration in the Arabic tongue: that he may spread and shew during his journey to all our esteemed Mussulman brethren, with whom he may come in contact: and especially to those high dignitaries in towns —and others who are chiefs of tribes, etc. for the purpose of shewing him their hospitality and protection: as also to recommend him to others in power in case of need.

'Such favours shall not be forgotten from our heart. Moreover to one who deserves esteem and respect: in conclusion we pray for his journey and return: with our greetings and Moslem Salamat, in the name of all the people of Iran.'

Date, etc.

The letter itself was a most beautiful example of the flowing Arabic character, and ought to carry much weight in a country where many people can neither read nor write.

After this came the question of complexion. This was a more intricate question than male readers would fancy. After diligent investigation I found that there was no choice between a powder whose transient properties were at the mercy of every sneeze and fingermark: and walnut-stain, which would yield a good lasting tint, and expose me in travelling home to the suspicions of every passport officer and gendarme, and perhaps to disowning by my friends.

Fair hair being irreconcilable with walnut skin, the hair must be thrown in with the arms, feet, and neck, and stained too. So I went to a chemist and asked confidently for a large bottle of walnut juice to stain my face. The chemist said he had none, adding that I was no doubt aware the colour would last for some weeks. I said I was afraid it would. He then asked whether a powder would do, such as was used in most private theatricals, and lasting fairly through an evening. I said that the play in which I was to take part would last for several days at least, and I saw that the chemist regarded me as about to evade the ends of justice.

I sought a seedsman, in the hope of getting some dried walnut leaves. He kept none, and didn't believe anyone else did. I might get some by waiting till the summer, when the leaves were on the trees. As it was not satisfactory to me to wait till the summer, I went to a chemical colour manufacturer, and, oppressed with a natural bashfulness—increased by the consciousness that I was leaving the country under suspicious circumstances —asked for a brown dye which would last for several days, but not for several weeks. Fancy dress ball, sir? he said. Yes, fancy dress, I said. Try this powder, he said; it will wear through the evening. I said I had to wear my dress for some days, and probably to sleep in it: and, seeing the chemical colour manufacturer did not believe me, I went sadly away.

I came to a dyer's, and asked him to give me the best thing for dyeing myself brown. We never sell our colours, the dyer said: everything must be dyed on the premises. It was not convenient to me to get dyed on the premises, so I went to a theatrical barber and wig maker. He had no idea where I could find walnut juice. Besides, he said, it won't come off your hands or head till the skin wears off. I was on the point of telling him that that was not of much consequence, as I was going to a place where the head itself might come off in a day or two: but the idea seemed so dark and sanguinary, that I was afraid he might get me watched by the police. Eventually I bought from him a hair dye and some chocolate-coloured cosmetic: and as I hesitated to carry on this compromising sort of search any longer, I started on my travels in despair.

Sitting in the hotel at Marseilles on the day of our sailing, drinking strong coffee, a profound idea came into my head: I smeared my hands experimentally with coffee—a rich brown—and felt that it would be a success. The scent was strong, but not inappropriate.

The reader will understand how, after anticipating a certain amount of enjoyable excitement and mischief, I was sensible of extreme disappointment on learning that I could go to Kairwân with an escort of soldiers, and under the protection of government, and how I was saddened on receiving the following kind note from Mr. Wood, on the morning of my departure from Tunis.

'My dear Sir: I beg to enclose a letter addressed to the Governor of Kairwân by the Prime Minister, and to inform you that telegraphic instructions have been sent to the Sub-Governor of Susa to furnish you with an escort. I will also telegraph to our Vice-Consul at that port: and I beg to suggest that, on approaching the city and before entering it, one of the Ispahis should go forward with the letter to the Governor, that he may make arrangements for your reception.'

CHAPTER XVIII.

Departure from Susa—The Sahel—Bedouins—A Discovery in Natural History—Drought—M'seken—The Great Plain—Footprints of Pilgrims—The Great Minar—The Walls—Enter Kairwân—Observations—Maledictions.

WE swung out of Susa very early in the day in spite of some lost time. The landscape consisted of a succession of rolling hillocks and brushwood: we saw old Arab buildings, among them a curiously buttressed cistern, and traversed olive woods which had been cleared of their undergrowth for firewood. The country around us was the Sahel, a province extending from the foudoûk of Birloubuita, forty-five miles north of Susa, to twenty miles south of Susa, and stretching from the seacoast twenty miles inland to the mountains we can faintly see in front of us.

Its almost exclusive product is the olive: the village of Hergla—the name sounds very like Heraclea—sixteen miles to the north of Susa—is noted for the purest oil in the Regency. The health of the inhabitants of the Sahel is vigorous: the air is fresh and wholesome in every village.

We saw the white domes of Zawi a mile away to our left among olive woods, and, passing gardens and hedges of prickly pear and olives, came among the houses and mud walls of Moureddîn, one hour and a half distant from Susa. We met a flock of lambs in the village— more perfect than even Syrian lambs, with black faces and feet, and lovely fleece. We saw a piece of an old column in reduced circumstances—once in a temple, now an olive crusher. We shuddered at the filthy black pools where, within a few yards of the house, the refuse liquid from the oil mills is collected. We reached a cistern in which we had counted upon refilling our *barada*: and, our muleteers having emptied those vessels in anticipation, we became suddenly exposed to the apprehensions of thirst.

We reached considerable olive groves, protected by hedges of dove-coloured thorn. Across the rough sandy track at short intervals were channels to carry the rain-water, dug by some poor Arab, anxious to lose no drop of what was life to his crop, and for which this season his labour had been in vain. In places the way became rocky. We overtook armed Bedouins with white camels travelling to Kairwân, and met numerous camels and asses laden with esparto for the seaport of Susa.

On the great plain, sweeping away to the mountains of Oussalat, were the squat brown tents of the Bedouins. To the north we could see the fine peaks of

Zaghwân—known to the Romans as Zeugis—and of Djebel Resass. We were travelling towards the *mughreb*, the sunset.

Our shâoushes were fine-looking men, dressed handsomely and in excellent taste: one with a red *djubba*, a white *haïk* about his head and shoulders, a dark blue burnous, and bare brown ankles. The other wore a chocolate-coloured *djubba*, with pale green embroidery, a white *haïk*, and light blue burnous. They were mounted on mules, the best of all beasts for Eastern travelling, where trotting is fatiguing and galloping often impossible. The swift ambling pace of the mule takes the traveller over the ground at a surprising rate. A *shâoush* is a serjeant, commanding perhaps fifteen or twenty Bedouin tents. They are the mounted gendarmes of the interior.

The clouds gathered overhead and a few drops of rain fell. We asked one of our guards if it were going to rain. I don't know—God knows, he said quietly, as if any speculation by him would be irreverent. Near the Bedouin tents on the plain were occasional patches of corn, which slightly cheered the landscape.

One or two mongrel greyhounds came to snarl at us. These are used for hunting the jackal. This amusing beast, whose cry resembles an infant's wail, is found in numbers in the Sahel. When got into a corner it becomes plucky enough, and fights like a dog. Gazelles, too, are plentiful here, and even between Susa and Moureddîn they are seen grazing like goats. They are hunted with horses and greyhounds, and are difficult to catch. The young gazelles are easily tamed, and become very domestic. The fox, too, exists in numbers on the plain: the Arabs eat its flesh and consider it excellent.

Then there are hedgehogs and porcupines, especially towards El Knais, five miles to the left of our road. They are hunted, so the shâoushes told me, with dogs, at night, and are capital food—very fortifying. This prickly pork is not forbidden by the Koran. Some porcupines weigh as much as twenty pounds, Perruquier said. He added that they are hard to catch alive, as they are not amusing to take hold of. Also that you might knock a porcupine about the head with a hammer, and he not think anything of it; but he is very tender and sensitive above his legs and feet, where one blow will disable him. The porcupine runs fast, almost as fast as a dog. The dogs know them well, and don't fancy them, but dance round yelping and snarling. Sportsmen in search of partridge on Djebel Resass often chance upon porcupines. I was told that a hedgehog will readily attack and kill a snake. Seizing him by the body, it holds him, while the snake in his frantic writhing, tears himself to pieces on the hedgehog's bristles.

We saw a prodigious worm or caterpillar nearly

as long as a porcupine, and with thirteen or fourteen hundred legs, so Perruquier said. We agreed that he must be very nearly the largest worm in the world: and as neither the shâoushes nor I had ever read of this caterpillar in natural history books, we believed him to be something quite new, and gave him the name of *Eruca Perruquiensis.* Besides the above creatures, there abound on the plain of Kairwân hares, partridge, and quail; so that a sportsman or naturalist should have a good time here.

After travelling for two hours and a half we sighted the Lake Sidi el Hâni, or Lake of Kairwân—a considerable sheet of water, three miles distant—but we soon lost sight of it among hillocks and rising ground. In another hour we saw on a hill, darkly covered with Barbary fig, the double marabout of Sidi el Hâni. Round the western and southern shores of the lake stretch the tents of the Oulad Zlass. This lake is fed by drainage and rain: its waters are brackish. There are only three considerable streams in all the Sahel—the Wadi Gimmal, into which we had formed unjustified hopes of Perruquier's having fallen—the Wadi Hamam, which we shall cross on our journey northward from Kairwân—and the Wadi Hamdûn.

What with the scanty natural supply of water and the precariousness of the rainfall, the failure of the crops in the Sahel is lamentably frequent. This and other causes have contributed to the dwindling away of the population from two hundred thousand to barely half that number.

Within nine miles of Susa is a noted town of the Sahel—a sort of miniature Kairwân—M'seken by name, proverbial for the jealousy, bigotry, and exclusiveness of its inhabitants. Not many years ago the inhabitants attempted to murder two Maltese, but the town was fined and the ringleaders were punished. The shâoushes said there was no longer any danger in visiting it, and our muleteer had been more than once within its walls.

After four hours and a half of quick travelling, we saw some white buildings and a minaret among trees— rather hazy and low in the plain. Beyond rose a grey serrated range of mountains, and the sun was declining behind them. It was the Holy City of Kairwân. We could see herds of camels grazing on the plain, and blue smoke rising from the Bedouin tents. The hills grew darker as the sun sank, the plain grew purple, the stillness of evening was coming on, and we wondered if we could arrive before the gates were closed. Fortunately the twilight is long on this vast plain and its exceeding level surface, extending as it does from Zaghwân to the borders of the Djerîd.

The track became enormously broad; the hard dry mud was impressed with countless hoof and footmarks. The caravans and pilgrims of centuries had used it. The city disappeared from time to time, as we traversed hollows where the horses' feet sank in still liquid mud. We could hear the bleating of the lambs in the dark brushwood enclosures of the Bedouin *doûars*, and wild forms looked out from the low black tents. We drew rapidly nearer, and the city began to develop itself. We could see to the right, outside the city, a great garden and a white-domed mosque among its trees. The shâoushes told me it was the garden of the late Kaïd.

The city walls were brownish yellow, with crenellated outline: to the right, above a long smooth stretch of wall, rose the tower of the most sacred building in all Africa—the shrine of the veneration, fanaticism, and bigotry of twelve centuries. In form this *minar* recalled those of Cordova and Seville, but it was more squat. It seemed to be of brownish brick for a great part of its height, and of a creamy white above. Everything was very silent, no hum came from the city. The Bedouins had lighted great fires on either side of the track, and thick smoke rose from them. We could distinguish shepherds with a flock of sheep ascending the slope in front of the eastern gate, and entering the city by the dark round arch. We could distinguish the brown bricks in the city wall, and above the crenellated parapet the yellow houses, domes, and minarets.

We advanced rapidly, leaving to our right a large white-domed marabout, to our left a sloping hill covered thickly with Barbary fig. To the right, below the city walls, extended wide gardens of the same dull green shrub. Among the figs to the left was another marabout, its dome fluted like a water-melon. By this time we were close to the city walls, and the tall half-round towers which project at even distances round it. It was a long, high wall, very complete and erect still, like the Great Wall of Damascus or the Moorish wall of Cordova. The domes of the mosques rising above it had convex flutings.

We saw no people about save the shepherds entering the eastern gate. We left this to our right hand, passing round for some distance under the wall, and between the wall and a great enclosure with cemented floor. This was a cistern, measuring maybe a hundred and fifty yards by a hundred yards, to collect the rain-water on which the city depends—but it was empty now, and as dry as a threshing-floor. Occasionally rain-water fails in the summer, and is not unlikely to do so this year. There were some buildings of *attob*, or mud, outside the city wall: and here we came among the inhabitants. One look back over the great dull plain behind, and we were in a suburb of Kairwân.

There were strange looks cast at us, but we passed quietly on to the gate Bab el Djuluddîn and entered the crowd. I had been cautioned not to approach the city till soldiers should be sent out: but one shâoush we had outridden, and there seemed nothing gained by loitering outside for him. The remaining shâoush I sent on to the Kaïd's house to carry the Prime Minister's letter and my respects, while Perruquier and I sat among the crowd.

There were the customary groups of men and boys idling at the close of day, and they came to see what evil chance had brought Christians among them—perhaps the first they had seen in their city. They stared at us, wondering who we were and what the deuce we wanted. Wonder gave place to superstition. What has Allah sent the unbeliever here for? they asked one another. I understood the ordinary forms of Arab compliment, such as *kalb, khanzîr, kafir*, and Perruquier translated the rest while I wrote them down in my note book. The dog! a white-robed man said, how dare he come into our city? Then they began to grow angry, and some of them scowled and spat at us from a distance. May the good God suffer the walls to fall and crush him! a man said.

They drew nearer. Some among them were quiet and respectful, but others seemed almost unable to contain themselves. The Kaïd has gone to the Castle to visit the soldiers, said a Moor with a grey beard. Your shâoush has followed him, and he will soon be back to receive you. We were close to the Kaïd's house, and could not present ourselves till he was ready to receive us, it being contrary to Oriental etiquette and law to do so. A boy, after examining me for some time, brought up a companion. See, he said, the Infidel's hat: is it made of wood? It was a round-topped black felt hat, and the young Moors were possibly calculating its brick-proof capacity. No one, however, raised a stone, and we sat tranquilly among them. There is a cheerful omen, said my interpreter. A man who had not spoken before looked at us and said, They will never leave the city. Inshallah! said his nearest neighbour: Please God!

Our reception was about as cordial as Linnæus' welcome by an old woman in Lapland, who addressed him with mingled pity and reserve in the following words: 'O thou poor man! what hard destiny can have brought thee hither to a place never visited by anyone before? This is the first time I ever beheld a stranger. Thou miserable creature! how did'st thou come, and whither wilt thou go?'

The soldier had been gone for half an hour, and we still sat among the crowd. I told Perruquier to give a handful of tobacco to a youth near, to see what he would do. Don't touch it! roared his companions; it is polluted with swine's flesh. Their unaffected dislike and contempt were novel and interesting, and their insults were so conscientiously and heartily offered that we could only receive them with good nature. They were more to relieve their utterers' feelings than to provoke us.

It was enjoyable to have reached the city, untrodden as it had been, save at rare intervals, by Christian feet for twelve centuries—the shrine which its inhabitants had contrived to keep sealed and almost unpolluted by foreigners and unbelievers. Strangers had come at distant intervals, but disguised and careful in manner. Here were two of the dogs in their ordinary native dress, sitting where they had no right to sit, and smiling at the hardest things they could say. Curse them! they would break out now and then—the swine!

Hasn't he a very large head? asked one little boy. Yes, and an ill-disposed countenance, said another. What can Allah's purpose be? I wrote down word for word as they spoke, and the act of writing puzzled and annoyed them more. At length our soldier reappeared. As we turned our backs the crowd raised a howl of execration. They had hoped that after delivering our message to the Kaïd we would leave Kairwân. Christians in the city! they yelled. Malediction!

CHAPTER XIX.

The Year of the Hejreh 1292—The Kaïd's House—Sidi Mohammed el Mourâbet—Hospitality—A Pervert—Supper à l'Arabe—Fanatical Mosquito—Visit the Kaïd—The Bazaars—Curiosity and Precautions—The Tunis Gate—A Horse Sale—My Bodyguard—Progress to Citadel—Soldiers—Civility—The Walls—Rough Usage.

IT was the twenty-fifth day of the month of Safar, in the year 1292. Thank goodness I had got away from the nineteenth century at last. Here was a refuge from telegraphs, railways, hotels, and financial commissions. We pulled up and alighted at the house of the governor, Sidi Mohammed el Mourâbet. A pleasant-looking man, stout and grey-haired, stood at the open door and wished me *Marhâba*, Welcome.

I went in with him. We passed through a large anteroom into a hall with grated windows. There were divans at the sides and end of the room, which was rather empty otherwise. The walls were tiled like the floor, and the wooden ceiling was painted in gaudy colours. Several attendants followed us in and stood respectfully about. My host made me sit beside him, and I told Perruquier to express my sorrow for having inconvenienced him at so short a notice. He shook me kindly by the hand, assuring me that it gave him much pleasure to see me, and that he would do his best to make my visit agreeable. It was not the governor himself, but his brother, Miralai or Colonel Mohammed el Mourâbet, a member of one of the oldest families in Kairwân, a mild amiable man, who was suffering from asthma.

He told Perruquier that any arrangement I might be pleased to wish for should be immediately made, and that he was to be informed of any desire of mine, that to the best of his ability it might be gratified. He said his brother, the Ferik or General, was absent in the Djerîd, collecting the revenues, and that he would be sorry to have missed the chance of entertaining any one recommended by General Khaireddin. He was expected back in Kairwân in ten days.

The Kaïd—for in his brother's absence my host acted as such—asked if I would prefer remaining in his house or occupying one by myself: assuring me that either arrangement would be equally convenient and gratifying to him. Believing this plan would cause less restraint to both of us, I told Perruquier to say that I should enjoy staying with the Kaïd very much, but that I should enjoy staying by myself more than I should enjoy staying with him.

The Kaïd ordered rooms to be prepared in a house hard by, and went out himself to see to the arrangements, leaving his attendants and Perruquier with me in the reception room.

In Kairwân, I had been told, was a renegado, a Frenchman, who had adopted Islamism, and who occupied himself in instructing the Kaïd's children. His perversion had taken place in Tunis, but he was shy or jealous of his new faith, and to avoid comment or curiosity he had sought refuge in the sacred city of the Moors. His habits and dress differed, I was told, in no way from those of the Moors about him, and he was unwilling to be identified. He was probably some shopkeeper or barber, I fancied, who had changed his faith to serve some small private interest.

When we came in sight of Kairwân, I instructed Perruquier to seek out the Frenchman and become as friendly as possible with him, and I provided him with a quantity of expensive tobacco with which to conciliate the renegado's rugged spirit. Our deep purpose was to obtain, by the means of tobacco and napoleons, drawings and measurements of the mosque, which it was said to be almost certain death for a Christian to approach. Perruquier, who had a ready intelligence, was to invite him to the café, and between the coffee, the tobacco, and the napoleons to form a quick and valuable friendship. The renegado had spent some months in Tunis prior to his change of faith, and was well known by sight to Perruquier. He was to cough when the renegado should make his appearance: and then Perruquier and I rubbed our hands and thought we had prepared a good bait to catch the renegado.

As we sat in the lamp light there came in a dear little boy, plump and jolly, about three or four years old. Without any hesitation he came up and sat on my knee, and when I gave him a yellow rose from my coat he was very pleased, and we grew very friendly. Quite frank and at home, he sat with me for a quarter of an hour, and told me that his father was the governor and that my host was his uncle. When it was time for him to go to bed, he kissed me, and said, May your sleep be sweet, and may you rise up with happiness!

The attendants had left, and we sat for some time longer in the empty room. I asked Perruquier to ascertain what the projects were for our food and lodging. I will ask for a glass of water, he said, and enter into conversation with one of the servants. The servant went in good faith for the water, and then told us that dinner was already prepared, and that my rooms were being put in order.

The attendants of the Kaïd returned. A tall, intellectual-looking man, with a white turban, an ordinary Arab cloth dress in good taste, and a beard closely cut in the Arab fashion, advanced to one of the tapers and lighted a cigarette, while the light fell upon his features. Perruquier coughed. It was the Frenchman.

A man of perfect Oriental manner and composure, he was one of the last in the room one would have picked out as a European.

Soon the Kaïd returned, and, taking me by the hand, led the way to my new quarters. Here was a suite of three small comfortable rooms, furnished with divans and mattresses, and in the inner room the Kaïd and I took our seats, awaiting the supper. The *Mudabbir*, or Minister, sat near us, a well-bred man, dressed in pale grey cloth with silk braiding, and having a close-pointed grey beard and sharp features. For twenty years he had never left Kairwân: had not travelled as far as Susa. He is an example of the life of the rest of the inhabitants of this city. For twelve centuries shut up and insensible to the progress of the outer world, they have no ambitions or curiosity, no enterprise, and relatively little information. The great world has been rolling on while the Moors of Kairwân, anxious only to be left alone and to maintain the exclusiveness of their shrine and city, have slumbered on, unconscious of outer changes of thought and circumstance.

Empires have risen and fallen, new continents have been discovered and peopled: the map of the world and the whole system of civilisation have changed, but Kairwân has been indifferent to it all. The source from which issued many kingdoms, both on this continent and in Europe, Kairwân has remained practically unaffected by their destinies. Her ancient splendour has in great measure disappeared; her independence and exclusiveness have alone prevented her complete decay. Reduced in size and wealth, Kairwân is still an intact holy Moorish city.

I was getting desperately hungry, and if the servants had not come to announce supper I should have devoured the Kaïd himself, for all I know. It was the year 1292, and I don't suppose I should have minded. The worthy gentleman led me to the table and wished me a good appetite. Near me sat my interpreter, and at the other end of the table sat—after much persuasion—the shâoushes who had escorted me from Susa. They wished, poor fellows, to wait till I had finished, but I saw no prospect of being finished for hours, and made them join us. The Kaïd had sent numerous attendants and a handsome array of dishes from his own kitchen.

After supper the Kaïd and Mudabbir sat with me and we had a long chat. In the course of it the Kaïd was called out, and he returned leading by the hand a mild-faced, pleasant young Moor, who saluted me cordially and then affectionately kissed the Mudabbir. It was the Kaïd's son, who had just arrived from Tunis by horse, having travelled the distance in two days. He had been studying the Mohammedan law in Tunis, and had not seen his father for many months. The Mudabbir's family had been in Kairwân, he told me, for six hundred years : the Kaïd's family almost since the city's foundation. They were of the famous sect who once governed Moorish Spain. El Mourâbet or Almorâvide—the name signifies one devoted to the Faith, as either warrior or saint. Sidi Mohammed el Mourâbet is Governor of Kairwân, of the Sahel and the Djerîd.

The chief religious functionaries here are the Bashi Mufti, two Muftis, and a Kadi. The Oujak, or corps of Hambas, are commanded by an Agha, a Kahia, a Khogia, and a Bashi Shâoush. In former times the Kaïd of Kairwân was almost absolute. Within a century—in the reign of Hamouda Pasha—the Kaïd had a dishonest baker of the city thrown into his own oven ; and when the Bey sent to remonstrate with him, the Kaïd simply replied that he had shown a good example. The Kaïd wished me good night, the Mudabbir did the same. The shâoushes, who never left me night or day, slept in the outer room. Delightful soft mattresses were spread for me on the floor, and I fell asleep and dreamt that I was the Scherîf with a green turban who discovered the coffee plant on the mountains of Yemen, in the year of the Flight 700.

I had not slept for many hours when I awoke, harassed by a single fanatical mosquito. The lights were out, and Perruquier was snoring near the door. I will not attempt to describe the variety and ingenuity of the schemes I formed for catching this mosquito.

Sometimes it seemed that he was within my grasp, and I arose with a light heart to squeeze him against the wall, but he always eluded me. Sometimes I simulated sleep and listened to his guarded hum while he watched me. Sometimes I struck my face a violent blow, willing to sacrifice everything to despatch the mosquito, but to no purpose. Eventually the mosquito defeated me, and I buried my head under the soft quilt.

I will cite for the reader's benefit a recipe copied from one of the most worthy and popular English papers. The writer of it had suffered grievously from mosquito bites, and had hit upon the following remedy: Oil of pennyroyal, 2 dr.; oil of cedar, 2 dr.; glacial acetic acid, $\frac{1}{2}$ dr.; pure carbolic acid, 1 dr.; camphor, 3 dr.; castor oil, 3 oz. He thinks this should be effectual. I should think so too. It ought to kill an elephant. The reader had better suspend his purchase of this preparation till I have completed certain chemical studies upon this subject. One of the chief ingredients I intend using is nitro-glycerine, and the preparation is to be called the Annihilator.

On the second day I was awakened early by the punctual Perruquier, and found that the Kaïd's servants had already prepared breakfast for me. It was an excellent Eastern meal, ending with a dish of *assida*, a kind of flour porridge eaten with honey, usually offered to parting guests. Whether this was a delicate hint on the part of the Kaïd's cook, suggested by the ravages made upon the supper, I don't know, but I had no intention of leaving for at least a day or two. After breakfast the attentive and hospitable Kaïd, with his officers, called: and after a visit of ceremony, which I had previously instructed Perruquier to frame some delicate excuse for cutting short, we all went downstairs into the street together. The Kaïd led me to his own house: we smoked a cigarette together, then we issued from his door. He accompanied me for a few yards, as far as an archway crossing the street, and then at my request left me with the soldiers and attendants.

There were two or three members of the Kaïd's household, in turbans and long robes, white stockings and yellow shoes; my handsomely dressed shâoushes from Susa, Perruquier, and several soldiers. Surrounded by this bodyguard, I made an imposing progress through the city. They watched me jealously, clearing a path and thrusting aside individuals disposed to be too forward or curious. They seemed to feel much more anxious than I did, and appeared to contemplate the possibility of my attracting stones or a knife. Probably the man who might succeed in reaching the Infidel with either would be entitled to the thanks of his spiritual advisers and deserve well of his city.

The people were dressed much as in Tunis, but not so richly or tastefully. They wore turbans and *aftâns*, sometimes the burnous, and more frequently the *djubba*, as in Sfax. They were mightily curious, and some of them rather insolent and angry. What in the name of God does he want here? they would ask, starting up from their occupations to crowd round the soldiers, who carefully kept them at a distance. We passed on our left a small white mosque, that of the Bey, with a square tower. On each side of the tower, at one third of the height from the top, ran an inscription in brick standing in bold relief. It was in quaint square old type, and probably either conveyed the title of the mosque, or else the Confession of Faith—There is but the one God. I was sorry to be too ignorant to read it, and quite ashamed of Perruquier, who is half a native. He said he couldn't read those particular characters, but when I questioned him searchingly afterwards, he confessed that he could not read any Arabic characters at all. So I cannot help regarding Perruquier as a fraud.

In a wide space in the street near the entrance to the bazaars was a sort of market place, where there were provision shops, and money changers, from whom we got some small money. There were grocers' shops, with esparto baskets full of beans, seeds, and roots; coppersmiths who left their red copper vessels and hammers to look at the stranger. This street was tolerably broad for a Moorish city. We passed butchers' shops, blacksmiths', and others, having a little arcade of pillars running in front of them. At length we came to the Bab el Tunes, or Tunis Gate. The curiosity was general: a throng of idlers accompanied us, kept at bay by the faithful bodyguard.

The Gate is a tower, having a Moorish horseshoe archway of alternate black and white marble, with a red keystone: its sides are faced with beautiful old marble pillars. A running scroll of ornament and inscription frames the arch, and the angles above it contain lovely arabesque designs. Above the first arch is a second, moulded in the wall, and overhead is the crenellated parapet of the wall. The whole gate forms, as almost every one of the city gates forms, a fine example of the best Mauresque design. In front of the gate were the customary loungers of every Oriental city, and by the wayside sat three blind beggars. This was the moment, I said to Perruquier, for doing the handsome thing: and Perruquier with munificence placed some copper in the hand of each beggar.

Beyond the outer doorway of the tower, which has a plain horseshoe arch in red and white stone, runs a tolerably broad passage, taking a turn to the left, and lined with shops of gunsmiths or armourers, and old iron and implement stores. Then comes another arch with beautiful inscribed lintels of white marble, and we emerge into an outer market place under the walls, where country produce is sold and fairs are held. Here was an animated scene: there were carpet sellers with their goods thrown over their shoulders, calling out for buyers: sellers of fodder heaped up on the ground, baskets of red chiles, esparto panniers of vegetables, pottery from Nablus: white-robed Arabs from the country, and Bedouins with goats for sale.

One Bedouin had a young horse: three hundred and fifty piastres he wanted for it. It was a thin and weedy-looking beast, but Perruquier fancied it. If Monsieur would lend me the three hundred and fifty piastres, he said, I would feed the horse up and gain a hundred and fifty piastres on the purchase. Young and inexperienced in the world's wiles as I was, it still occurred to me that were I to advance Perruquier the money, the chances were that it might be a clear gain to him of five hundred piastres; so I commenced running the horse down. I assured him that the animal was feeble, misshapen, and very likely to become subject to stringhalt and the strangles. This alarmed Perruquier, and he concluded not to make a bid, much to the dissatisfaction of the crowd, who thought it just like Christians to look at a horse and decline to buy it. What, then, do they want here, the unbelievers? was the talk of the outer market.

We strolled from spot to spot, the faithful army, formed in a hollow square, always on the watch. Round the outer market place were small houses and one or two *foudoûks*. We went out and watched a simple but efficient apparatus for making esparto ropes. They are used by the Barbary seamen, and also by the boatmen of Italy and Sicily, being very good substitutes for hempen ropes. They are worth ten pounds a ton. Those which are exported from Susa are excellent, those of Tripoli not so good or carefully made. We saw mats, too, made of esparto: some stout and rough like hemp or cocoanut mats, others thin, delicate, and in pretty patterns. Among the Bedouins we saw the huge flapping straw hat of the Djerîd and Wadai, decorated with ostrich feathers. It takes from the Arab dress much of its grace and dignity.

We passed from one group to another, examining and making notes of everything, and watching with amusement the various shades of expression on the faces. The bodyguard were very unceremonious—men and boys were thrust on one side as if their gaping or scowling were injurious to me. We returned past the gunsmiths and through the gates, turning to the left, and passing along the streets to the old Kasbah. Men and boys would stop and turn to join the procession. The guards seized one by the arm. Pass on, they said: thou hast seen his face, it is enough for thee.

The Kasbah, now called the Keshlah, is a rectangular fort, having a large open court and low barracks round it. We went in without restraint among the soldiers. At the gate was the Kaïd's son, who saluted me with the courtesy of his family. All round the quadrangle were groups of soldiers, some idling about, others under arms and doing musketry drill. Many were Arabs from their tribes in their own picturesque attire. An officer approached in uniform with the star of the *Nischan Iftikhar* on his breast: he received me civilly and begged me to look round. My guards explained who I was, and how kindly the First Minister had recommended me. The Kaimakam led me to the military gate of the Keshlah, which was bound and faced with iron, and the soldiers threw it open.

Beyond it lay the open plain, and towards the suburb Sayiha Jebliyeh, among the trees of the late Governor's garden, stood a white mosque and the College of Kairwân. To the right, a mile away from this, lay the little village of Dar al Mana—House of the Obstacle or Prohibition—beyond which point Jews are forbidden to approach the city. I asked the Kaimakam if I might note down all I saw. Certainly, he said. He called a soldier to him from the detachment at drill. You did not present arms as the stranger entered, he said. See that you do it as he goes out. As we passed, the soldiers stood to their arms, and their guns went up with a rattle. Round a cistern in the quadrangle lay skins and kegs for water. The garrison were being replaced by troops from the Bardo, who had just arrived. The officer wished me a civil farewell, accompanying me into the street, and we moved on in the direction of the Great Mosque.

All round, within the city walls, runs an empty street, with houses here and there demolished, to make waste places, no doubt for the purpose of giving free circulation round the fortifications. Where they were to any extent ruinous, the walls were being repaired and plastered. They were constructed of small brown bricks, measuring in section three inches and a half by two inches—there being no stone or quarries in the neighbourhood. Through the bricks ran, in places, lines of tile or white bricks, apparently for no other purpose than ornament.

At times in our progress a man or a boy would allow himself to use the offensive word *Kafir*! Unbeliever! in a mocking voice, or boldly call out *Kalb*! Dog! Then two or three soldiers would go for him, and cuff or beat him till he howled. Sometimes they would drive him into a corner and stone him. I remonstrated with them now and then, representing that the punishment was in excess of the offence. Let him leave us to deal with them, they said to Perruquier, if he wants to be safe.

CHAPTER XX.

The Great Mosque—Sketches—The Khasinah—Decaying City—Its Former Size—The Bazaars—Slippers—Marabouts—The Mosques—Tombs of the Saints—Curiosity—An Aspiration—The Suburbs—Djemma 'l Zitûna—*Yahûdi*—Postern Gate.

WE saw over the low roofs the great tower of the mosque, and in a few more paces came upon the famous edifice.

In the north-eastern angle of the city, in a wing of the city, in fact—which without it would not be far from the form of a hexagon—stands the great quadrangle of the mosque.

It is in a clear space of ground, withdrawn from the confusion of the narrow streets, and distant from the city walls round it perhaps fifty or a hundred yards. On the north-west side nothing stands between the mosque and the walls. On the north-east side stands a collection of little houses or huts: on a portion of the south-east side are a few small houses and washhouses. The south-west side has a tolerably broad lane, with houses on the opposite side. The mosque enclosure is a high level wall, flanked by massive buttresses with

EASTERN ANGLE AND PORCH OF THE GREAT MOSQUE.
Dome or Mihráb to the left.

From the Author's Sketch.

sloping tops. The northern and southern walls are each adorned by two handsome domed tower gateways, and two plainer entrances, also in towers, rising above the level of the wall. At the eastern end of the quadrangle rises from a hexagon the dome of the *Mihrâb*: from the west wall rises the solid and imposing *Minar*. Everything, save the lower portion of the tower, was snowy white, standing out against the blue cloudless sky. This was the mosque of Kairwân—the shrine and tomb of its founder, Okhbah ibn Aghlab, and the spot chosen from its sanctity as the last resting place of the Kings of Tunis.

I began by making a sketch of the north-west elevation, and the *Minar* rising about midway along the wall. This massive erection, measuring ten yards on each side of the base, runs up with a slight taper to a height of about sixty feet, in brownish brick. Round a gallery here runs a line of round headed crenellations. From this platform rises, perhaps twenty feet, a smaller tower, with arched panels, and having a porch from which the mueddins issue on to the gallery. Round the parapet of this upper tower were attached a number of black objects, which proved to be lanterns. The birthday of the Prophet, *Leylet al Moolid*, was approaching, and the devout Moors of Kairwân were making ready for it. There rose from the second platform a little tower of belfry form, with an arch open to each of the four winds, and through which the sky appeared. A cornice of brickwork supported the plain fluted dome, and from its centre rose a tapering pinnacle, with the Crescent of Islam upon its summit.

As I was sketching, some people approached. *Kafir*! one cried, whereupon he was stoned by the guards. Some children passing stopped to look at me. Are you not ashamed, cried the Hambas, to stare at the guest of the Kaïd? The bodyguard was reinforced by two soldiers, and kept the lane clear, turning people back, while I moved on and sketched the south-west face of the mosque.

The domed gateways had delicate marble columns, with acanthus capitals; let into them. Of the four entrances on this side, only that by the Great Porch was habitually open. There was a small door for the mueddins in the blank wall. Down the opposite side of the lane ran houses, the doors of which were studded in designs with nails, and having in front of them small sloping platforms of tesselated brick.

I sketched the south-east end of the mosque. It was a high and solid wall, strengthened by buttresses. It had been recently restored, plastered, and whitewashed. From the centre rose the fluted dome of Okhbah's sacred *Mihrâb*. In the centre panel of the hexagon supporting it, was a rose window with coloured glass. To the left of the *Mihrâb*, and projecting thirty feet from the wall, were the porch and entrance of the Bashi Mufti, the high priest of the district. The northern side of the mosque had a general resemblance to that of the southern.

Having gained a general idea of the exterior, and after a leisurely scrutiny of the interior through the wide open doors, we moved on towards the bazaars. At the south-eastern angle of the mosque there stood facing it an ancient mosque, El Khasinah or the store, with a colonnaded court. It was used as a lime store then, and half a dozen perspiring negroes were carrying sacks of lime and whitewashing themselves with the dust. Shall we go in? I asked the soldiers. No, they said; it was once a mosque.

We proceeded through the mean and shabby quarter which lies between the mosque and the bazaars, the Arbat Medîneh, or Quarter of the Mosque. At almost every corner and angle of the walls were columns with beautiful heads, of grey granite, and of marble, grey, red, and white. The number of columns in Kairwân was simply surprising: every interior we looked into, every corn mill or magazine, seemed to have rare old pillars carrying its vaulted roof. The houses generally were poor, and many of them decaying. Kairwân, like Cordova, is still too large for its shrunken population.

The legend is that, eleven hundred years ago, the

city contained thirty quarters, each as large as the present city. One might travel for a whole day without reaching the farther side of it. So vast was it, that children used to carry a small label of wood or silver, given them by their parents, with the name of their quarter engraved upon it, that they might not go astray. Another legend says the city was a square, measuring eighteen miles in every direction. (!)

We passed Dar el Kaïd, the house of the late Governor, a large building, with a gallery across its front, and a tiled roof supported on grey marble pillars. We came to the bazaars, and strolled slowly from one to another. They were vaulted in brickwork, and were cool and dark. We saw the Soukh el Sarajîm, whence come the slippers of canary-coloured morocco leather for which the city has been famous for centuries, and which it taught Cordova the art of working. The dye of the Kairwân workers is said to be unrivalled: but I think that nowadays they get their colours from Tunis, where I saw slippers made fully as good in colour and better in shape. I have heard on good authority that they import the leather from France and Italy.

We went to the woollen bazaar, where they sell the white and grey *barracan*—the prevailing outer garment of Barbary. In the calm, quiet alleys of the cotton and silk bazaars were well-dressed respectable citizens. Unlike those of Tunis, the costumes of Kairwân were of a predominating white colour, very becoming to dark countenances. Many a striking group I saw in the quiet vaulted passages: some of the faces were placid and indifferent, others curious and surprised. We saw but few women: they are scarcer in the streets of Kairwân than in any of the Oriental cities.

Every now and then appeared a marabout or saint, only half clad perhaps, and carrying a drum to make a fool of himself with. These were the most likely folks to attempt to make my visit unpopular, guided as these creatures are neither by religion nor by reason. Hungry predatory fanatics, or else drivelling idiots, they commit the grossest follies and excesses under the plea of sanctity or inspiration, and are tolerated to an inconceivable extent by the best classes of Moslems. This is one of the weakest features in the powerful and impressive Faith of Islam.

We came to the Djemma 'l Barôta, in the grocers' bazaar. There are in Kairwân six mosques of a considerable size: and almost countless smaller places of worship and saints' or dervishes' tombs: in some streets one might pass a dozen within fifty yards. The chief mosque is, of course, Sidina Okhbah—Djemma 'l Kebîr—the Great Mosque. Then comes Djemma 'l Zitûna, the Mosque of the Olive Tree, outside the city wall, facing the Bab el Djedîd, or New Gate. Next is the Djemma 'l Telatha Biban, or the Three Gates. Then

Djemma 'l Bey, the only Hanefite mosque in Kairwân, and which stands in the Soukh. Facing it, and behind the stuff bazaar, is Djemma 'l Malek. Lastly, Sidi Bou Aïssa, where scorpion, glass, and cactus eating take place on holy days.

In the streets leading to the Great Mosque are marabouts' and saints' tombs—scarcely distinguishable as such—to a surprising extent. Great numbers of holy and devout people came to lay their bones in the religious capital of the Moors, and many were canonised. Besides, in a city devoted so long to religion, it is natural that pious and learned men should collect, that over a space of a dozen centuries their places of sepulture should multiply enormously, and that tombs of the faithful should cluster near them. There exist still, though in a ruinous state, the tombs of the Aghlabites, the conquerors of Sicily, Sardinia, Corsica, and Crete; they are among the most venerated monuments of Kairwân. The tomb of Schanoun, the great Kairwân theologian, who died in the year A.D. 862, is also to be seen.

We passed from street to street, continuing the object of much curiosity and some remark. A quiet, respectable woman, closely veiled, as she went by said something in a gentle voice. There is a good-natured wish at last, I said, turning to Perruquier. Do you know what she said? he asked. She prayed that the Great God might not inscribe your name in His book.

There are weavers, in the quiet bye streets, who make haïks and barracans of undyed wool: and near them are charcoal burners and sellers of firewood. We went out by the Bab el Djedîd, and rambled among the suburbs, which are poor and small, and of which the gardens seem to produce nothing but prickly pear.

There are two chief suburbs, Sayiha Jeblieh to the north, and Sayiha Kubliyeh to the south. These are simply mean and scattered collections of small mud houses, and the estimate of inhabitants attributed to them, five thousand, must be twofold what they contain. The outer cities, or suburban annexes, Raccadah, Abassiyeh, and Mansourah, have disappeared.

We went to the marabout of Sidi Abou el Awib, which has a melon-shaped dome. Here lies El Awib, the companion and bosom friend of Mohammed, with three hairs of the Prophet's beard placed upon his heart. In Tunis I was told he was the Prophet's barber, and that he was buried in the Great Mosque. Then to the Mosque of Sidi Amir Abada. At the sides of its ruinous plaster archway are two very old columns indeed. This marabout or mosque has six domes. The streets at this south-west angle of the town are especially dirty and decaying. In the city walls the plaster has half fallen from the small flat bricks. This is the Arbat Kharfan, or Quarter of the Aged, where the aged of Kairwân, I was told, used to live. There are three other quarters,

Arbat el Mar, or Bazaar Quarter: Arbat el Medineh, or Quarter of the Mosque: and Arbat el Bey, the Quarter near the Mosque of the Olive Tree.

We went to the Mosque of the Olive Tree. It has on each face of its square *Minar* an inscription as follows:—

each face, if I am not mistaken, the same, executed in characters of raised brick, and forming a rather remarkable band round the tower. I have already mentioned the similar decoration of Djemma 'l Bey. Col. Playfair, a very high authority, who saw them shortly afterwards, tells me the above are in no sense intelligible characters. I am satisfied he suspects me of having copied them incorrectly. The city wall resembles at the same time those of Damascus and of the Kremlin. The crenellations are narrow, and rise perhaps three feet above the parapet: the bricks are as often red as white.

What did that pretty little boy say just now? I asked Perruquier. He said, May you be seized with some irritable disease! *Roumi! Yahûdi!* hissed some others. Foreigner! Jew! One boy who took a pleasure in thus mocking us is not likely to take a pleasure in it when the next Roumi comes to Kairwân, for one of the soldiers took him by the ears and throat, lifted him up, and flung him on the ground. *Yahûdi* is a term of special contempt. The dislike of the Mussulman for the Jew is very curious—more strong than his dislike for the Christian. The Christian has power, which the Mohammedan recognises, and perhaps admires: but the Jew seems to have no qualities that command his respect. In many respects similar—both Oriental races, inhabiting the same regions, and thrown much together—the Mohammedan seems to have no affinity or sympathy with the Jew. Nowhere is this more noticeable than in the old capital of the Jews.

We went through a *khaukhat*, one of the postern doors through the walls. Low winding passages, like the entrance to a tomb, five feet in height, they are barely of width to admit a man. Each angle is faced with a marble pillar, worn smooth by passers through. The *khaukhat* is never closed or guarded by day or night, unless in times of disturbance: and when next we go to Kairwân in disguise, we will go in the evening and pass in quietly by one of the *khaukh*. There are three of them in all—one to the right, on entering, of the Bab el Tunes: one called the *khaukhat* of the Kharfan Quarter, near the southern angle of the city: and a third to the right of the Bab el Djuluddîn.

CHAPTER XXI.

Moorish Calendar—Chronicles of the City—Okhbah—Conquest of Spain—Ibn Aghlab—The City's Decline.

An Arabic Calendar, published in this Regency, gives the following as among the facts in their annals considered most noteworthy by the Moors:—

Memorable circumstances anterior to the Hejra.

	Solar years
Creation of Adam	6212
The Flood	3974
First King of Egypt	3548
Birth of Abraham	2580
Conquest of Egypt by the Persians	1108
Conquest of Egypt by Alexander the Great	916
„ „ the Romans	612
Birth of Christ	582
Discovery of Glass	484
Construction of Santa Sofia, at Constantinople	334
Year of the War of the Elephant, being the year in which the Prophet was born	53

Memorable facts subsequent to the Hejra.

Hejra of the Prophet, which corresponds to July 12, A.D. 622	1
Death of the Prophet	10
Khalifat of Abou Bekr	11
„ Omar	13
Foundation of Bussora	14
Capture of Damascus under Omar	14
„ Egypt „	20

ANNALS OF THE MOORS.

	Solar years
Khalifat of Osman	24
Conquest of Africa	26
First Siege of Constantinople	39
Building of first Mosque in Constantinople	49
Commencement of the Walls of Kairwân	50
First Mussulman Coinage	75
Capture of Carthage	79
Conquest of Andalusia	92
Completion of the Walls of Kairwân	146
Extinction of the Companions of the Prophet in Africa	148
Dynasty of Mólahabites in Africa	151
,, Aghlabites ,, ,,	184
,, Fatimites ,, ,,	297
,, Obeidites ,, ,,	297
Foundation of the Russian Empire	362
Dynasty of the Sanhagites	365
Foundation of City of Algiers	366
Dynasty of Saljukites	432
Death of Ibu Raschik of Kairwân, author of the work *Omda*	463
Dynasty of the Ajubites	567
Conquest of Syria by Saladin	573
Dynasty of Hafsites	603
Commencement of Ottoman Dynasty	688
Taking of Constantinople	857
Siege of Vienna by Suliman I.	935
Death of the last of the Abassides	950
Death of Dragut Pasha at Malta	971
Succession of Hussein Ben Ali—founder of the reigning dynasty—to the throne of Tunis	1117

These are the Chronicles of Kairwân.

In the year of the Hejra 27, Abdallah, grandson of Abou Sarh, with twenty thousand Companions of the

Prophet, invaded Africa, devastating its northern provinces as far as Numidia : and eventually accepting from the inhabitants three hundred talents of gold as the price of his withdrawal.

After seven years the Saracens returned and established themselves in those regions of Barbary : in the year 45, or A.D. 667, the Emir briefly known as Okhbah ben Nafi ben Abdallah ben Kaïs el Fahhri was appointed by the Khalif Othman governor of the newly acquired provinces.

Okhbah chose this spot as the site of his capital— being central for warlike operations, and secure from maritime attacks; and here he laid the foundations of a magnificent city. In the year 677 Okhbah was recalled, and his envious successor, after attacking Western Barbary, returned to destroy and raze Kairwân.

In 684 Okhbah returned to power, and swept the country as far as the Great Ocean, into which he plunged with his horse, declaring that the sea alone could stop his career. Following his troops, whom he had sent back to Kairwân, he was slain in an ambush, with three hundred Companions of the Prophet, by Kassila, king of the Berbers. Kassila then occupied Kairwân, and established his government and laws. These aboriginals, Touâregs and others, who still exist in the Atlas and mountainous districts of Barbary, are regarded by the Arabs as direct descendants of Ham by Canaan. Long preceding the Saracen invaders in this country, they have witnessed its successive changes without losing their individuality by intermarriage or their independence by war.

In 689 the Khalif Abd el Malek proclaimed a holy war: Zohaïr ben Kaïs entered Africa, met Kassila at Oss in the neighbourhood of Kairwân, and in a murderous battle the Berber king was killed. Zohaïr soon returned to Damascus. I went, he said to the Khalif, to fight in the holy war, and I fear the seductions of the pleasures of the world. Intercepted by the Byzantine fleet on his way to retirement in Egypt, Zohaïr was slain by the Infidels. May God shed on him the treasures of His mercy: adds Ebn Khaldoun, the Arabic chronicler, who tells the story.

Zohaïr's successor in Barbary was Hassan ben Nouman, who, after setting out from Kairwân to assault and destroy Carthage, was overthrown by the Berber queen Kahina, and driven into Cyrene. Hassan, reinforced, marched against Kahina. What do the Arabians want? said the queen to her army. To occupy cities, and take the gold and silver they contain, whilst we want but fields and pastures: I see no means of stopping them but to so ravage the country that they will have no motive for seizing it.

This policy was carried out without hesitation. Barbary, which had been a succession of towns and villages from Tangier to Tripoli, was laid waste. The unlucky inhabitants, it is not to be wondered at, threw themselves, at the first opportunity, into the arms of the Saracens. In a great battle the heroic Kahina was killed, the Berber power was crippled, the tribes submitted to the *kharadj* or capitation tax, and agreed to furnish a contingent of twelve thousand soldiers.

In 708 Musa ibn Noseïr was appointed, by El Mansour—the Sword of God—governor of the Mughreb. This warlike Emir, setting out from the capital, reduced Numidia, Mauritania, and the country of the restless Berbers.

Then comes the greatest chapter in the book of history of the Moors, the feat of the natives of Kairwân, with which this city's history is wrapped up, and without which its sketch would be incomplete. Julian, the Gothic chief, governor of Barbary, and since known as the Apostate, invited the Arabian Emir to invade Spain, that fertile country where the Gothic kings had reigned and prospered for two centuries and a half. Among the warriors of Kairwân was a gaunt, swarthy, one-eyed veteran, scarred with wounds, and revelling in the love of war. Tarik departed on a voyage of discovery, and his report so inflamed Musa's enthusiasm, that he wrote from Kairwân to the Khalif in these words: A new land spreads itself out and invites our conquest: it equals Syria in its fertility and climate, Yemen in its temperature, India in its fruits and flowers, and Cathay in its precious minerals. What is to prevent this glorious land from becoming the inheritance of the Faithful? God is great, cried the Khalif on reading this: and Mohammed is his Prophet. Then he authorised Musa to undertake the conquest.

One dark night, as Irving so well relates, Tarik conveyed his soldiers from Tangier to Tarifa, where he burned his ships. How shall we escape, cried his followers, if fortune should be against us? There is no escape for the coward, replied the one-eyed Emir: and the brave man thinks of none. But how shall we return to our homes? Your homes, said Tarik, are before you. Tarik assaulted and took the rock of Gibraltar. Signior, wrote its Gothic defender to Roderick: the legions of Africa are upon us, but whether they come from heaven or earth I know not. They seem to have fallen from the clouds, for they have no ships.

Then followed the battle of the Guadalete, one of the most bloody and decisive on record. Tarik inspired his troops by the account of a revelation of Mohammed. Fear not, Tarik, the Prophet had said: I will be with thee on the morrow. The field was strewn with the flower of Gothic chivalry, Roderick disappeared, the Gothic power was extinguished, and Spain lay open to the Moors of Kairwân.

The turbaned horsemen, with their flashing scimetars, overran the peninsula, reducing fortresses and annexing vast provinces. The honest, fearless, and noble Tarik forbade wanton plunder and cruelty. Soldiers of Mohammed, he said, spare the vanquished: spoil not the poor and unresisting. All this was bitter news to the Emir of Kairwân—where were his African successes in the blaze of Tarik's victories? So he wrote to Al Mansour, without naming Tarik: The battles have been terrible as the day of Judgment, but by the aid of Allah we have gained the victory.

Leaving his son Abd el Aziz to govern Kairwân, he hastened to share in the glory of the conquest of the land of the Goths. Tarik meantime had reached Granada and its Vega, destined to be for ages the earthly Paradise of the Moors. Cordova, the ancient Kurtuba of the Phœnicians—the birthplace of that most wonderful of all philosophers, Seneca—had fallen: Toledo had been betrayed by the Jews, Tarik had subdued the mountains of the Sun and Air: and Seville was the only great city of the South which remained for Musa to capture.

What a devil of a man, said the citizens, when they saw Musa's grey beard, to undertake such a siege when on the verge of the grave! Surely the city can hold out longer than the life of this old man? Abd el Aziz arrived with a reinforcement from Kairwân, and Seville fell. The spoil of the city was rich and vast.

Musa then followed Tarik to Toledo, and a bitter

quarrel ensued. Musa taunted Tarik with his recklessness and wilfulness, and deprived him of his command. I have done the best I could to serve God and the Khalif, said the blunt Tarik, whose one eye burned like fire: my conscience acquits me, and my sovereign will do me justice.

The Moorish armies under Musa and Tarik, whom the Khalif reinstated, then subdued the districts of the Ebro, the Pyrenees, and captured the cities of Saragossa, Barcelona, and Narbonne. Musa's self-glorification was unspeakable; he became renowned throughout Islam as the great Conqueror of the West. His quarrels with Tarik continuing, the Khalif summoned both of them to Damascus. The single minded Tarik set out at once: Musa first established his three sons as governors of Cordova, Tangier, and Kairwân, and departed to Damascus with a vast collection of slaves, retainers, and spoil.

Tarik became the idol of the Damascenes, and Musa for his jealousy and selfishness, in spite of his great qualities, fell into disgrace. He was even scourged, and thrown into prison. He received one day the news of the simultaneous murder of his three sons, and died broken-hearted. Abd el Aziz had given proofs of a large and generous mind: he had recognised the true means of making secure the conquests of Islam, namely the establishment of just institutions and of the pursuits of peace. On these solid principles the Moorish Empire in Spain was founded; it endured for seven hundred and seventy-eight years, and gathered strength, wealth, and glory beyond measure.

Abd el Rahman, Khalif of Cordova, was seized with a mighty ambition to conquer Gaul. Under renowned chiefs the army of the Crescent entered France, and marched with fearful rapidity upon Bordeaux. Sacking that city, it proceeded, after a bloody encounter on the Dordogne river, into Touraine: and in the year 7:3 of Our Lord, or little more than thirty years after Tarik had set forth from Kairwân, the Standard of the Prophet floated from the ramparts of Tours.

Between Tours and Poictiers, the Frank king Charles Martel met the Saracens, and in a battle—one of the most solemn and prodigious in history, lasting seven whole days—the tide of Moslem invasion was broken. Abd el Rahman more prudently turned his mind to thoughts of peace, and the magnificence of Cordova became his monument.

In the year of Redemption 756, the city had attained such a size, wealth, and splendour that, as Richard Ford's delightful book says, the description of it reads like an Aladdin's tale. Its glory, accumulated under seventeen successive Sultans, culminated in the eleventh century. It contained three hundred mosques, nine hundred baths, and six hundred caravanserais.

Among its million of inhabitants were philosophers, poets, physicians, chemists, astronomers, mathematicians, engineers, architects: this patient, ingenious race had acquired a refinement and culture scarcely ever surpassed. At this time the provinces of Cordova, Catalonia, and Murcia were one vast garden. Granada had half a million of inhabitants, and its Red Palace was one of the marvels of the age.

Then came civil wars. Ibn Abdallah, son of a lamplighter of the Mosque of Kairwân, persuading the Moors to regard him as a saint, incited the new faction of Almohades against the governing sect of the Almorâvides. The Spanish monarchs were not slow to profit by this: they organised a crusade against the civilisers of western Europe.

The Grand Soldan, the head of Islam, was vexed at these constant assaults upon the flower of the Faithful, and wrote to remonstrate with the Catholic monarch. He uttered, says an old Spanish chronicler, opinions savouring of damnable heresy: for he observed that although the Moors were of a different sect, they ought not to be maltreated without just cause.

In the year 1235 St. Ferdinand captured the imperial city of Cordova, and inflicted the first heavy blow on the Moorish power in Europe.

Twelve years later Seville fell, having been for nearly five centuries and a half in the hands of the

Moors: and in the following century the capture of Granada completed the downfall of one of the most religious, enlightened, ingenious, chivalrous, and industrious races that ever established themselves in Europe.

Much was due to the example of the parent city Kairwân, the type on which Cordova was founded, and the source from whence she derived much of her learning and culture. What Cordova became, Kairwân had been: and, in the refinement and intelligence of the existing inhabitants of this country, we can recognise traces of that high but almost vanished civilisation. Kairwân must have been a wonderful city: Cordova and Granada are noble in their ruins.

The last days of the Moors in Spain are inexpressibly sad. Distracted by civil wars, torn from their famous strongholds, the cities they had created, and the rich lands so dear to them, they made a last stand in the city of Granada. The iron ring of Christian armies closed in upon them: the Moors fought as they had always fought, but now it was for their own existence, for the scenes of their infancy, their glories, and their homes—and it was in vain.

Broken-hearted, the king, the viziers, and the nobles exclaimed, Allah Akhbar! God is great: the will of God be done! and they went to the Spanish monarchs and resigned their last hold on Spain. Exiled, persecuted, tortured, they drifted sadly over into Africa.

The thread of the chronicle recommences with Musa's successor. The Berbers having, some years after Musa's death, defeated the Khalif's army in the Mughreb, Kolthoum ben Ayad was sent to the seat of government in Kairwân, where he collected his army. He was slain in battle in the West, his Syrians fled into Spain, and the Africans and Egyptians took refuge in Kairwân.

The Berbers, soon after this, were beaten at Gabes, but rallying again, three hundred thousand strong, they attacked Handhalah, Emir of Kairwân, under the walls of this city. When the citizens and warriors saw the vast army of the Khouaridj, or Touâregs, they fell to praying. Encouraged, they fell upon the Africans at the dawn of day, and, routing them with awful carnage, slew, it is said, no less than a hundred and ninety thousand.

In 748 Handhalah was supplanted by Abd el Rahman, and retired into Syria. The new Emir made a successful raid against the Berbers of Tlemçen, and in the year 757 he despatched expeditions against Sicily and Sardinia. Picking a quarrel with his sovereign El Mansour, Abd el Rahman declared himself independent.

Assembling the people in the Great Mosque here, he presented himself in sandals and a robe called *khazz*: and mounting the *membar* he praised God and the

Prophet, while he cursed the Khalif. He declared El Mansour's injustice and tyranny: and, flinging off his sandals, said it was thus he repudiated his suzerainty. Calling for the *khilat*, or black robe of investiture granted by the Abassides or Black Khalifs—the Ommiades were the White, and the Fatimites the Green Khalifs, so called from the colour of their own robes and those of the members of their court—Abd el Rahman had it burnt. He proclaimed these acts throughout the Mughreb. For two years only was his ambition gratified: he was assassinated by his two brothers.

Elyas, one of them, and Habib, Abd el Rahman's son, succeeded him. Dividing the kingdom, Elyas chose the province of Kairwân, and sent in his submission to El Mansour. Upon this, Habib marched against Kairwân, took it, and slew Elyas in single combat. Why, said Habib, should so many of our faithful subjects perish in our quarrel? Let us fight alone. If I die, I shall rejoin my father: if I kill thee, I shall avenge him.

These Emirs were mere Mohammedans, and knew no better. Their Most Christian Majesties nowadays, with the advantages of eleven centuries of civilisation, when they covet a neighbour's territory, enter it with God's name upon their lips, and, sending their soldiers to be slaughtered, withdraw their own sacred persons out of harm's way.

Habib being defeated by the Berbers, the people of Kairwân offered the city and its sovereignty under the Khalif to Ibn Djamil the Berber, who refused it. He did not refuse, however, to ravage the city, sack the mosques and pollute them. He was eventually killed in the Aures Mountains by Habib, whom he had pursued thither.

Kairwân, its provinces, and all Saracen Barbary in 763 fell into the power of the Werfadjoumah and their chief Abd el Malek. When the garrison of the city issued to defend it, Arabs who were in the Berber army cried to their countrymen to join them.

Only a thousand Moors of Kairwân, among the most renowned for their religion and uprightness, remained faithful to the Kadi, and died fighting at his side. Conducting their government with gross cruelty, the Werfadjoumah were driven out.

El Mansour sent El Aghleb ibn Salem to restore peace in the Mughreb, but he was killed in battle and replaced by Omar ben Hafs. During his absence at Tobna, which he was fortifying, the indomitable Berbers seized Kairwân. Omar ben Hafs had recourse to his wealth, and, by distributing large bribes among the chief insurgents, succeeded in demoralising their army.

The next incident in the city's history was its siege for eight months by Abou Hatem, chief of the Ibadhieh, with a hundred and thirty thousand men. Omar, bent on victory or death, made a furious sortie and lost his life. The long siege had reduced the city's treasury to the last dirhem, the granaries to their last sack, and the inhabitants to the necessity of eating dogs and beasts of burden. The Africans destroyed the city walls, burned the gates, and retired to the Atlas.

El Mansour sent Yezid ibn Hatem to restore order, with sixty thousand Arabian warriors, who defeated the Africans in the Country of Palms, giving them no quarter. Yezid proved himself an able and just administrator. He rebuilt the Great Mosque, established numerous bazaars, and assigned to each trade a distinct quarter: in fact, remodelled and half rebuilt the city.

On his death, Rouh ibn Hatem, his brother, governor of Palestine, came to replace him, and, thanks to Yezid's policy, he had a tranquil administration up to his death. When Yezid was sent to the Mughreb, and Rouh to govern the Sind, it was said to the Khalif, Surely there is no chance of these brothers being buried together. However, Rouh and Yezid sleep side by side in this city.

After many bloody disputes, Horthomah ruled next in Kairwân, a mild and conciliatory Emir, who built, a year after his arrival, the great Castle of Monastir. He is said to have built the sea-wall of Tripoli. He received Haroun el Reschid's permission to retire to

IBRAHIM IBN EL AGHLAB.

Irak: and his successor was driven by insurgents out of the province.

Ibrahim ibn el Aghlab, who had established himself as independent ruler of Zab and Tobna, made his appearance, and recovered Kairwân from the insurgents. He wrote to the Khalif, offering, on condition of his appointment as hereditary Emir of Kairwân, to forego the yearly subvention from Egypt of a hundred thousand dinars, and to contribute, instead, forty thousand dinars. El Reschid accepted these conditions, and Ibrahim became the founder of the dynasty of the Aghlabites.

Mohammed ibn Mokatil, mortified at his displacement by El Aghlab, endeavoured to recommend his own cause to the Khalif. Why, said the Commander of the Faithful to him, should I prefer thee to El Aghlab, to entrust to thee again the government of Africa? Is it because of his bravery and thy cowardice, his strength and thy weakness, his submissiveness to my will, and thy spirit of revolt?

El Aghlab built, close to the western side of Kairwân, the fortress city of Abassiyeh, which he inhabited with his court. No traces of this kind of Moorish Escorial or Bardo, save the reservoirs, remain. The name Abassiyeh is frequently found on coins of the period of the Black Khalifs.

Arabic geographical works describe five spots bearing the name of Abassiyeh. A sand-hill near Mecca, a town of Upper Egypt, a quarter of the city of Baghdad, a town near Koufa, and lastly the city built in the environs of Kairwân by El Aghlab.

This stronghold became the habitual abode of the Aghlabites, who reigned here in great magnificence. Here Ibrahim, after he had established the Faith of Islam throughout the Mughreb, constituted himself Khalif of the West, and received the envoys of Charlemagne, who came to solicit permission to carry to Europe the body of St. Cyprian, buried near Carthage.

Ibrahim had his armoury and treasures removed by night to this palace, and surrounded himself with a bodyguard of trusted Saracens and Berbers. On discontent arising among the Africans, he quieted them with money. He pardoned the citizens of Tripoli, who had revolted, and shut up their governor in a mosque.

In 817 Amran of Tunis took the city of Kairwân, and invested the city of Abassiyeh during a whole year. Amran tried to suborn the Kadi, and induce him to surrender the Khalif, but the governor was incorruptible.

The Moors of Tripoli revolted twice in the succeeding years, and El Aghlab only succeeded in subduing them by engaging mercenary forces from among the Berbers. After a reign of twelve years and a half, the first of the Khalifs of Kairwân died. His son and successor, Abdallah, treated the citizens so cruelly that a santon prayed publicly to heaven for his destruction. Abdallah was promptly seized with ulcer in the ear and died.

His brother, Ziadet Allah, ascended the throne, a man of harsh and intemperate mind, unlike his politic father, and who shed his soldiers' blood on the slightest pretext. El Mansour, chief of Tabnada, took Kairwân, and shut up Ziadet Allah in the royal city, but by a desperate sally the Berber was routed. Ziadet then destroyed the walls and gates of the city to punish the citizens, who had shown themselves sympathetic to Mansour: some say he was foolish enough to destroy also the bazaars. He almost demolished, but afterwards restored, the Mosque.

After various successes in Barbary, the Khalif sent an expedition to Sicily, which met the Byzantines and routed them. Subsequently the Saracens had to be succoured by a fleet of three hundred vessels.

The wars of Ziadet and his successors in Sicily and on the Italian peninsula present very monotonous features. They resulted in the annihilation of Byzantine power in the island.

Abou Ibrahim had a passion for building. He constructed of stone and lime no less than ten thousand strongholds in the Khalîfat of Kairwân, giving them gates of iron. He also enlisted Ethiopians in his army, in which he took a great interest. Mohammed, who took his place, lost various places in Spain, but captured Malta.

Civil wars were of constant occurrence during the next reigns. In 877 Ibrahim ibn Ahmed, a dignified, just, and firm ruler, pacified the country. He built on the coast of Africa a succession of towers, so that fire signals could be transmitted from Ceuta to Alexandria in a single night. He also surrounded Susa, the seaport of Kairwân, with a wall.

In 885 he laid the foundations of the suburban city Raccadah, and in the same year took up his residence in it. This town had a circuit of fourteen thousand cubits: no purer air, more agreeable climate, or richer soil existed in Africa. The Moors used to say that in Raccadah one was happy without cause, and gay without motive.

A number of emancipated slaves having revolted and seized the old citadel, they were disarmed: some were scourged to death, some crucified, and others immured for life in the dungeons of Kairwân. Shortly after this a severe drought occurred: and, in the lamentable famine resulting from it, the inhabitants in some instances devoured one another.

In later life Ibrahim's generous qualities disappeared, and he became a cruel, senseless tyrant. Surrounded by disaffected subjects, he shut himself up with his bodyguard of blacks in Raccadah, which he fortified with a deep trench.

His army took Tunis from certain insurgents and were on the point of putting twelve hundred prisoners to death: news of the victory, however, reaching Ibrahim, in a note fastened under a bird's wing, he sent for the prisoners, and had them paraded in triumph through the city of Kairwân. In a fit of exultation over one of his triumphs, Ibrahim cried: Why did not the Almighty witness in person so complete and glorious a victory? One of his acts was to crucify Mohammed, governor of Tripoli, whom he had hated from childhood for his good qualities and profound learning.

Ibrahim, who one day had lost his napkin, put to death for that circumstance three hundred servants. He was seized with a black sickness which daily excited him to fresh murders: his servants, wives, and children were butchered, tortured, burnt: the story seems a hideous romance, but it is well authenticated.

His grandson, Ziadet Allah, murdered his father, brothers, and uncles, and, taking alarm at a rising of the Berbers, fled from Raccadah with his family and treasures into Egypt. He died of poison: and, says the Moorish historian, thus was extinguished the family of the Aghlabites and their glory eclipsed: God alone is Eternal.

Wars with Morocco occupied much of the next century. Sicily continued an object of contention. Obeid Allah, the first of the Green Khalifs who reigned in Kairwân, amongst other feats pillaged Sfax and attacked Tripoli. He ravaged Lombardy, took Genoa, and Sicily in the next fifty years became practically an independent Moorish state.

After 1086 Islam ceased to dominate in the island: but Roger, Count of Sicily, by his able and considerate administration, establishing equal faith and rights, caused the first real union between the East and the West, the Crescent and the Cross: Islamism and Christianity being equally tolerated and practised.

From this period the glories of Kairwân begin to fade, and its history becomes subservient to that of the Moorish Khalifat in Spain. At one time it was destroyed by Yussuf, sovereign of Morocco: at another governed by Mehdi, the restorer of Afrikieh, the False descendant of the Prophet. Sometimes allied with the Cordovans, sometimes with the Emirs of Granada, Kairwân— which had given birth to both those glorious kingdoms, furnished them with warriors, saints, artists, and learned men, had taught them to conquer and to civilise, to extract wealth and use it in erecting temples to the glory of God, and palaces for men's glory such as the world had never seen—Kairwân, the mother city, the cradle and shrine of Islam in Africa, began gradually to decay.

When the Moors at length lost those noble possessions in Europe, in this old sacred city and its provinces they found a refuge: and here they wait with the keys of their ancestors' homes in Spain, till their destiny becomes fulfilled.

DECLINE OF KAIRWÂN.

We hear incidentally of the city in the sixteenth century, when Dragut of Tripoli conspired with the Ulemas of the Great Mosque against the King, and entering the city by night put him to death: but the real history of Kairwân ended with the dynasty of the Fatimites, or towards the close of Saxon days in England.

They have all vanished now, Fatimites and Aghlabites, Black Khalifs and White, Raccadah and Abassiyeh, the great city's wealth and palaces: only the solemn old Mosque remains, in the spot where Okhbah first placed it, with its Kibleh still pointing to the Prophet's city, which preceded it as a sanctuary only by forty years. Lo, says the Moorish historian, resignedly, at the close of his chronicle, God is He who rules the nights and the days.

CHAPTER XXII.

The Frenchman — Servants — Soldiers — Ride round Walls — A fine Barb — The African Mecca — The Haj — The Kaïd's Predecessors — Colleges — The Renegade of Kairwân.

I HAD on the second day an interview with the Frenchman. He had volunteered a few remarks to Perruquier in French, explaining that he had been partly educated in France: and one afternoon he came into my room and began to talk on various subjects in indifferent French. He made an unnecessary apology for his familiarity with the language, and his little slips and defects in grammar were most amusing. He became very friendly, and talked in a most interesting way of Kairwân and its customs. He promised to find for me an old native of Kairwân, a barber, who should take me to every corner of the city: and who, having been employed some time in the French Consulate in Tunis and lived in Algeria, could speak tolerable French. In course of time the barber, Hassan ben Ali, presented himself, a bright, friendly old fellow, strongly resembling the Moor in the frontispiece, who assured me that nothing inside or outside of the city should escape me.

The Frenchman—Sidi Haji Mohammed—to whom I suggested with delicacy the possibility of getting a plan of the mosque, told me rather coldly that the Moslem injunction for the mosque was to pray and not to look about. Besides, in the Great Mosque was written up a warning against counting, or measuring its proportions: whoever should do so would lose his sight. There was no irony in the Frenchman's manner as he spoke, but I wondered how far he was convinced of this. To turn the subject, which was getting on to delicate ground, he explained how warm the Prime Minister's recommendation had been, and what a high regard he entertained for General Khaireddin.

After an elaborate Oriental meal sent by the Kaïd's orders, that worthy gentleman came in and paid me a visit. My rooms were comfortable, very simply furnished, and numerous well-dressed attendants would loiter in from time to time. In Moorish households many servants attach themselves merely for the sake of their food, and receive no remuneration. All dishes appearing first on the master's table, the number and extent of them there appears surprising.

Soldiers in Kairwân and the capital have, or rather used to have, a precarious remuneration. Their pay was very moderate, and sometimes they didn't receive it punctually. When I was first in Tunis, for example, it was about eighteen months in arrears. So the nominal amount of six piastres or three shillings per month might almost be regarded as an income of six piastres a year. Matters of this kind, however, are slightly better managed now: but what with irregular pay and their allowance of coarse black porridge, the poor soldiers do rather badly. They are often to be seen knitting or doing some little kind of work: and on our first visit to Tunis, the most active and enterprising assistant we had in the pursuit of old curiosities, was a soldier who temporarily excused himself from duty.

The necessaries of life are not dear here or in Tunis—the prices being publicly fixed by the *amîns* of the bazaars from time to time. So the poorer classes get things at their proper value—such as meat, bread, vegetables, oil, eggs, butter, cheese, honey, besides all kinds of fruit which are sold by weight, such as apricots and plums. Fish, fresh butter, fowls, and groceries are not sold by weight, and are a matter of bargain.

The Kaïd asked me what I should like to do with myself on the second day: and, as I expressed a wish to ride round the city, he had three horses brought to the door at the appointed time—one for Perruquier, one for the Kaïd's servant, and one for myself. Perruquier had the Kaïd's son's horse: mine was the Kaïd's own, a splendid iron-grey Barb, with a cream-coloured embroidered saddle-cloth over the high peaked Arab saddle, and so powerful and spirited that I felt he could have fled with me to the Desert whenever he pleased. Perruquier's horse was also a fine grey, with red velvet trappings and gold embroidery.

We sallied forth by the Bab el Djuluddîn, and rode to the westward all through the suburbs or outer villages of Kairwân. There is a noticeable want of fruit and flowers: the utmost efforts of the gardeners seem to result in nothing but prickly pear. Indeed, my personal belief is that if date seed, poppy seed, and pumpkins were sown in these gardens of Kairwân, they would all come up as prickly pear. The houses are poor and unimportant without exception. It was a glorious, hot afternoon. We had no soldiers with us: our two shâoushes remained in the house to sleep, the lazy rascals.

There was but little life outside the walls, and we passed from one spot to another without exciting more than a passing interest. We rode between mud walls and prickly pear hedges and over dust heaps, keeping the city to our right hand. Beyond the green of the enclosures stretches, north, south, and west, the vast plain, skirted in all directions save the seaward by mountains. We passed the Mosque of the Olive Tree, the outer market place, the Bab el Tunes, the Keshlah and its gate: then a long straight reach of wall broken midway by a ruined fort: past waste ground, and—what is generally but little better—a Mohammedan burial place. We rounded the towers at the north-east and eastern angles of the city, within which points lies the Great Mosque, with its far-seen *Minar*: then up the long turreted curving south-east wall, and past the Bab el Khaukh to the Bab el Djuluddîn, whence we had issued to make the circuit.

Kairwân is, and always has been, a city of pilgrimage: and in the Mohammedan faith seven journeys thither still rank with one to Mecca, and equally entitle the pilgrim to the name of Hâji. Thus Perruquier and I have the right to regard ourselves as ·143 of a Hâji each, which circumstance affords us a certain satisfaction. The green turbans of the Prophet's descendants are tolerably plentiful in Kairwân, but not so thick as in Sfax. There are probably more openings for amassing piastres in Sfax, and the Scherîfs forsake the sleepy and half dead city of Kairwân. In spite of the advantage of a local Mecca, numbers of pilgrims travel from Barbary to Arabia. The caravan which used to traverse Tripoli and the deserts of Cyrene is a thing of the past, and the Faithful travel on the decks of a *markab nâr* all the way to Djeddah: then on camels or on foot till they see the flickering lightning playing over the Prophet's tomb at Medina, or till they kneel to drink of the sacred well in the Great Mosque of Mecca.

The evening was very cold, and we discovered during

dinner that the windows of our dining-room were not glazed. We no longer wondered at the freshness perceptible to the backs of our necks and tops of our heads on the previous evening. The Kaïd's servants brought in on long trays numerous dishes having basket covers, decorated with coloured cloth, such as I saw the black women working at Tripoli. We had soup, cold fowl, roast mutton, roast veal with herbs, sausages stuffed with herbs, *assida*, a kind of flour porridge eaten with honey, *kouskousou*, rice pudding scented with otto of roses, and of course water to drink.

The Kaïd came in as usual to spend the evening, and we had a long amusing talk about Kairwân. I asked him if his grandfather were not Sidi Othman el Mourâbet. He said, Yes, with surprise. I asked if Sidi Othman had not a fine stud of horses and other animals in his stable. The Kaïd asked Perruquier how it was possible for me to have learnt these things. I told him that in England we were compelled to employ ourselves diligently in reading, especially about other people and other countries, for fear we should become grossly ignorant: that with many of us it was a matter of pride to be extremely well acquainted with our neighbours' affairs, and that our ladies strove to anticipate one another in the dissemination of news. He wondered at this.

I put one or two historical questions to the Kaïd,

rather beyond his scope, which so alarmed the genial man that he fairly stampeded, wishing me a pleasant night's rest. Afterwards the Mudabbir came in, a good-looking, well-informed man. He told me that the once famous colleges of Kairwân are declining, though there is still a very creditable theological college near Dar al Mana, the mosque there belonging to it. Kairwân became the principal seat of the study of the Mohammedan law and doctrine. The educational institutions were renowned throughout Islam. They were magnificently endowed, and from their libraries came some of the Oriental MSS. most valuable in Europe, and unobtainable elsewhere. These magnificent libraries of the Early Middle Ages are dispersed, but there remain in the city great numbers of curious manuscripts and books, many theological, and even books of travel illustrated. With a little patience some might be got.

Most Arabic scholars know, but I did not know before, that when a boy is set to learn the Koran he commences with the Fatthah, or first chapter. Then he goes to the last chapter, then to the last but one, and so on backwards through the book, the chapters increasing in length up to the second chapter, which is the longest.

I was sitting on one of the divans, writing, when the Frenchman—or, as I ought to call him, Sidi Hamet el Haji—came in, and, looking to see that no one else was present, sat down cross-legged on the carpet in front of me, and thus addressed me in the purest French: You were astonished, sir, this morning to hear such good French spoken in Kairwân. I can hardly say that I was, but I said that the circumstance had filled me with surprise.

Well, sir, he went on, I have perceived from your conversation that you are un homme d'intelligence et de cœur—the worthy Sidi Hamet was not un homme de pénétration—and I desire to make to you a communication which I have made to no one before. Know that I am a European, a Frenchman, I may almost say half an Englishman, for I come from Normandy, the home of our common ancestors. My family—he went on rapidly and with emotion—are still living in Normandy, for all I know. My father was a banker and connected by marriage with a large manufacturer of Rouen. I studied in Paris, and took the degree of Bachelier ès lettres. Owing to circumstances, into which I need not enter, I attached myself to the monastery of La Trappe, remaining there for three years. At La Grande Chartreuse I also spent some short time. I cannot describe to you how those few years' experiences shook and uprooted my faith in Christianity and Catholicism, or how great are the meanness, the hypocrisy, the imposture of such a system. Sickened and disillusioned with this mockery of religion, I left my country, resolved to seek some simpler, purer way to another world.

Forgive me, he said, interrupting himself, if I have said anything which can hurt your feelings or convictions. I came to Tunis. I was received by the Prime Minister, the distinguished and successful Khaireddin, who himself came to the Regency a Christian of the Greek Church. He treated me generously and as a friend, and I have become attached to him as a father. Under his auspices, and after anxious consideration and preparatory study, I resolved to adopt the Faith of Islam. I gained sufficient acquaintance with the Arabic tongue, and in Tunis was formally admitted a Mussulman.

I came directly to Kairwân, and yours is the first European face I have seen here. I resolved to wipe out and forget the old life with its associations, and to devote myself to the study of my new faith and of the philosophy of life. Determined to abandon everything that could suggest or recall the past, I became simply and purely a Mussulman. In habits, in dress, and even in thought, my wishes, my associations, my affections, have become Mohammedanised. I am surrounded by friends who have given me evidences of the truest affection, such as I did not before believe the Arab mind capable of. My happiness is consulted, and I see about me examples of philosophy and true religion.

I occupy myself in instructing the Kaïd's children,

to whom I have become fondly attached, and now for the first time in my life I have learnt to realise what happiness is. I live in the most absolute calm and tranquillity of mind, unruffled by circumstances: the past is blotted out—all I ask for the present is peace. My life is to me the realisation of practical philosophy. I have nothing to disturb the peace of the mind or the balance of the intellect.

My perversion was the cause of astonishment to many, and each one endeavoured to invent some motive for it. According to one, it was the fulfilment of an ambition. But where is there room for ambition in Kairwân? According to another I was attracted by the sensual features of the social life and religious faith of the Mohammedans, but on adopting the Faith I made a vow of chastity and poverty. Should I be offered a wife I would not refuse one, but I want neither riches nor pleasures. I want the philosophical enjoyment of a quiet spirit.

I have tired you, he said, stopping. On the contrary, I said, what you have told me is very interesting and remarkable. I asked whether he thought he found in the Mussulman faith any higher inspirations than in that of Jesus Christ. I do not, he said; it is in the practice of their faith that Christians fall short, as compared with Mussulmans: and the imposing extravagances which have grown up under the auspices of the priesthood—I speak of my native country—have rendered the worship of Christ a theatrical mockery. The influence established by ignorant and intriguing men over the minds of their flocks is unjustifiable, and the result is mere superstition. In the Koran there is sufficient to take a man to heaven, if he follows its precepts and his own conscience.

I asked if he had any curiosity to hear of his family or friends. Absolutely none, he answered. None to hear of events in the outer world? None whatever. Had he the curiosity to hear of my experiences and return home? No, he said, politely: not even that; I wish to know of nothing outside of this city. I will not for anything risk the distraction of my thoughts or the absorbing of my interest. One thing I ask: should you ever write an account of your travels in this country, send me, I beg, a copy of the book. And should it be in my power at any time hereafter to receive here, protect, and serve any friend of yours, believe me I will not fail to do so.

He rose to go, and I accompanied him. I will not forget you, he said, though we may not meet here again. We are both travelling along the same road, I said. Yes, he added, and let us hope that it will lead us to where we may meet hereafter. Espérons. He grasped my hand on the doorstep, and went out into the darkness.

He had spoken with such energy and conviction, and so much as a cultivated and intellectual man, that it was impossible not to be struck. The perversion of some barber or shopkeeper, such as I expected to find in the apostate of Kairwân, would surprise no one. Some small mercenary motive might have explained it: but this was a man brought up in the so-called centre of the intellect of Europe, and it was hard to believe him actuated by anything short of conviction.

It is of course easy to suggest reasons. Emulation of a career such as Khaireddin's, a Circassian by birth, brought as a slave to Tunis, and now the most influential man in the Regency. It might be an ambition to advance to eminence in the Mussulman religion, where it is clear his eloquence and force would powerfully impress the worshippers in the mosques. Who knows? he might aim at the foundation of a new sect, a compromise, or a Christian-Mohammedanism, combining what he might consider the advantages in both Faiths. He might have chosen this as the only means of studying in its completeness the Faith of Islam.

But, whatever views he might have, he was too clever a man to work without a purpose: and the earnestness with which he was mastering the doctrines of his new creed might excuse the suggestion that tranquillity of mind and forgetfulness of the past were not the only things aimed at. I confess he impressed me, by his intelligence as well as by his good breeding and friendliness. Such was the Renegade of Kairwân, a man of whom I should not be surprised to hear in Barbary at some time hereafter.

CHAPTER XXIII.

The Bazaars—A Bargain—Mosque of the Three Gates—Tombs—
Measure the Great Mosque—Fanaticism—Details of Exterior—
Sacred Well of Kafâyat—The *Minar*—The Courtyard—The Prayer
Chamber — Its Interior — Columns of the Great Mosque — An
Intrigue—Writing on the Wall.

THERE was still much to do in the city : to map out and sketch—subject to the popular will—the Great Mosque, and to make a plan of the city walls. It would have been unseemly, too, to leave Kairwân without any souvenir, so I started with the old barber, Hassan ben Ali, for the bazaars. We went to the shop of Haji Hamouda, *amîn* of the bazaar, near Djemma 'l Barota, where carpets, woollen stuffs, silks, &c., were sold. Hamouda was also *amîn* of the jewel and silver trade, which seemed to be almost privately conducted in Kairwân. Owing to the absence of Jews and Christians, there is not a silversmith's shop to be seen, and the absence of ornaments, rings, &c., is quite noticeable. The carpets of Kairwân are celebrated for their fineness and beauty : they are, however, made solely by women, and it is consequently impossible to see the process. The finest carpets sold in the bazaars of Tunis are those made in Kairwân.

In the little shop of the *amîn* I took my seat, and Hamouda, a well-dressed, good-looking, and courteous man, bade the crowd stand at a little distance. He found me a handsome pair of old bracelets, with the silver-mark of Tripoli upon them, and a silver earring of picturesque form. A man came up to offer me a few old Roman coins, which I said I was willing to buy. He then told me he had a great many more in his handkerchief: and, as the crowd was growing a little forward, we withdrew to the Kaïd's stables, which were close by. The Moor showed me a bag containing more than a hundred and twenty Roman coins, several of silver, and was satisfied with what I gave him for them. He told me that he had been collecting them among the neighbouring ruins during the last twenty years.

We went off through the streets beyond the bazaars and came to a soap manufactory, a dark building below stairs, where were tanks full of melting grease and oil. The barber, who should be a good judge, told me the soap was excellent. We saw it in all stages, from the boiling down to the cooling and cutting into slabs. Then we rambled down an unfrequented-looking street to the barber's shop, a neat, clean little cupboard, where were small hand-glasses stuck round the walls. It

CHAP. XXIII. THE MOSQUE OF THREE DOORS.

faced an open space close to the Djemma 'l Telatha Biban, or Mosque of the Three Gates: and we next visited that beautiful old building, probably of the thirteenth century, externally by far the most striking in Kairwân.

It has a plain façade, with a triple gateway, the arches of which are supported by marble columns. The windows are double arched, the single minaret is poor and cramped. What tiles there are, are of the beautiful Oriental green melting into blue, in delicate patterns. But the chief feature is the rare old carved stonework, which gives it the air of the front of a fine old Crusaders' church. It runs above and about the arches, extending across the front in broad bands of successive text and ornament, in solid deep beautiful chiselling. First a line of running foliage two feet in depth, then a band of Kufic or early Arabic characters, free and bold, then a row of alternate panels of carving, each containing a single rose or a leaf pattern. Then text and carvings alternately, and finally the moulding and corbels of the cornice. The carving is of the finest, and the designs are most rich. The front was well worth sketching, but too elaborate for a rapid drawing, so we moved on to the Mosque of Kader Awi. Round the white minaret ran the broad text I have described on the Mosque of the Olive Tree.

We saw the marabout of Sidi Mohammed 'l Awâni,

with a white melon dome, and with the jambs of its doorway minutely carved in a coarse cream-coloured marble. On either side of these uprights are tiled surfaces. We saw tombs of saints by the dozen: many of them seemed simply placed in houses which had been long tenantless: for there was little to indicate beyond the little flag, or the grated window through which the sarcophagus could be seen, that they were other than dwellings of the living.

We came by a quiet lane to the Great Mosque, where we spent two or three hours in measuring and sketching. The soldiers, a few of whom had joined us, barred the approaches, and warned off or threw down intruders. *Ma maléh!* not good! the people would say, as they saw the unbeliever taking the proportions of their sacred building. The sun shining in the cloudless blue sky fell upon the dazzling white walls of the mosque, and perspiration stood on the soldiers' dark faces. The great doors of the courtyard and of the prayer chamber were wide open, and there were so few worshippers inside, and so few people at hand, that I should probably have entered but for fear of compromising the soldiers, and of making any further rambles about the city risky and perhaps impossible. As I saw, too, pretty clearly all I wanted, it would have been an idle satisfaction to go in for the sake of saying I had been there.

Before starting for Kairwân, Mr. Wood told me how a little Jewish boy, a few months before, was playing with some companions in the bazaars of Tunis. A Moorish boy took the Jew's cap, and ran off with it through the courtyard of the Mosque of the Olive Tree. Quite heedlessly the lad ran after him to recover his cap, and as he came out by the opposite door he was put to death. Tunis is much Europeanised, and the inhabitants are relatively enlightened and liberal.

I was walking one day with Perruquier past an arcaded gallery of the same mosque near the grocers' bazaar. A few gracefully dressed Tunisians sat in the gallery. I said something to them, and they smiled. I am coming up, I said playfully, pointing to the stone staircase. In an instant the smiles vanished, and a shopkeeper behind me sprang growling from his seat. Perruquier explained that I was not quite so simple : and when I drew my finger across my throat to suggest a violent death, and shook my head, they laughed again.

At the southern angle of the mosque wall was built in a charming little white marble column, having a capital of acanthus of hart's tongue form: but one-half of the capital having been broken off, it had been replaced by another acanthus head with saw edges, like a swordfish's snout. Outside the south-west door of the prayer chamber lay a beautiful fallen capital, now used as a seat, of white and bluish marble, the decoration being of a highly ornate fretted acanthus. I commenced the measurement of the south-east end, which extends eighty-five yards in length. It is the wall of the prayer chamber itself. Midway along it is the porch of the Grand Mufti, the spiritual governor of Kairwân. He is, in one sense, of more consequence than the Kaïd, who on state occasions goes to visit him. His antechamber stands out from the building, and none but the Muftis have access by this way to the mosque. Above this porch there rises from the prayer chamber its only dome, that over the sacred old *Mihrâb* of Okhbah.

The sides of the mosque measure each one hundred and forty yards. At a distance of thirty yards from the eastern angle of the prayer chamber stands the finest of the entrance towers. It has an outer horseshoe arch, and an inner one which contains the door opening direct into the prayer chamber. The exterior is a finely proportioned piece of Saracenic work: it has a row of arched panels along the upper portion of its sides, and the dome and interiors of arches are in plaster fretwork. In the angle it forms with the great wall stands the marabout, a simple white domed cube, of a holy woman, Lilla Rahanna. Forty yards from the southern angle there is in the wall a pattern of diamond form in slightly projecting bricks. This is the mark of the limit of the chamber of prayer, or rather of the colonnade which runs across its front.

THE HOLY WELL.

Almost midway along the north-east wall stands the sacred well of *Kafâyat*, or It is enough. It was here before the city existed : its water was used in the building of the walls, and in times of drought it has served —and is still said to suffice—for the wants of the whole district. Five years ago, when rain failed, the well, I was told, maintained its character, and all Kairwân drank of it. It is enclosed by a low circular wall, of a yard and a half in height, built of rough stone. The aperture measures ten feet across, being faced with pieces of aged marble shafts, yellow, red, and white, worn into deep channels and furrows. A rusty iron frame serves as a lowering apparatus. This well is said to communicate with the holy spring at Mecca : indeed a pilgrim who once let his drinking cup fall into Zemzem, found it in Kafâyat on his way homeward ! The only other well in Kairwân is that called Bir el Bey.

As in the south-west wall, there are four gateways in the north-east wall, of an interesting Saracenic style : but only the principal one is used. At the northern angle is a pink marble column, let into the masonry.

The north-west end, measuring seventy-five yards, or ten yards less than the opposite end, has rising from it the great *Minar*. The brick and plaster of this massive tower are defaced by marks of gunshot, fired by the Government troops during the insurrection, when they retook the city from the insurgents. A rusty gun, possibly from the same interesting period, lies at the foot of the *Minar*. There is an opening near the tower—communicating with underground cisterns in the courtyard—by which, in case of overflow, the water can escape. On either side of the *Minar*, within the enclosure, is a store room. Within the southern colonnade, entered by a private door from the street, is the chamber of the Mueddins. Facing the southern angle, and near the main entrance, is a bath, entered by a plain doorway faced with marble, where the Faithful come to wash and pray before entering the mosque.

The prayer chamber occupies the south-east end of the enclosure, running across the building eighty-five yards, and measuring about forty yards from the *Mihrâb* to the wall facing it. The two great porches open directly into it on either side, having heavy wooden doors, unpainted, and with large rusty ornamented iron hinges.

This leaves a quadrangle, measuring a hundred yards, by eighty in average width. Round this runs the double colonnade, about thirty feet wide, consisting of two rows of grey marble columns in pairs, carrying a simple roof. The courtyard is paved with white and grey marble, defaced and broken in places, and a little grass-grown.

In the arcade which runs along the front of the prayer chamber facing the quadrangle, the arches are double,

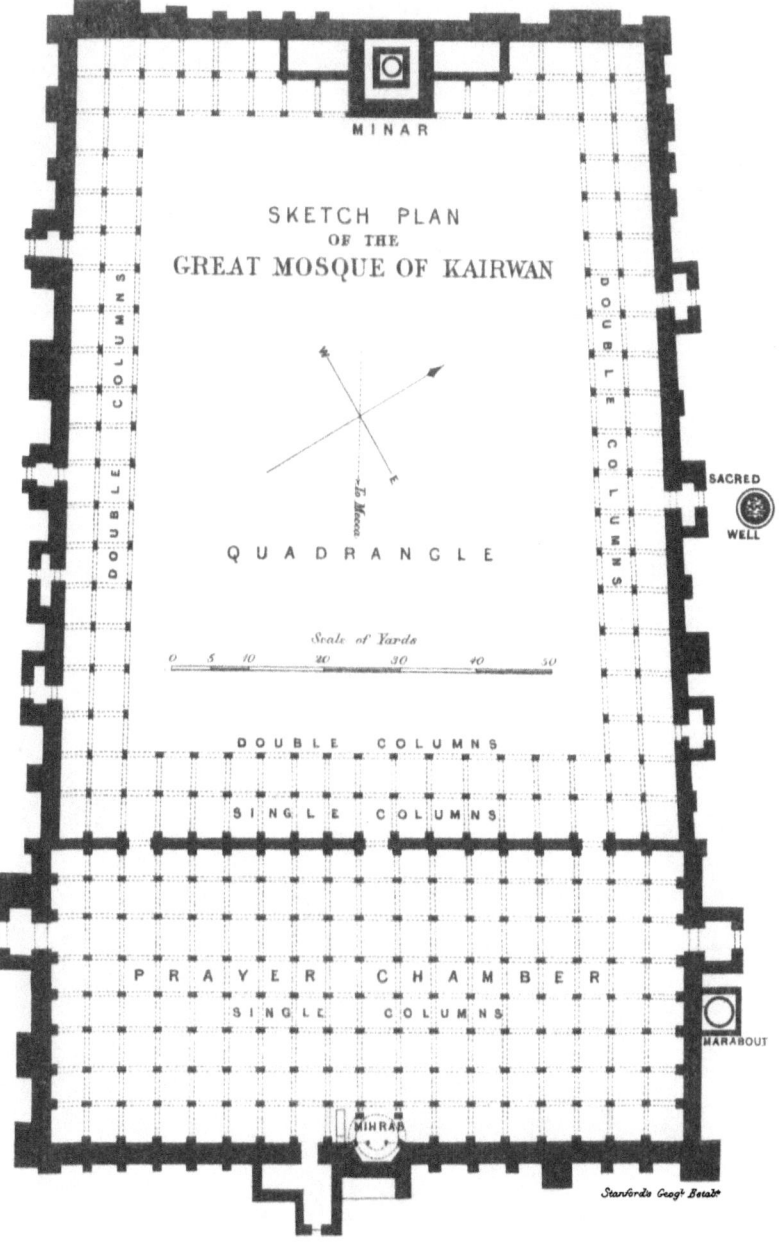

London: John Murray, Albemarle Street.

rising one upon another, as in the Mezquita of Cordova, and supported by fine old columns of various proportions and colours. Pillars of rich colours flank each of the three doorways under this arcade. Some are of old dusty red marble, fluted; others of various colours. The doors are beautifully inlaid and arabesqued in elaborate patterns, and have decorative hinges.

The interior of the prayer chamber is imposing and fine. Nine ranks of nineteen massive columns each, many of them dark marble, many of white marble with rich Corinthian capitals, and exceedingly fine and old, carry the whitewashed double arches of the roof. The walls are whitewashed, and on the floor are mats of straw. Some parts of the vaulting were being restored, and where wooden supports were giving way they were being replaced by iron. The dome of the Mihrâb is vaulted in stone. It took a whole week to pierce a hole for the staple to carry the lamp. The lamps of the mosque are series of large iron rings, diminishing upwards, and carrying, in numerous little glass cups, the oil and wicks.

There were no ostrich eggs—the symbols, as the genial author of My Winter on the Nile says, of that credulity which can swallow any tradition. In the eastern angle stands the *Kubbeh* or Chamber of the Tomb, containing, I was told, manuscripts and old weapons. The *Kibleh* or Shrine, is faced with rare old red marble pillars. The *Membar* is of dark wood, elaborately carved. The last rebuilding took place in 827, and in the year 1082 El Bekri stated the number of the columns in the mosque to be four hundred and fourteen. I believe this to be near the truth. I reckoned the total number of columns in the prayer chamber at one hundred and seventy-one: in the court about two hundred and forty-four: in all four hundred and fifteen. On the exterior of the building and enclosure are about twenty.

The great dim interior was fine and striking after the glare of the sun, and the few Moors kneeling at their prayers were probably very fervently asking their lord Mohammed for a malediction upon the Christian dog at the door.

I was curious to confirm my calculation of the number of columns in the mosque, and one evening, calling the old barber into my room, I thus commenced: O Barber, it is said that none has yet counted the columns in Sidina Okhbah. That is true: it is forbidden. Traveller: Thou, who hast lived among the Roumi and learned their tongue, art free from superstition. Barber: True, O traveller! Traveller: Dost thou know a man in Kairwân willing to bring me the number of those columns? Barber: It is written on the wall in the Great Mosque, Cursed be he who shall count these columns, for he shall lose his sight. Traveller (indirectly):

The Franks reward services. Barber: It may not be, the danger is too great. Traveller: The curse would not fall upon him who counted but the ranks of columns: so many ranks from east to west, and so many ranks from south to north. Barber (after some hesitation): It is forbidden to regard the columns at all. Traveller: The curse does not apply to the arches and the vaulting above the columns. Barber (stroking his beard): That might be. It is true there is no mention of the arches. Traveller: Is it understood? Barber: *Wallah*!

And then the old ass went straight to the Mufti of the mosque, the Scherîf Hamuda, and blated out what he was going to do. My son, said the Scherîf, beware. It will bring good neither to the stranger nor to thee. One man attempted it and lost his sight: and a second and a third did the same. Be warned, and leave the matter alone.

CHAPTER XXIV.

Foundation of Kairwân—Its Mosque and Kibleh—Its Vicissitudes—Cordova—Constructions—Raccadah—The Last of the Aghlabites—The New Mecca.

WHEN Okhbah ibn Nafi had formed the resolution of building Kairwân, he led his followers, among whom were eighteen Companions of the Prophet, to the spot he had chosen, in a deep forest where no path existed. What! they said, when he asked them to set to work: wouldst thou make us build a city in the heart of a pathless forest: and should we not have to fear wild beasts of all kinds and snakes?

Okhbah then cried aloud: O ye serpents and savage beasts, know that we are the Companions of God's Prophet! Withdraw from the spot we have chosen: any of you that we may find hereafter will be put to death.

The Mussulmans then saw with wonder during the entire day, the wild animals and venomous reptiles withdrawing and carrying off their young, a miracle which converted many Berbers to Islam. They say that for forty years afterwards not a snake or scorpion was seen.

Okhbah then made the circuit of the spot, offering prayers to God that science and wisdom might prosper there: that it might be inhabited alone by God-fearing men and those serving Him with love: finally, that the city might be preserved from the assaults of the powers of this world. Then they traced the streets and tore up the trees.

The first care of Okhbah was to choose the position of the citadel and the mosque: the former is said to have comprehended the site of the ancient Phœnician fortress Camounia. There was much variety of opinion regarding the Kibleh, it being rightly believed that the inhabitants of Africa would adopt the Kibleh of this mosque: and Okhbah was urged to determine its position with the greatest care.

The Arabians remained long engaged in observing the rising of the sun and of the stars, in summer and winter, without coming to a determination. Okhbah, becoming uneasy, addressed himself to the Most High for inspiration. One night, during sleep, he had a vision, and a voice from on high addressed him in these words:—

O thou! beloved of the Master of the worlds, when the morning is come, take the sacred Standard upon thy shoulder: thou wilt hear the Tekbir sound in front of thee while none other can hear it; the spot where the chant shall end is that which must be chosen for the

Kibleh : there the throne of the Imâm must be placed. God Most High will protect this city and this mosque. His religion shall be established upon solid bases, and till the consummation of time unbelievers shall there be humiliated.

At these words Okhbah arose from sleep, bewildered at such a revelation : he performed his ablutions, and repaired to the still unbuilt mosque to pray, accompanied by the chief inhabitants. As soon as the dawn came he prostrated himself, and hearing before him the Tekbir sounding, asked those about him if they heard it too. They replied, No.

He took the Standard upon his shoulder, and followed the sound of the voice. It ceased when he reached this spot, where now stands the pulpit of the Imâm. Immediately he planted his banner, and cried : Henceforth this is the spot whither ye shall turn in prayer.

The palaces, mosques, and habitations rose with rapidity : the enclosure measured three thousand six hundred fathoms, and it was completed in the year 677. Inhabitants flocked thither from all parts, and it rapidly became a powerful capital.

The accuracy of the site of this Kibleh is regarded as such that the Imâm—turning neither to right nor to left to allow for possible inaccuracy—turns direct to the Kibleh.

El Bekri says the mosque was razed, all but the

Mihrâb, and rebuilt by Hassan ibn Nouman in the year 69 of the Hejra. He embellished the Mihrâb, transporting thither the two superb columns, which still exist, of red stone marked with yellow stains, once taken from the ruins of a Christian church, and for which the Byzantine Emperor had in vain offered their weight in gold.

The legend in Kairwân is that no person guilty of mortal sin can pass between these columns. In the Mosque of Omar there is a similar tradition, Paradise being forbidden to him who cannot pass his body between a certain pair of columns.

In 727, the mosque was reconstructed on a vaster scale. Fifty years later, Yezid ibn Hatem demolished and rebuilt it, sparing the Mihrâb as before: and when in 827, Ziadet Allah ibn Ibrahim razed it, for the third time, and was preparing to destroy the Mihrâb, it was objected to him that all his predecessors had spared Okhbah's work. He then preserved and masked it with a wall, rebuilding and remodelling the rest of the mosque.

This was upwards of a thousand years ago, and in spite of time and wars this sacred old building has never since been destroyed by Mohammedans or desecrated by Christians.

When Abd el Rahman III. declared himself independent Khalif of the West, Imâm, and Commander of the Faithful, he resolved to build a mosque in Cordova, grander and more magnificent than any other. In the year 778 he commenced it, assisting with his own hands in the work, and in twenty-five years it was completed. Its court measured a hundred and thirty-five yards by seventy, its prayer chamber a hundred and thirty-five by a hundred and twenty.

Twelve hundred columns of rare marble, taken, like those of the Kairwân mosque, from Greek and Roman ruins, divided the prayer chamber into nineteen naves and twenty-nine aisles. The columns were brought from Nîmes and Narbonne, Seville and Tarragona, some from Carthage: while others, together with glorious mosaics, were sent from Byzantium.

The massive buttressed walls of the Mezquita, as the mosque was called—from *mesgad*, to prostrate oneself in prayer—were penetrated by nineteen gates: the Puerta del Perdon, the most beautiful of all, opening on to the Court of Orange Trees. The chapel, or recess of the Mihrâb, the abode of the Spirit of God, which held the Alkoran—the sacred book written by the hand of Othman, covered with gold, pearls, rubies, and chained to the desk of aloe wood—was, and still is, indescribably rich and beautiful. Round the small octagonal chapel, the Kibleh, where the God of Islam used to reveal his presence, the Faithful used, as in the Kâba of Mecca, to crawl seven times.

In the *Maksurah*—the privileged enclosure where the Khalif, the Muftis, and Imâms alone could enter—stood the throne of El Mansour, on wheels, carved in precious woods with figures and images, under a special dispensation from the Khalif—the sculpture of images being forbidden by the Mohammedan law.

Such was the temple built by the Moors of Kairwân, sixty years after their establishment in those rich plains of Cordova. The mosque surpassed those of El Aksa, of Kairwân, and of Mecca in beauty, and ranked next to them in sanctity. A pilgrimage thither was regarded as one to Mecca or to Kairwân. The Mosque of Seville, modelled to a certain extent on the Mezquita, was completed four centuries later, and only forty years before the Christians took Cordova. Its sacred Minar—the Giralda—measured fifty feet across at the base, and rose to the height of two hundred and fifty feet.

The proportions of this and of the Mezquita rather dwarf the imposing and venerable Shrine of Okhbah and its Minar. But in the prayer chamber at Cordova, the relatively small size and corresponding crowding of the eleven hundred columns and their arches, take a little from the space and dignity which characterise the older mosque here. No doubt Kairwân never endowed its mosque so lavishly as did Cordova, but its proportions and space render it both solemn and grand.

The treasures of Kairwân were at one time of countless value. Tarik found at Toledo twenty-five crowns of the Gothic kings, of fine gold, garnished with jacinths, amethysts, diamonds, and other precious stones. He also found at the city of Medina Celi an inestimable table, which had formed part of the spoil taken from Rome by Alaric King of the Goths. It was composed of a single emerald possessed of talismanic properties—wrought by genii, so it was said, for King Solomon the Wise.

Musa found at Seville, among other sacred spoils, a cup made of a single pearl, brought by an early King of Spain from the Temple of Jerusalem, at its destruction by Nebuchadnezzar.

The foresaide two captaines *Tarik* and *Muse*, says Leo, with all good successe proceeded euen to Castilia, and sacked the citie of Toledo: where, amongst much other treasure, they founde many reliques of the saints, and the very same table whereat Christ sate with his blessed Apostles: which being covered with pure gold and adorned with great store of precious stones, was esteemed to be woorth halfe a million of ducates: and this table *Muse* carrying with him, as if it had beene all the treasure in Spain, returned with his armie over the sea, and bent his course toward Cairaoan.

Ziadet Allah ibn Ibrahim, after thirteen troubled years, finding himself in tranquil possession of Africa, set himself to repair by peaceful labours the evils of war.

He used to say that he had been permitted to accomplish four things which entitled him to Divine mercy on the day of Judgment. To rebuild the great mosque at a cost of eighty-six thousand dinars, in lieu of that built by Yezid ibn Hatem: to build the bridge of Abou el Rebi, and the castle of the Marabouts at Susa: finally, to appoint so worthy a Kadi as Ahmed ibn Mahriz.

Among the numerous constructions due to Abou Ibrahim Ahmed, Nowairi cites: the reservoirs at the Tunis Gate, the porches and cupola of the Great Mosque, the cisterns of the Abou Rebi Gate, the mosque of Tunis, the walls of Susa, and the great reservoirs of Abbassiyeh.

These were his last work: he was very ill while they were yet unfinished. At last a vase of water was brought him from thence. Praised be God! he cried, who has suffered me to see this work completed. He died, says the chronicler, after these words: it was one Tuesday, the tenth of the month Dhi 'l Kaada, 249. He was only twenty-nine years old.

The Aghlabites are still held in grateful remembrance throughout this country for the similar works they established in many different spots.

From the circumstance that the great reservoirs referred to lie to the western side of the city and within a short distance of the city wall, we can gather that the city or palace of the Abassiyeh extended westward from the neighbourhood of the present Tunis Gate.

'Outside the walls of Kairwân,' says El Bekri, 'are fifteen cisterns built by Hescham and other princes: the greatest, however, by Abou Ibrahim Ahmed, grandson of Aghlab. They stand near the Tunis Gate, are of circular form, and very considerable.

'In the centre of the chief cistern stands an octagonal tower crowned by a pavilion with four gates. On the south side of the reservoir wall there abut vast colonnades. To the west of the same reservoirs, which receive the waters of the winter torrent Wad el Merkelil, Ziadet Allah built a palace: and to the north a beautiful pond.'

These works were executed with extreme magnificence. They are the only monuments of the Aghlabites' work that remain: their necessity has been their safeguard. Only certain of them have been kept in proper repair, the requirements of the city being much reduced. El Bekri found in this province of Afrikieh two monuments which were unequalled by anything else, these reservoirs of the Aghlabites, and the palace city of Raccadah.

I think it possible that in the considerable traces of buildings, extending upon rising ground eastward from the north-east angle of Kairwân, and along an old watercourse or trench—possibly that dug by Ibrahim—we may look for the site of Raccadah.

Such a position would be in full view of the great shrine, whose finest porch lies in this direction, of the once rich plain to the northward, and of the refreshing sight of the mountains of Oussalat. It would also have been an outlying fortress on the road from the coast, and the cistern Elmawahel would have supplied it.

Moorish writers refer to a third royal city outside the walls of Kairwân, known as Mansourah. It may have been one of the suburbs, possibly the present Dar al Mana.

This is the story of the escape of Abou Modhar Ziadet Allah, the last of the Aghlabites. Word was brought him to Raccadah that his army, under the Emir Ibrahim, had been routed. Idle and voluptuous, he had lost all hold upon his citizens' loyalty, and feared to tell them the truth.

Sending to the prisons of Raccadah, he had numerous prisoners executed, and their heads paraded through the city as trophies of a great victory. Meantime, he secretly and precipitately prepared for flight. News of his army's defeat had reached him after midday prayer: before the mueddin's cry to evening prayer was heard, he had left Raccadah with his family and treasures—his household following by torchlight—and all taking the direction of Egypt.

When the truth became known, Raccadah was pillaged, the palaces ravaged, and the very soil of the gardens—which might have concealed treasure—was turned over during six whole days. Ibrahim returning found his master fled and the inhabitants in a tumult. Vainly he urged them to join him in the defence of the city, to provide him with either money or soldiers.

We are not valiant in war, O Ibrahim! they said candidly, neither will we trust thee with our riches. If the bravest warriors and the resources of the public treasury could not bring thee victory, there is no chance of success with us and our private means. As Ibrahim scornfully upbraided them, they commenced to stone him: but he escaped and fled to Tripoli, where he joined the last of the Aghlabites.

When the gentle and pious Handhalah resigned the government of Kairwân, he called together the Kadi and the more notable citizens. Opening the public treasury he took out one thousand dinars, which he counted before them. Be witnesses, he said, that I have taken from the city only what is necessary for my journey.

Bruce says: 'There is a tradition among the natives of Alexandria that it has often been in agitation to retire to Rosetta or Cairo: but divers saints have assured them that Mecca being destroyed—as it must be, they think, by the Russians—Alexandria is then to become the Holy Place, and that Mahomet's body is to be transported thither: that when that city is destroyed, the sanctified reliques are to be transferred to Cairouan in the kingdom of Tunis. Lastly, from Cairouan they are to come to Rosetta, and there to remain till the consummation of all things, which will not then be far distant.'

CHAPTER XXV.

The Gate of Greengages—Measure the City—Ruined Bastion—Call to Prayer—The Citadel—A Mob—Leylet al Moolid—Elma wahel—Imprecations—Form of City—An Incident—Opinion of the Bazaars—Prepare to Leave—Farewell to the Kaïd—Last Night in Kairwân.

I WENT to make a plan of the city walls, round which we had already gone twice. Traversing the Quarter of the Mosque, we issued on foot from the city by the Bab el Khaukh, or Gate of the Greengages—like all the others a double arch in a tower. The inner gate is a lofty horseshoe arch supported by two marble columns: the capital of one is a beautifully carved thistle-shaped acanthus. Outside the columns, jambs of white and grey marble carried a lintel of the same. Above the arch was a tablet in white marble, engraved with the names of the gate and its builder and the date of its construction. Beyond the vaulted chamber or passage, the outer archway is similar in form. On its left side is a yellow stone column having an acanthus head in marble, which does not belong to it. Facing it is a red marble column. This is the finest of the city gates.

Within this gate, and extending along the ramparts towards the Bab el Djuluddîn, lies the Dyers' Quarter—a succession of low, flat houses, with their doors and walls and the ground in front of them stained deeply in red and blue. The gates of Kairwân are five: the Bab el Khaukh, on the eastern side: the Bab el Djuluddîn, facing to the south-east: the Bab el Djedîd, to the south: the Bab el Tunes and the Bab el Keshlah, to the west.

We passed along the city walls, taking the angles and measurements as we went. The wall runs in a sloping curve, with half-round towers at intervals, till it reaches the eastern angle and turns suddenly to the north-west. The space outside here is waste land, having one or two marabouts, a small powder magazine, prickly pear bushes, and, running towards the east, traces either of the old wall of the greater city of centuries ago, or of the outer city, Raccadah. From the square tower at this angle the wall runs two hundred and fifty yards in a straight line to the north angle, where is another square tower. This face of the city wall looks over a few mud walls and hedges of prickly pear, but no dwellings.

The wall now turns to the south-west and runs six hundred yards straight to the Keshlah. Midway along the great wall are the ruins of a vaulted mud and brickwork bastion, projecting sixty yards from it. On its platform are a few old rusty guns, and in the city wall at its back are the traces of a gate which once led to the fort, but is bricked up now.

We sat down to rest in the fort, looking over the wide plain which lost itself in haze to the northward. Beyond the college and by the trees of the late Kaïd's garden, two miles off, we could trace the course of the river Roumel. Doubtless the city once extended thither, for the Moors were too intelligent to avoid such a blessing as a river: they were admirable hydraulic engineers.

It was hard to picture round these dilapidated walls and on this lonely plain the vast and populous city of old—to recall, in these wastes of mud walls and melancholy prickly pear, the splendour and luxury which made this spot the wonder of Africa. Palaces, gardens, treasure houses, colleges, shrines, fortresses, were here, peopled with the intellectual and mighty race, the illustrious Moors.

As we rested, there came from the great minaret the high tenor call of the Mueddin. There was something plaintive in the cry from the decayed city on this golden afternoon: it seemed like a lament for the lost glories of Granada, of Cordova, and of Kairwân.

At the foot of the walls, and among the tombs of the little ruinous cemetery, we found the ice plant growing freely, all covered with its transparent globules. We should recommend it to the camels of Kairwân on such a glowing day as this.

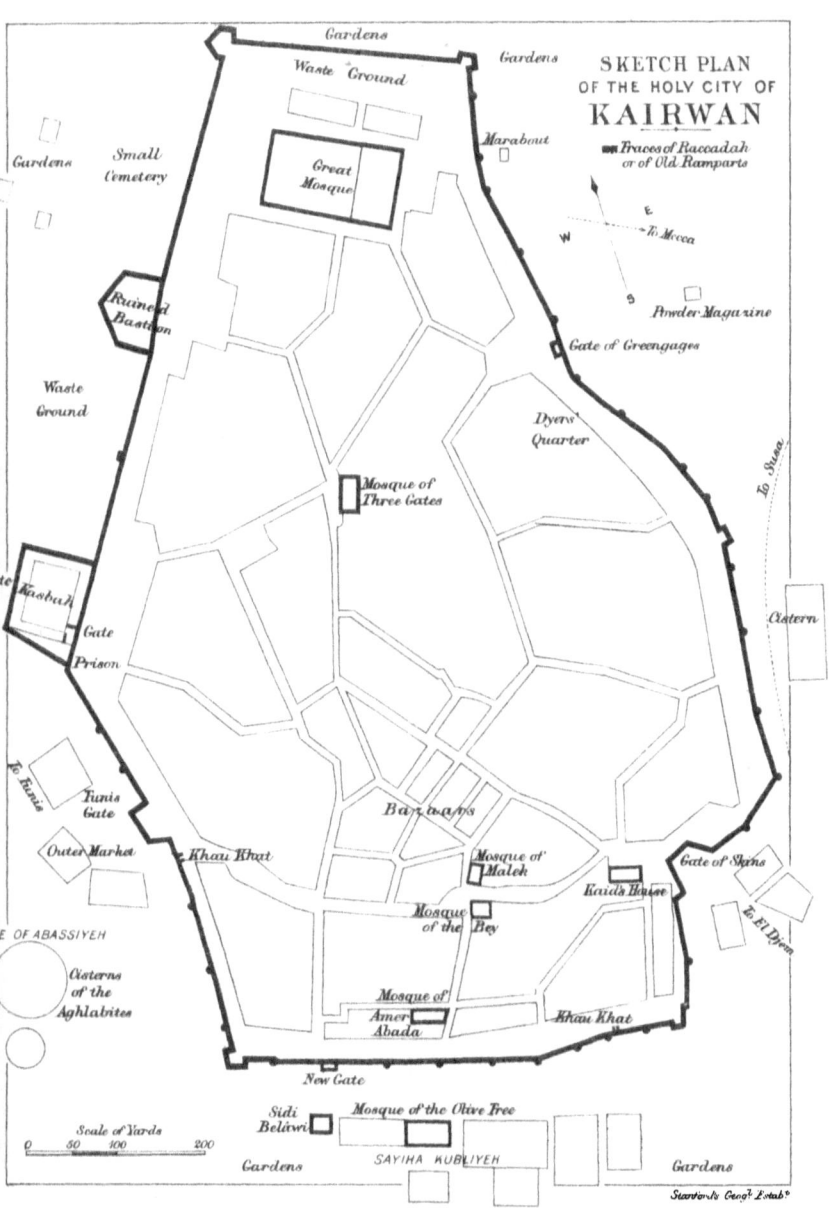

London: John Murray, Albermarle Street.

We moved on to the Keshlah, of which the quadrangle projects eighty yards from the main wall, and which is entered by the gate I have before referred to. The wall then turns to the south for five hundred yards, making a sudden bend at the Tunis gate, and half encompassing the outer market place.

The appearance of an Infidel in his ordinary dress, with a large sheet of paper, on which he was recording his measurements of their venerated wall, caused dissatisfaction among the people: and they began to collect round me. I had sent Perruquier and one soldier to the silversmith's to get the bracelets, the other soldier and the old barber remaining with me. As we went on the Moors followed, not liking the proceeding. First there was a crowd of fifty, then of a hundred: finally I had a mob of a hundred and fifty marching in silence on my heels. Whenever I halted, to make the measurement from tower to tower or to take an angle, they halted too. The whole thing was exceedingly funny.

First went the old barber, then the soldier, then I, then the mob. At a sudden pause they would almost run over one another, and come crowding to look over one another's shoulders, wondering what the tall lunatic in the Frank dress was about. Every now and then came a murmur suggestive of the Arabic word for brickbats, and I still think that if one of them had picked up a stone, many more would have done the same. It seemed a droll thing to be marching round the walls of an old sacred city in Barbary, with a crowd of men about me, satisfied in their consciences that I had no right to be there, and yet none of them molesting me. The boys and youths were disposed to grow insulting. We traversed in this way the broad southern end of the city: the wall is turreted at intervals, the so-called suburbs lying under it to our right. We passed the Mosque of the Olive Tree, the Bab el Djedîd, the *khaukhat* of this quarter, and rounded the south-east angle near the Bab el Djuluddîn.

From this gate the walls curve gently round to the Bab el Khaukh. We passed the great dry reservoirs, mentioned already, to our right hand. Of these the Arab historian Abulfeda writes: 'Incolæ urbis Kairwân bibunt aquam pluvialem quæ hyemali tempore colligitur in piscina magna dicta Elmawahel, id est cisterna.' They are used for prayer gatherings on the solemn feast days, such as that of L'Hayd Saghîr, the three days' rejoicing after Ramadhan—or the Leylet al Moolid, the anniversary of both the Prophet's birth and death. This occurs on the twelfth day of the month of Rabîa Awwal— corresponding this year to our April 18. As the Arabic months revolve through the year, like the precession of the equinoxes—only they retrograde, and accomplish their circle in thirty-three years and a half—the Prophet could never have known with any accuracy, unless he kept an astrologer, when his birthday was to come off.

Here the crowd, who had fancied I would enter by the Gate of Skins, which would lead me to the Kaïd's house, began to think that I was not going to stop, but circumambulate the walls without end. They began to draw back and curse or insult me: and when I had gone fifty yards further they stopped and raised a cry, a kind of groan and yell in one, which their pent-up feelings gave a remarkable vigour to. This encouraged passers-by, and they too cried and hooted: *Kalb! Khansir! Kafir! Yahûdi!* There would have been no satisfaction in putting twenty or thirty to death where all were equally interested: and I reflected, too, that I had no special African evangelising mission which would have justified me in making war on my own account—so I went tranquilly on, and terminated my labours where I had begun.

We entered by the beautiful Gate of the Greengages and returned by the Dyers' Quarter to the Kaïd's house. I have no doubt that the crowd fully expected me round again later, like the sun, and that they waited for my next revolution, with little piles of stones and fragments of brick and mortar laid by.

Sir Grenville Temple says: 'The city is surrounded by a crenellated wall, and its suburbs by another; it seems to form a square.' He makes a mistake—not a common event with him—for the suburbs are surrounded by no wall: indeed, they are so poor that no one would ever think them worth surrounding with a wall. As to the form of the city, it is a little squarer than a tomato, but not so square as a pear. I found the total circuit of the walls to be about three thousand five hundred yards: when Moëz ibn Badis rebuilt them in 444 of the Hejra, their measure was eleven thousand yards.

I found Perruquier at the Kaïd's, in a state of high excitement. He had been threatened in the bazaars, and had to escape to the house. I at first wondered at the success and celerity of his flank movement, but afterwards recollected that he had served in the Mobile Guard during the defence of Paris. But for the experience acquired in the exercise of his military profession, the ex-Mobile might have fallen a victim to the immortal principle of the pursuit of knowledge—a principle to which I was ready to sacrifice his life, and he mine.

Anecdote.—Perruquier, having in his boyhood received some slight instruction in the form of drill, was out one day during the siege with several comrades, going through musketry drill. Present arms! said the corporal. You are wrong, he said, as Perruquier presented arms in a manner that seemed unusual: do it again. I shan't, said Perruquier—you are wrong yourself. Perruquier was brought before the adjutant. You are disobedient? said the adjutant. The corporal doesn't know how to present arms, said Perruquier. Let me see you both do it, said the adjutant. You are appointed caporal instructeur, he said to Perruquier: Corporal, you may return to the ranks.

It appears that, as Perruquier sat in the bazaars, a fanatic with a drum made his appearance, and at the sight of the Kafir went off into uncontrollable hysterics. Malediction! he yelled. Christians in our city! There is no justice. God will punish us. A curse on them! A curse on them!

The caporal instructeur had other information too. He had heard of a vast subterranean city, thirty-six kilomètres from Kairwân, forming large mounds and containing vaulted chambers. We called in the attendants, who confirmed all he said. They had not been there, but were satisfied the underground city existed. Finally two men came in who had been there. The city was called Ain el Hammam, or the Well of the Bath. On second thoughts its extent was not great, and, on questioning, it was possible the buried city might represent a series of cisterns or baths. It happens that eight leagues or nearly thirty-six kilomètres from Kairwân, there are the warm baths of Hammam Truzza—the Turzo of Ptolemy—where are hot springs, much frequented formerly by Moors from all the Regency. They are described as vaulted chambers full of sulphureous vapours.

It appeared there was in the bazaars a pretty generally favourable opinion regarding my visit. He may be a worthy Infidel, the Moors said, whom it has pleased the Prophet to send here, that he may see our faith and be converted. The Kaïd and Mudabbir came to pay a farewell visit. The Mudabbir told me that there was no wish for a telegraph line to Kairwân. That from Susa was not distant, and news came quite fast enough for the Holy City of the Mughreb. A railway would, of the two, be less unwelcome.

The Kaïd asked me when I wished to leave. I said, Three hours before sunrise on the following day. The gates are not opened until six, he said: but I will order them to be kept open for you. Eventually we decided to send the cattle to a *foudoûk* near the outer market, and to pass out ourselves by the *khaukhat* of the Bab el Tunes. The Kaïd asked what escort I should like. I said I cared for none. He insisted: said it was necessary, that he was responsible for my safety, and at last I agreed to take two horsemen. I will write an acknowledgment, he said, which I beg you, for my satisfaction, to hand to the soldiers when you send them back. Take them as far as Tunis if you like.

After expressing many kind and hospitable wishes the Kaïd rose to go. He took me by the hand, and we walked to the door together. He would scarcely allow me to accompany him downstairs: and when we wished one another good-bye, the warm-hearted, genial man threw his arms round my neck and kissed me repeatedly.

We called in the two shâoushes of Susa, the old barber, the soldiers who guarded me in the city, the house servants, and all who had done me any service, and made them suitable gifts. Then we lay down for a short night's rest—the last night in the singular city of Kairwân.

CHAPTER XXVI.

Issue from the City—Traverse the Plain—Camp of Bedouins—Interview with Bedouin Ladies—Halt under Olive Trees—Ruined Tomb—Nablus—Hammamet—The Foudoûk of Birloubuîta—The Dakkhul Promontory—The Lead Mountain—Suleiman—Gulf of Tunis—Hammam 'l Anf—Rhades—Enter Tunis.

It was a quarter past two when Perruquier awakened me and lighted the candles. The packing was soon done. Our sergeants, sleeping in the outer chamber, I awakened, to wish them good-bye and to give them an acknowledgment of my safety for the Governor of Susa. A servant lighted us downstairs, and we went out. It was moonlight, and the stars shone faintly as we passed through the silent street. We came to the *khaukhat* of the Bab el Tunes, and, stooping, passed through the wicket. We saw nothing of the horses, which were to have been waiting for us here, and the servant's shout re-echoed from the wall. Everything was very quiet. The grass market was empty, and we began to think it not impossible that the horses had left for Susa.

We had had a slight misapprehension with Severio Valentino, the muleteer. He had been understood to say that unless I started on the previous evening he would not take me to Birloubuîta: and I was understood to say in reply that unless he started whenever I pleased, somebody was likely to take him to the Kaïd's prison in the Keshlah. After this, Severio explained that no malice was intended. Perruquier and the servant set off to hammer at the doors of the various *foudoûk* and to shout: and it seemed rather a foolish occupation to be here at three o'clock in the morning under the dark high walls of Kairwân. The footsteps died away: it was very cold, and all I could hear was the wind whistling in the muzzle of my gun. At last the horses were found: the gates of a *foudoûk* were thrown open: two shâoushes on horseback galloped up: a few Arabs, muffled up and bearing lanterns, came out to see us start, and we set off from Kairwân at a rapid trot.

After an hour we came to a low ruined bridge across the Wadi Kantara, so broken and dilapidated that, but for its moral effect, it might as well not have been there. Mists were rising from the low marshy ground and old river bed on either side of it, and water stood in pools among the rushes. We traversed the low plains of the Bilad Souatir, the shâoushes, with their white hooded cloaks and guns, riding in front of us. We left to our right a range of low hills. Presently a shâoush's horse fell with him, not hurting him much, however. Shâoush, perhaps, not much accustomed to night expeditions, and caught napping. After three hours we pulled up. I handed to the soldiers the Kaïd's receipt for my body, a backshîsh, and, sending a message of thanks to the Kaïd, dismissed them.

The daylight had been advancing for some time, the sun rose, and we pushed merrily on. After four hours and a quarter we traversed the dry bed of the Wadi Beni, the clay banks of which were all baked and cracked by the sun. Round us stretched broad fields of long-eared barley, glistening in the sun and shivering in the wind. We met a caravan of Arabs, with camels laden with pottery from Nablus—dishes, vessels, pots, jars, and bottles, all slung in nets from the pack-saddles. One Arab wore the prodigious straw hat common in the Djerîd.

After five hours and a half, the track turned off sharply towards the coast: we were still in the great plain of Kairwân. We passed to our left hand the ruins of Djebel 'l Emfida. There was a Bedouin *douar* near the track, hedged in by a rough thorn fence: and camels were browsing among the barley. The country became rather richer, and the crops were considered worthy of protection by scarecrows—such scarecrows, however, that the Barbary wild fowl must be far simpler than our worldly-minded and predatory crows.

After six hours and a half we passed—half a mile to

its right—the marabout of Sidi Takroûna, with two domes. To the left of the road stood a small ruined building of rough stones. Four miles to our right we could see a white building on the Susa road, not far from the coast. Soon we turned to the northward. To the left stood a ruin, and a marabout, in form like a Syrian tent—Sidi Wahid Allah. To the right of the track lay a low pool or swamp. Bedouins met us, driving a flock of black goats, kids with coats silky as spaniels', and a herd of dun cattle. The Arabs' faces were almost black with exposure. Half a mile further stood a *douar* of twelve tents.

Shortly after this we pulled up at a round cistern containing a few feet of water. A Bedouin family were grouped round it. The women had tattooed chins, and one wore a neck ornament which I should have liked to buy, but, alas! I had scarcely any money left. The girls were not tattooed: one had a pretty face and dark eyes. I gave them all the small money I had, and they were very pleased. After ascertaining whence I came and whither I was going, they inquired whether I had a wife. When they heard that I was not blessed with a mother-in-law, they wished me a wife with immense black eyes. As we moved on they wished me repeatedly a fortunate journey, and hoped that their saint, the servant of the One God, might take me under his especial protection.

After seven hours we sighted the blue and stormy Mediterranean, about four miles to our right. We saw a few marabouts, and passed, a mile to our left, the Sisters of Kuda—three round-backed hills, over which the strong wind was chasing black shadows. We approached two olives, the first trees we had seen since leaving Kairwân, and threw ourselves down for a rest and food. Perruquier went off with the gun. After a single discharge he returned, and when I asked afterwards whether he had hit anything, he said he had killed a lark. I asked what he had done with the body. This Barbary Samoyede had plucked and eaten it warm.

There stood, a quarter of a mile from the track, a small ruined building, with remains of others: beside it, to the right, were stones and evidences of buildings strewn about. The olive trees were tossing their branches in the strong wind blowing from the sea, which cooled and refreshed us. Twenty English miles yet lay before us. After an hour's rest we set off again, the horses going well and all the better for the halt. We passed quantities of oleander growing in shrubs of considerable size. To our right lay a long stretch of yellow sand, and patches of turf so level that Perruquier, the muleteer, and I might have had an excellent game of lawn tennis if there had been more time to spare. There came past, from time to time, a caravan of camels—some having loads of palm baskets and brushes closely packed upon their humps.

After nine hours and a half we reached a curious round tower on rising ground, built in brick and faced with yellow stone in horizontal ribs, standing alternately in and out, and giving it the form of a strongly-bound coffer dam. Shaw says that two leagues west by south from Hammamet was Menarah, a large mausoleum, twenty yards in diameter, built like a cylindrical pedestal, with a vault beneath: several small altars, supposed by the Moors to have been lamps for mariners, stood on the cornice. No altars remain now, but the building stands in sight of the sea, and might well have served as a tomb and beacon. Half a mile to the right were yellow ruinous buildings.

In front we could see the snowy town of Hammamet—the Dove—the ancient Heraclea, the frontier town of the inland district or Zeugitania, and the last town northward of the seacoast Province of Byzacium. A mile from the shore and a few miles east of Hammamet, lies the industrious and thriving little town of Nablus—close to the site of the ancient Neapolis—which sends its pottery into many parts of the Regency.

Hammamet was distant about three miles from our halting place. We could see its brown castle by the water, the white houses sloping up the hill behind it among a dark stretch of lemon woods. A steamer lay at anchor loading lemons, which form the principal export of the town, and which go all the way to America. We had entered upon the Susa road; there was far more traffic than on the plain, and very thankfully we trotted into the courtyard of the white Foudoûk of Birloubuîta, about fifty-five miles distant from Kairwân.

We started in good time, having sent the Susa horses back, and travelling with those which had been sent from Tunis to meet me. We left the Dakkhul promontory to our right, and made almost due northward for Suleiman, passing for miles through brushwood and juniper bushes, over a sandy track, and gradually ascending. We came up among the hills: in the fields little goldfinches in yellow and brown plumage were fluttering about. Perruquier was pleased to see the chardonnerets in such numbers: he said they sang well in cages. I wondered whether they sang better in cages than out of them, and whether Perruquier would sing well in a cage.

Two hours from the Foudoûk brought us near the village of Kroumbeliyeh and the olive woods through which it is approached. It has a moderate-sized mosque. We passed trees of the caroûb or locust, bushes of oleander and of yellow broom in blossom. The Arabs use the charcoal of the oleander wood, mixed with tobacco, and apply it as a fomentation in cases of rheumatism. In the mountains of the Dakkhul, to our right, there used to be many wild boars: the orchilla weed also grows plentifully there. Perhaps I shall be doing the reader a service by explaining that this weed is used as a dyeing material.

To our left, seven miles away, we saw the massive peak of the Lead Mountain, Djebel Resass, towering above the hills. Two miles and a half to our right, low down on the plain, was the little white town of Suleiman, with five minarets. It lies on the Wadi Khalifa, and is inhabited by descendants of Andalusian Moors, who, I believe, still retain in a great measure the Spanish language. We can see Cape Carthage now, twelve miles off, and the white patch upon it—Sidi Bou Saïd. After three hours' journey we approached the southern shore of the Gulf of Tunis. We passed fields of aniseed, and hawthorn in blossom, with its sweet English scent. Not a very wholesome scent, the Moors think, for a sleeping room, and likely to cause headache. There were ruins to the right and left of the road: by the former stood a single palm tree.

The dwarf palm grows freely about. This country is strewn with ruins: its population and resources must have been immense. In another half-hour come more ruins to the left. Beyond an olive wood, and in the side of the steep hill are great caverns, once quarries, hewn in the yellow stone. We can tell our distances easily: the telegraph poles are placed just a hundred mètres apart. We see the Island of Zembra now, away to the north-west. Great numbers of camels pass us, many of them muzzled—biters, no doubt. We round a spur of the hills on our left, and reach, after having travelled rapidly for four hours and a half, the little white town of Hammam 'l Anf, the Bath of the Nose or Headland.

Through it runs a fair road. What I have hitherto called a road, was a simple horse or waggon track over the hills or plain. The Bey and General Khaireddin have country houses here. The road is one evidence of the career Tunis has entered upon—one of progress, which is likely to be as materially profitable as artistically fatal. In half an hour from Hammam 'l Anf we reached the River Milianeh, a constant stream, which we crossed by a stone bridge. We passed the large Foudoûk of Shoukh el Rhades, the ancient Ades, where Regulus defeated the Carthaginian Hanno. To our left were the hills where Hanno was simple enough to post his elephantry, and the hard-headed Roman profited by his error. The journey came to an end after travelling forty-five miles from Birloubuîta. We entered Tunis by the Bab Alîwa an hour after sunset.

CHAPTER XXVII.

A Hammam—A Negotiation—Leave Tunis—Footsteps of Bruce—A Touch of Nature—Sad News—The Last of Perruquier—Cape Carthage—The Malta Channel—A Swell—Cagliari—Amphitheatre—Antiquarian Museum—A Visit from Sards—The Colony of Tunis—Leghorn—An Incident—Genoa—Paris.

AFTER a good night's rest I rose early, and, lightly clad, made for the baths. Entering the dim and steaming chamber, I went to the dressing room, where, propped up against the wall, and swathed mummy-like in numberless towels, were two benevolent-looking Moslems enjoying the repose. Hullo, said one of them, it's Mr. Rae. This Mussulman was Colonel Playfair. He was refreshing himself after his journey with Dr. Playfair and Lord Kingston to Zaghwân, which had been a great success.

I was led away into the hot chamber. In this cheerful apartment, of which the temperature stood at I am afraid to say what, for fear I should be suspected of untruth, and of which the steam I inhaled seemed to scald my interior, were cells. One of these I shared with half a dozen of the most prodigious cockroaches on record. It is clear the cockroach needs steam to bring him on, and then he develops finely. At table d'hôte I asked a pleasant Englishman with whom I had had many conversations before leaving for Sfax, whether the English bank established here was likely to be a failure. Well, I hope not, he said: I am the manager.

In the street leading from the consulate to the bazaar I met a Moor. I knew his face well: he had more than once offered me confidentially, as a good thing, some antiques in carnelian, of recent Neapolitan work. He now held out two or three rings. Yes, I said: very handsome, I have seen them already—Italian. No, no! he exclaimed. These are, but not this! picking out a Sard intaglio set in gold, with the figure of Hector bearing off the arms of Patroclus. Traveller (dissembling): Italian—(hands back ring). Merchant (seizing his beard): Mashallah, no! Traveller: Two francs! Merchant: Seventy francs! Traveller: Five francs! Merchant (making as though about to hurry away): Sixty-five. Traveller: Twenty. Merchant (returning): Sixty. Eventually I gave him three Tunisian gold pieces, worth about fifteen francs each, and was very glad to get the ring.

This is an immense charm in Oriental life, this uncertainty, this competition of intelligences at each point. It is an every-day training in insight, self-control, command of feature, in estimating expression as a clue to thoughts in others, in judging of the best expression for concealing thoughts in yourself, and in tact with which to take advantage of manner and admission. The repose in an Oriental's countenance, especially when he is departing from the truth, is creditable and worthy of example. We are too fussy and emotional, and allow our expression and words to betray our meaning: thus we fall an easy prey to the self-possessed Oriental. And yet we call him a heedless, thriftless fatalist.

One story told of Bakkoush in Tunis, was this. Many years ago, one of the Bey's ministers, in a thoughtless moment, promised him the order of the Nischan. Upon going to claim it, he was refused. Bakkoush intimated that he was willing to accept either the order or a sum of money, but that failing both he must complain to the Bey. Eventually his feelings were assuaged by a handsome present. This is not so good as the story of the German soldier who had distinguished himself in the war with France. He was offered his choice of the Iron Cross or twenty-five thalers in money. He asked the intrinsic value of the Iron Cross. They told him about four thalers. Well, he said, I tell you what I will do: I will take the Iron Cross and twenty-one thalers.

I prepared to leave Tunis. Colonel Playfair, his brother, and Lord Kingston were to sail in the *Corsica* for Susa: and there commence their journey by land into the interior. I will make no excuse for referring to the result of this journey in the shape of an interesting and valuable work, Travels in the Footsteps of Bruce. Bruce was the pioneer, but his journal was never published: his drawings have only now been brought to light, and we may consider the journeys of Bruce and Colonel Playfair as one. The drawings of the ruins as they existed a hundred years ago, and the account of their present state, link the past with the present, and form an admirable archæological picture of perhaps the most interesting region in Northern Africa. Colonel Playfair's previous wanderings through the Provinces of Algeria in the track of Bruce had been most extensive and laborious: those on which he and his genial companion were now embarking represented a circuit of some hundreds of miles through this Regency.

From Susa the travellers proceeded to El Djem, whose Amphitheatre rivals that of Rome: thence to Kairwân, whither I had only preceded them by a fortnight. From Hammam Truzza to Sbaitla, Hammada, Zanfour, Teboursouk, El Baja, and finally through the untravelled region of the lawless frontier tribe, the Khomair, into Algeria. Conciliated by good-humoured amusement, and by Lord Kingston's unfailing precision as a shot, the Khomair were taken by storm with a pot of jam.

They would hardly part with the travellers. They offered them lands, wives, sheep, and begged to be allowed at least to escort them to the end of their journey. There are little weaknesses which make the whole world akin. Chocolate is the way to one person's heart, green figs to another's: black currants are the high road to the affections of the rugged Khomair. I may be allowed to express a hope that his journey will tempt the author of Mr. Murray's Guide to Algeria to make known in a similarly interesting way the byeways, cities, and ruins of this adjoining province of Barbary.

A year after this I was grieved to hear from Mr. Bury, an English merchant well known in the Regency, that the poor Arabs of the Sahel were starving. Rain, as had been anticipated and dreaded, absolutely failed. The crops of corn, olives, and vegetables came to nothing. Poor creatures, men, women, and children, roamed like caravans of shadows up and down the country, seeking for work and for food. Unless the Government, as they readily can, take such matters up, this terrible affliction, too probably, will be followed in a year or two by typhus or some other deadly scourge.

We all went down by train to Goletta and put off to our respective steamers, which were to sail at the same time. Perruquier came into the cabin, and I gave him a tolerably good character—a better character, I am bound to say, than he strictly deserved—and dismissed him. Apart from his merits, I could not help afterwards regarding this recommendation as thrown away: for by the side of Perruquier's recommendations of himself to future travellers, mine could only sound mean and flat.

We steamed out of Tunis Bay, under the cliffs of Cape Carthage, sighted the palms and buildings of Biserta, and ere nightfall were out in the Malta Channel. The *Lombardia* lurched and swung in the heavy swell from the gale of the previous days: and the saloon was soon emptied of passengers. In the morning we were moored in the little harbour of Cagliari.

There had sat opposite to me at dinner, and had strutted about the deck till it grew too rough, a swell: an Italian swell, of the highest Tuscan order. His wristbands of snowy linen covered his hands to his knuckle-joints, and were fastened by prodigious solitaire buttons bearing a coronet. The cuffs barely left room to display a diamond ring. His finger-nails were on the same scale as the cuffs, and would have been the envy of a mandarin: between the two longest he generally carried a cigarette. Upon his nose he wore daintily a double eyeglass. His collars were tall and vast, so that he could barely put his hat on: in fact, everything about him was on the same imposing scale.

The heels of his boots were tall and tapering: he sauntered with his toes well turned out. His clothing inclined rather towards the English fashion, and when on deck he was not himself till he bore on his head an enormous round Highlander's bonnet, standing well up, and having a large red tuft in the centre.

This picturesque creature invited me to go and spend the day with him on shore, and we strolled together up the steep streets of this sort of seedy and decaying Malta. The fortifications, apart from the natural strength of the place, are of little value. The panorama from a terrace garden above is very beautiful. We came to the post office, and my companion took from his pocket a pocket book decorated with a coronet. Do me the pleasure, he said to the clerk, to look for a letter addressed to the Conte Bianco. When the clerk handed him his letter, his bow and smile were beautiful. Grazie tante! Thanks, so many! he said. This was his favourite expression to anybody from whom we asked our way or anything else. Grazie tante, I take, therefore, to be a term in use among the more select nobility of Italy.

I took him to lunch, and he protested with much elegance against my paying. We went to a glove shop, and he was in despair because the provincial shopkeeper had only gloves with three buttons, whereas, as he told me, he never wore any with less than four. I took him past the barracks, where some recruits were hard at drill, down to the Roman Amphitheatre, near the Convent of the Capuchins. The Conte Bianco was less at home here than on the pavements of the town, and we did not stay longer than was necessary. We went again through the streets, to the Cathedral, and to one or two silversmiths' who sold peasants' filigree ornaments. Then, as a little of this entertaining idiot went a long way, I gave him the slip and came on board the *Lombardia*.

I went to the Museum in the afternoon, which is a creditable little collection of gold work, very early iron ornaments, local Phœnician scarabæi, lamps in red white and black clay, some of them doubled-necked: many Sard idols in bronze, very rude and extravagant in form, like Mexican gods: some vast cinerary or grain jars, and pointed wine jars: many small urns in glass and earthenware, some containing bones and ashes, enclosed in earthen urns. There were old Phœnician glass vessels of all forms and in marvellous colours: Roman mosaic, sculptures, marbles inscribed in Latin and Phœnician characters, and many old gems. Sardinia is rich in ruins, tombs, stone monuments, and all those good things which make an antiquary's mouth water, and bring into the antiquary's face that look of languor which betrays the internal workings of his heart.

After dinner, as we sat on deck, there came on board four of the most primitive and simple peasants in the world, dressed after the manner of the Sards in black jackets, snowy white shirts, long tasseled tarbooshes, and having their faces closely shaved. One peasant, who must have been of a considerable age, wore a cloak of unwashed sheepskin. As they came on board they made low bows to me, whom they took to be the spirited proprietor of the steamer, and asked if they might look round. I took off my hat, and said with affability that they were very welcome: then they went about the deck softly, like cats on a new carpet, with a surprised and innocent smile. They examined all the objects on deck, and their questions were frank and void of compliment.

Contadino: Where does this thing come from? Traveller: From Tunis. Contadino: Tunis belongs to Emmanuele? Traveller: Not yet—by and by. Contadino: Ah, good. What's this? Traveller: A compass, to guide the ship. Contadino: That's odd—I don't believe it. What's this? Traveller: The rudder wheel, to turn the ship with. Contadino: I don't think so much of that. What are you?—turning to a young Tunisian in native dress—a boy or a girl? Tunisian blushes. Contadino, holding him up to ridicule: What a dress! I don't think much of him. What's that thing? Traveller: An Italian book. Contadino, examining the book upside down, and noticing the defaced paper cover: A book, eh? I don't think much of it. Their grateful bows when they took their leave were splendid: and on the whole they were a great success.

Talking of Tunis, there is a Cagliari newspaper, which bears the title of *Avvenire di Sardegna e Corriere della Colonia di Tunisi*, which is not a bad example of effrontery. There is a strong feeling, not always confessed, among the Italians for the annexation of Tunis. An ancient province, which their ancestors were the first to colonise, and which bears at every point the traces of those early settlers—geographically situated almost adjacent to their kingdom—connected by commerce, and containing a greater number of their countrymen, as settlers, than of any other European race—it does not seem an unnatural aspiration. When the Fiat Lux comes in the East, and the time arrives for making things comfortable in the Mediterranean; when Constantinople is secured to Turkey, Egypt allotted to England, Tripoli to Germany, Syria to France: the moment will have arrived for gracefully handing over Tunisia to Italy.

The *Lombardia* was loading numerous bales of cork, with which the island abounds. The sun had set two hours before, and we sat on deck chatting in the lantern light. At midnight we sailed, and by daylight were well along the coast. It is far less fine than the neighbouring island of Corsica, along which we coasted in the afternoon and night. At early morning we were at anchor in the harbour of Livorno. As the *Lombardia* was not to sail for Genoa before midnight, I transferred my effects to the *Pyroscafo Galileo Galilei*, lying alongside of us, which would sail at ten in the morning.

I went on shore to get a newspaper, which had been rather a scarce object of late. There was a good and characteristic incident in the *Gazzetta di Livorno*. Two gentlemen had met and quarrelled in a café. B had said that A was a rogue and adventurer: A had pulled B's nose. B challenged A to a duel. A, being a married man with a family, refused to go out. B sent Baron C and Captain D to A to provoke him into accepting the challenge, without success. Hereupon the Baron and Captain wrote a letter to the *Gazzetta*. After recapitulating with candour what had taken place, they went on to say: We therefore hereby declare that Sig. A is a dastard, devoid of the principles of honour, and that Sig. B, who has behaved as a man of courage and rectitude, issues from the affair with spotless honour. These gentlemen add their names in full: Baron C, &c., &c.; Capt. D, Commandante of so-and-so, in the service of S.M. il Ré d'Italia. Had I not lost the newspaper, I should have been happy to reproduce their names, as a further advertisement for two gentlemen anxious to be known as cowardly bullies and abettors of assassination. Thank Heaven, Englishmen don't thus understand the meaning of the word courage.

The *Pyroscafo Galileo Galilei*, a fine, powerful paddle steamer, steamed out along the coast in the warm haze of a Mediterranean morning. In the afternoon we entered the crowded and inconvenient harbour of Genoa. I left Genoa at midnight by the International Mail train.

It was a warm and lovely day as we approached the Alps. At Chambéry were the willow trees and poplars of that beautiful valley: and among the fruit trees and their rich blossom, watching the swift-rushing river and splendid ring of mountains, were the first French gendarmes. They cannot be Republicans, those men of stately aspect, and magnificent uniforms which grow not old nor shabby. Those padded bosoms must hide Imperialist hearts—those cocked hats can be the emblems of neither Liberty, Equality, nor Fraternity. We passengers slept peacefully through the night, and the International Mail train shot into the Lyons terminus at Paris within five minutes of its appointed time.

مكتوب

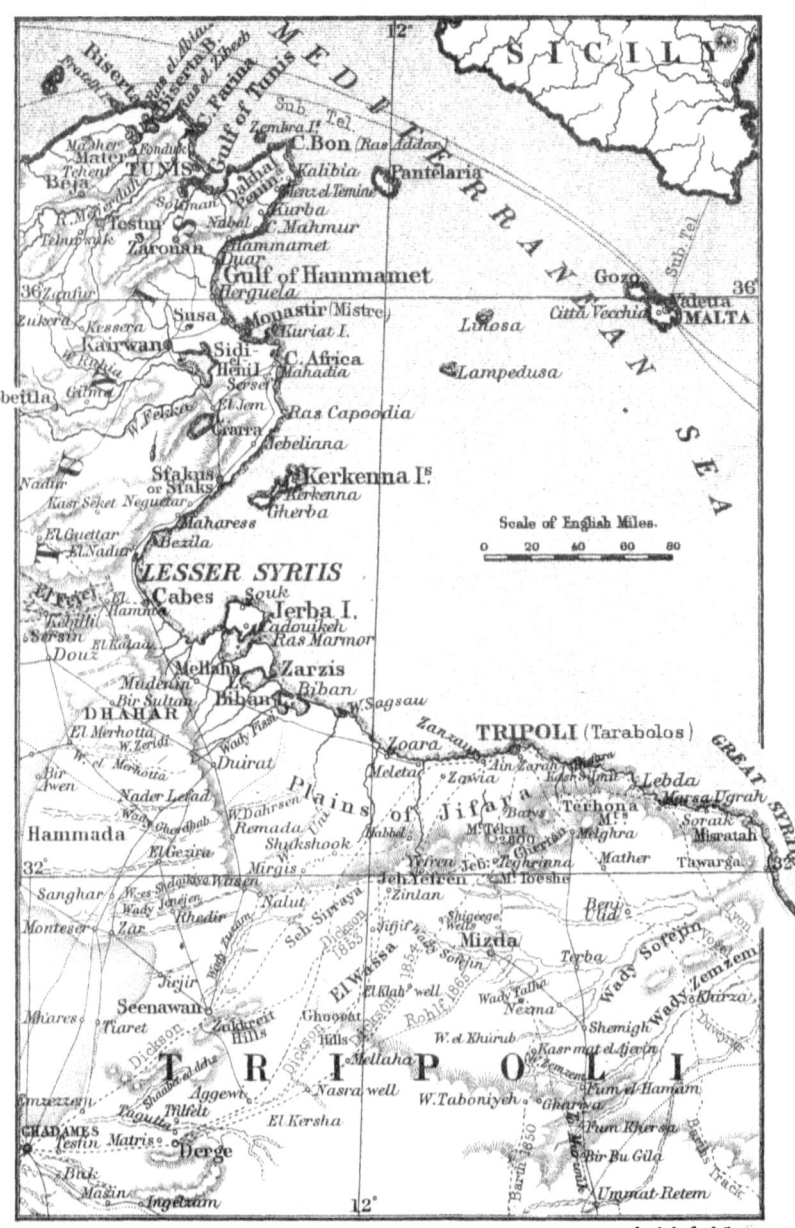

London: John Murray, Albemarle Street.

www.ingramcontent.com/pod-product-compliance
Lightning Source LLC
Chambersburg PA
CBHW021817300426
44114CB00009BA/205